WHY I AM
A FIVE PERCENTER

WHY I AM
A FIVE PERCENTER

MICHAEL MUHAMMAD KNIGHT

JEREMY P. TARCHER/PENGUIN   *a member of Penguin Group (USA) Inc.*   *New York*

JEREMY P. TARCHER/PENGUIN
Published by the Penguin Group
Penguin Group (USA) Inc., 375 Hudson Street, New York, New York 10014, USA · Penguin Group
(Canada), 90 Eglinton Avenue East, Suite 700, Toronto, Ontario M4P 2Y3, Canada (a division of Pearson
Penguin Canada Inc.) · Penguin Books Ltd, 80 Strand, London WC2R 0RL, England · Penguin Ireland,
25 St Stephen's Green, Dublin 2, Ireland (a division of Penguin Books Ltd) · Penguin Group (Australia),
250 Camberwell Road, Camberwell, Victoria 3124, Australia (a division of Pearson Australia Group
Pty Ltd) · Penguin Books India Pvt Ltd, 11 Community Centre, Panchsheel Park, New Delhi–110 017,
India · Penguin Group (NZ), 67 Apollo Drive, Rosedale, North Shore 0632, New Zealand (a division of
Pearson New Zealand Ltd) · Penguin Books (South Africa) (Pty) Ltd, 24 Sturdee Avenue, Rosebank, Johan-
nesburg 2196, South Africa

Penguin Books Ltd, Registered Offices: 80 Strand, London WC2R 0RL, England

Library of Congress Cataloging-in-Publication Data

Knight, Michael Muhammad.
    Why I Am a Five Percenter / Michael Muhammad Knight.
        p.   cm.
    Includes bibliographic references and index.
    ISBN 978-1-58542-868-7
    1. Knight, Michael Muhammad.   2. Five Percent Nation—Biography.   3. Authors, American—
21st century—Biography   I. Title.
    PS3611.N566Z46   2011   2011030039
    818'.603—dc23
    [B]

BOOK DESIGN BY NICOLE LAROCHE

While the author has made every effort to provide accurate telephone numbers and Internet addresses at the
time of publication, neither the publisher nor the author assumes any responsibility for errors, or for changes
that occur after publication. Further, the publisher does not have any control over and does not assume any
responsibility for author or third-party websites or their content.

146119709

FOR SADAF

CONTENTS

Once I went to the land of China.
Those whom I had not met
put the mark of friendship on my forehead,
calling me their own.
The garb of a stranger slipped from me unknowing.
The inner man appeared who is eternal,
revealing a joyous friendship, unforeseen.
A Chinese name I took, dressed in Chinese clothes.
This I know in my mind;
wherever I find my friend, there I am born anew.

—Rabindranath Tagore[1]

ONE

DEVIL IN DEEP SPACE: THE BIRTH OF AZREAL WISDOM

DON'T GET ME WRONG — before my first trip to the Allah School, they had me scared shitless. According to 50 Cent's old fence-man, there was a time when Five Percenters owned the streets like the Bloods and Crips. According to a State Senate subcommittee, Five Percenters were the ones who ran things during the 1971 Attica prison rebellion. In newspapers from the 1960s, I found references to the Five Percenters as terrorists who trained in martial arts with ambitions to kill white people at random. "If the Nation of Islam is a religion that finds converts in prison," Russell Simmons once remarked, "Five Percenters find their converts *under* the prison. That's how street it is." It all contributed to an image of Five Percenters as half-gangster, half-revolutionary, quasi-Muslim cultists, maniacs with names like Ruler Zig-Zag-Zig Allah. It was said to be a convicts' religion or a rappers' religion or not even a religion, but they had their own wild mythology of mad scientists blasting the moon from the Earth and believed that they were all gods and spoke in a secret language that somehow incorporated numbers. How does anyone work their way through that scene? In a tight situation, would this white boy even have the vocabulary to plead for his neck?

I remembered those thoughts while backstage after the Wu-Tang Clan show at Manhattan's Webster Hall, interviewing Brand Nubian's Lord Jamar in his dressing room and choking on the smoke from a passing blunt, Jamar telling me how he came into the knowledge. By that point, I had been building with the gods for a few years; if the Five Percenters were anything like their reputation, I should have been dead several times over. Lord Jamar introduced me to other gods in the room, and it was all peace, everyone smiling and shaking my hand, no one calling me a devil or putting swords to my neck. "I like your shirt," said one, pointing to Elijah Muhammad's portrait on my chest, rhinestones making the fez sparkle.

Searching the darkness backstage, navigating between orange-robed Shaolin monks and groupie girls, I found the Wu-Tang's "abbott," Ruler Zig-Zag-Zig Allah, better known as the RZA, and he said that we could build outside. Following him down the crowded stairwell, passing Masta Killa, I thought about art's intersection with spiritual authority. If this was medieval Iran, I'd be hanging around Sūfī orders, chasing after poets. Sometimes the line between poet and prophet gets thin, and sometimes it's not there at all. In the Qur'ān, God tells Muḥammad to remind his people that these words aren't mere poetry—but with a battle-MC's bravado, God also challenges poets to match the Qur'ān's verses.

The RZA toes that line, but only if you know what the hell he's talking about, and most don't. "The dumb are mostly intrigued by the drum," says his cousin, the GZA (also known as the Genius or Allah Justice). Encoded in the Wu-Tang's body of lyrics, buried deep under layers of references to Mafia culture and kung fu flicks, is a metaphysical matrix that never gets fully explained; you have to know before entering. At one point during this Webster Hall show, the RZA stopped the music and told the crowd that amidst hedonism and crime in the streets, one could also find wisdom. He then launched into an a cappella version of his song "The Birth." People didn't know how to take it. "Six is the limitation of the devil," the RZA recited, "and the million square miles of land that he settles." Unless you're *in* enough to get what that means, it means nothing. So his fans threw up the Wu hand sign and waited for the drums.

I couldn't have been the only one in the room to pick up on the verse, but it felt good to pretend that I was. That's a common experience in both art and mystical orders: the desire to search between the master's words, to know him better than any of the other disciples or fanboys. We believe that through our heavy intellectual and emotional investment, we earn greater intimacy with the poet or saint. Knowing that not everyone was qualified for the wisdom, classical Ṣūfī masters such as Ibn al-ʿArabī (1165–1240) would present their doctrines with deliberately complex language and arcane symbolism, offering privileged knowledge only for those who were willing and able to dig deep. In hip-hop, this approach also provides balance between two audiences. The RZA's specialized code allows him to address the initiated without alienating most of his fans.

If the RZA founded his own Ṣūfī order, I'd probably join it. Over the years, he has cultivated an authoritative, semimystical charisma, as though we should look to him for much more than music. Not many other MCs could write books on the philosophical underpinnings of their lyrics (there's no *The Tao of Lil Wayne* coming out). I had once heard a rumor that the RZA was taking time off from music to find a cure for brain cancer; for at least a few minutes, the idea seemed reasonable. It wasn't hard to imagine him in the lab—not the lab where he makes beats but an actual *laboratory*—wearing a white coat and goggles, mixing smoking liquids between test tubes.

AS WE WALKED down the street, I asked the RZA questions and jotted down his answers in my notepad. I was writing a book on the Five Percenters, I told him; excerpts had already appeared in the notes for Lord

Jamar's new album. The RZA shared his thoughts and we parted ways with "Peace" at the corner, in front of a giant tour bus with Method Man's face splashed across the side. The East Village was quiet at that hour, and I walked alone down Fourth Avenue reciting lyrics that most failed to catch:

> *Understand the equality, God in the bodily form*
> *Lettin' my knowledge be born*[1]

You have to know the code; in the Five Percenters' system of Supreme Mathematics, "Understanding" corresponds to the number 3; "Equality" corresponds to 6. "Born" corresponds to 9, so Understanding your Equality (3+6) leads to your knowledge being Born (9). Also, "Knowledge" corresponds to the number 1; to go from 1 to 9, or to make "Knowledge Born," means to make your Knowledge manifest in the world. Though it doesn't factor into the number play here, "God" happens to be the attribute for 7.

Here's how it would read mathematically:

> 3+6, God in the bodily form
> Lettin' my 1 be 9

Hip-hop is filled with these secret Five Percenter references, even from MCs who aren't Five Percenters. Listening to Jay-Z's freestyle with Big L, I would geek out on the part where Jay says, "Just like the gods, I start with Knowledge and follow with Wisdom, for greater Understanding." Knowledge, Wisdom, and Understanding correspond to 1, 2, and 3. In "Jigga My Nigga," when Jay-Z boasts, "The god, send you back to the earth from which you came," there's a double meaning for Five Percenter ears, since "Earth" represents woman.[2]

Five Percenter code appears most often with New York MCs of a particular generation, but even Lil Wayne uses it in "Tha Heat," when he says, "I'ma shoot your Arm, Leg, Leg, Arm, Head," playing on the Five Percenter understanding of A.L.L.A.H.[3] I don't think that the gods liked that one.

THE **KNOWLEDGE** WAS first born in 1964 with Clarence Smith, a decorated Korean War veteran doing his best in Harlem.

Near the start of the 1960s, Clarence's wife, Dora, joined the Nation of Islam and convinced him to follow her. The Nation's mosque in Harlem was headed by Malcolm X. Registering as a Muslim under Malcolm's instruction, Clarence Smith dropped his "slave name"; as the thirteenth man named Clarence to do so, he became Clarence 13X. The Nation of Islam's leader, Elijah Muhammad, presented himself as the Messenger of Allah, but his Allah was not the unseen, unknowable Creator worshiped in normative Islam. Such a being was only a "mystery god," a spook used by slave masters to deceive and control the masses. All black men were gods, taught Elijah; among them, the "best knower" was designated Allah. The Allah who taught Elijah was a living man with a physical body, who had come to Detroit from the holy city of Mecca on July 4, 1930. He was known by numerous names, most commonly W. D. Fard and Master Fard Muhammad. Because there was no "mystery god," Fard was not a "manifestation" or "incarnation" of a spiritual being's essence; Allah was a mortal man. Before Fard, another man had been Allah; and after him, someone else would take his place.

By 1964, Clarence 13X's intense study of Nation of Islam doctrine had led him to a breakthrough: not only was he a god, but he had every right to claim the name Allah for himself. The man that Elijah called Allah had disappeared without a trace exactly thirty years ago; at that point, Fard himself was only a mystery god, a ghost used to place Elijah on the throne. Clarence recognized himself as Allah, with no need for divine intervention by Fard or his Messenger.

Legend depicts Clarence as proclaiming his newfound understanding in the mosque, leading to his swift exile, but it's hard to say exactly when and why he left the Nation of Islam. Some have speculated that Clarence, a known lover of gambling, women, and marijuana, had a hard time with the Nation's strict moral codes. Akbar Muhammad, a high-ranking official in the contemporary Nation of Islam, has alleged that Clarence had been suspended for domestic violence. One of the Muslims who ditched the mosque with Clarence has said that they left to pursue street hustles.

The year 1964 was a chaotic one for Elijah Muhammad's followers, especially in Harlem, with Malcolm X's exodus from the Nation and rebirth as a Sunnī Muslim in Mecca. The FBI, which had been monitoring the Nation, initially believed Clarence 13X to have followed Malcolm after the split. In the summer of 1964, however, Clarence appears to have drifted between his former minister and the Messenger, hanging around Malcolm's organizations and also attending Nation of Islam rallies. Caught between sides in Harlem's Muslim Civil War, Clarence had no place to go. Dropping his X, he was back to living "in the grave" as far as the Nation was concerned; but he couldn't get into the Islam that Malcolm had found overseas, the old Islam in which God was back to being a spirit, not the black man. Hanging around Harlem's basement pool halls, Clarence continued to study the "Supreme Wisdom Lessons," a series of transcribed question-answer exams between Master Fard and Elijah Muhammad. Though the Nation guarded these lessons, allowing access only gradually to new converts, Clarence shared them with non-Muslims, the young hustlers and dropouts who might appreciate the main gist of Elijah's religion but weren't likely to wear bow ties and abstain from music or girls. Clarence added his own flavor, interpreting the lessons through his unique algebra, "Supreme Mathematics," upon which he'd expound while shooting dice on the corner.

He told the kids that there was no god in the sky; the only god who could save them was waiting to be found in the mirror. "Islam" as he gave it to them was not merely the name of a religion but an acronym for "I Self Lord And Master;" the power to change their world could be found within them. The black man is God, always has been, always will be. As the man who unlocked the secret for New York's runaways and throwaways, Clarence had proven himself as the best knower; the kids called him "Allah."

The new Allah and his cluster of teen disciples emerged in the local underworld as a growing sect, named for a breakdown of society in the Supreme Wisdom Lessons: as 85 percent of the population remained deaf, dumb, and blind to the truth, having been deceived by 10 percent, the "slavemakers of the poor," the remaining 5 percent consisted of "poor righteous teachers" who would liberate the masses from "mental death." Allah told his young gods that they were these messianic "Five Percenters" who would bring knowledge of self to "all human families of the planet earth," destroying religion and racism.

In December 1964, Allah was shot at one of his usual gambling haunts. For many of Harlem's fatherless kids in search of a black super-hero, his survival bolstered his claim to be Allah. After a disciple named Bilal made the *hijra* from Harlem (which Allah referred to as Mecca) to Brooklyn (which he called Medina) to teach his friends, the movement spread like wildfire through Fort Greene and the surrounding neighborhoods. The Five Percenters had not yet fully distinguished themselves from their Nation of Islam heritage; in that early period, they would greet each other as Muslims with *as-salāmu alaikum* ("peace be upon you"). One day, Allah asked Bilal what it meant, making the youth repeat his answer three times. Allah then asked him, "Why don't you say it in a language that you understand?" From that moment on, Five Percenters greeted each other with a simple "Peace."

As the Five Percenters began to set themselves apart from the Nation of Islam and Sunnīs, Harlem's Muslim civil war was still raging. On February 21, 1965, as Allah was still recovering from his wounds, Malcolm X was assassinated just two miles uptown. With a can of gasoline, unknown arsonists then brought down Mosque No. 7. In May, Elijah Muhammad named Louis X (Farrakhan) to Malcolm's former post. Allah led a handful of Five Percenters on a march from the mosque's remains to the Hotel Theresa, former home to Malcolm's Organization of Afro-American Unity and Muslim Mosque, Inc. Along the way, they allegedly smashed windows and assaulted a man. Taken into police custody and brought before a judge, Allah identified himself only as Allah, and declared that no one could put Allah on trial. Unfamiliar with the complexities of Nation of Islam doctrine and what the term "Allah" would have meant in this context, the judge suspected Allah of having delusions of grandeur and sent him to Bellevue Hospital for psychiatric examination.

While Allah waited for his trial, the Federal Bureau of Investigation began to take an interest in his movement. Allah's name was added to J. Edgar Hoover's Security Index, meaning that in the event of a national emergency, he could be transferred to a special prison camp without regard for the Constitution. After five months in Bellevue, Allah was found mentally unable to comprehend the charges against him, and sent to Matteawan State Hospital for the Criminally Insane— New York State's darkest pit of institutional torture, a "hospital" used to train prison guards, where inmates/patients were routinely beaten, raped, and murdered. Allah's classification as insane was better for the authorities than a guilty verdict; without a fixed sentence, he could be held at Matteawan "for his own good" until the end of time.

Prior to his incarceration, Allah's views on race had followed the Nation of Islam's doctrine: white people were devils, wicked by nature and beyond redemption, having been created by an evil scientist named Yakub to take over the world. At Matteawan, however, Allah took pity upon a white teenager who had been beaten and drugged into a coma by the guards. When the youth regained consciousness, Allah revealed himself as Allah, proclaimed the kid to be a "righteous man," and taught him the Supreme Wisdom Lessons and Supreme Mathematics. Allah named him Azreal, after the Islamic angel of death, and told him that his duty was to get the "wrongdoers."

Back in New York City, officials expected the Five Percenters to wither away without their Allah, but Allah's message was so brilliantly packaged that it could thrive on its own. The lessons traveled from basketball courts to housing projects to city parks to school yards and street corners, with every new convert pledging to teach ten others younger than himself. The Five Percenter message was at once simple enough to be easily digested by anyone—*the black man is God of the universe*—and complex enough, through its call to rigorous study of the lessons and Supreme Mathematics, to promise a challenging life of study and inner growth. It offered both freedom and discipline, politics and spirituality, salvific manhood and then *more* salvific manhood. By the time of Allah's release after more than twenty months at Matteawan, there were thousands of young gods waiting to welcome him home. They were willing to put the whole solar system on his shoulders, but Allah refused; he told the kids that they were not Muslims or Christians but true and living *gods*, each of them entitled to his name. "Sun," he told a youth who would later be called Allah B, "Know you are Allah, never deny yourself of being Allah. Even if the whole world denies you, never deny yourself, because it's your own doubt that can stop you from being Allah."[4]

This was around the time that Mayor John Lindsay sought alliances with informal neighborhood leaders, local figures apart from elected officials and clergymen, who could help him prevent riots and improve relations in the worst parts of the city. Lindsay's generals reached out to Allah, at the time the most feared militant in New York. Allah told them that he'd work with City Hall in exchange for his Five Percenters getting free bus trips to the beach, plane rides above the city, and their own school.

Through the Urban League Street Academy program, a Five Percenter storefront school was opened on Seventh Avenue and 125th Street, and Allah became one of Lindsay's most important street ambassadors. After the assassination of Martin Luther King, Jr., Allah and Lindsay marched arm in arm through Harlem to keep the peace. Afterward, a life-size photo of them hung in the school's front window, signed by each man to the other: "To Mayor Lindsay, the greatest Mayor we've got"; "To Allah, thanks a lot."

Lindsay felt a real affection for Allah, the mayor's former aides told me, but Allah had more than enough enemies: the Nation of Islam hated him for putting their secret lessons on the streets and elevating himself above Elijah, the Sunnīs hated him for calling himself Allah, the Black Power scene hated him for working with City Hall, the drug dealers hated him for preaching against drugs, the gangs hated him for preaching against gangs, the NYPD hated both Allah and Lindsay, J. Edgar Hoover viewed the Civil Rights movement as a communist conspiracy, and there were always gambling beefs. When Allah was shot again, this time in an elevator shaft, one could pick from a crowd of suspects. The assassination was never solved.

THOUGH THE STREET ACADEMY program eventually closed, the Five Percenters still have their building on 125th Street and Seventh Avenue, now called the Allah School in Mecca. Before Lindsay gave the property to Allah, it had been a barbershop that went to the city in a tax case.

I made my first trip there in the summer of 2004, not knowing what to expect; could white guys just show up and get lessons? All that I had in my favor was a name to drop.

"Is Azreal here?" I asked the god at the front desk. He led me back outside to the adjacent yard, where a white man in his mid-fifties was digging in the dirt. I told Azreal my name, and he told me that his middle name was Michael. We went to a bench at the nearby St. Nicholas projects, where he smoked while I interviewed him and looked out for cops. He told me about the hell of Matteawan and the love of Allah, the only father that he knew, and he promised that whites could be more than devils. Upon returning to the Allah School, I found myself in fruitful conversations with numerous gods about Islam, the nature of religion, and the mission of this man that they called Allah.

At the time, I was writing a road book in which I sought to capture the story of American Islam through riding on Greyhounds, sleeping in cars, hanging out in mosques, and having adventures with all the various sects and characters. The Five Percenters were a vital part of that story, but I had no idea that when I arrived at the Allah School, I'd find a tradition of serious depth—that I would actually encounter truth in their words that would have me rethinking my own Islam.

It's a common religious prejudice. We often assume that all of the genuine wisdom and useful stories rest in the old scriptures, while the new scriptures contain only made-up nonsense. When old scriptures seem unreasonable, we search for the deeper meaning, the buried esoteric truth; when new scriptures give us trouble, we dismiss them as the gibberish of lunatics and charlatans. When I mentioned the Nation of Islam to a Sunnī friend, he mocked their bizarre myths such as the Mothership, an advanced spacecraft that would someday release drone ships to bomb the white devil's kingdom off the map. His tone surprised and disappointed me; this Sunnī kid's religion, after all, had its own share of strange.

"But you believe that the Prophet flew into heaven on the Buraq," I answered. The Buraq was a creature commonly depicted as a flying horse with a peacock tail and woman's head. "Isn't that a bit counterintuitive?"

"It's allegory," he said. "It was the Prophet's *soul* that ascended into paradise, not his body."

"So why can't the Mothership be allegory?"

For some reason, this rarely occurs to people. But Allah broke down the Mothership as "mother's hip," so I don't think that it was really about flying saucers for him.

There was no shortage of strife between the Five Percenters and my own Sunnī background: for Sunnīs, members of the NOI/Five Percent tradition failed to grasp the awesome beauty and truth of Malcolm X's pilgrimage to Mecca, where he prayed with white Muslims and found transracial brotherhood in Islamic orthodoxy. The real issue, of course, would be the problem of Five Percenters regarding the black man as God—apparently a flagrant insult to Islam's most crucial principle, God's absolute oneness. But I was both white and Muslim, and did not feel offended on either count. Seriously, weren't white people devils? Do a Google Image search on "lynchings," look at the smiling white faces around the hanging black bodies, and tell me that you're not looking at Satan. Even in places like Rwanda or the Congo, where black people butchered one another, you could find white people at the root of their problems. Anyway, Five Percenters never mistreated me; I was welcomed with hospitality and even friendship, and more than one god told me that I was not a devil at all. Nor did the Five Percent really threaten my religion. Looking closely at their conception of the divine, I couldn't get worked up about Five Percenters calling themselves gods. They weren't claiming to have magical powers or infallibility; asking Five Percenters to explain their godhood in person, it never seemed nearly as ridiculous as it might on the Internet. Sometimes it even sounded like Sūfism. Meanwhile, even if I believed in the god of "mainstream" Islam, I wasn't exactly sold on the ways in which I had been taught to relate to him; I struggled with my own estrangement from organized religion, and the Five Percenters could speak to it in ways that I would never hear in a mosque. Between commentaries on white supremacy and religious authority, it seemed to me that Five Percenters had some devastating truths to share about America and the search for God.

December 19, 2004, marked the fortieth anniversary of Bilal's trip from Harlem to Brooklyn, the beginnings of the Five Percent's storied rise in what they called Medina. I went back up to the Allah School and interviewed Bilal, now known as First Born ABG ("First Born" represents a special position in the culture's history, and ABG stands for "Allah Born God"). The mission to Brooklyn had not received any academic attention, but it meant something to me. For the Five Percenters,

Bilal's subway ride had taken on the significance of that other *hijra*, Muḥammad's migration from the original Mecca to the original Medina. I understood the anniversary to be truly and deeply—I'm not sure if this is the right word, given the Five Percenters' particular thoughts on religion—"sacred."

As he shared his story with me, I considered this elder's role in the Five Percenters. It was an interesting time for the community; approaching forty years after Allah's assassination, some of the major characters were gone, but I could still find numerous elders who had been there during the early period, gods who had walked with Allah. As a Muslim, I understood their position through comparison to the Ṣaḥābas, the esteemed companions of the Prophet, who preserved his legacy by relating his sayings and actions to their own heirs.

I finished my Islamo-American road book, *Blue-Eyed Devil,* and from it grew a new project: a history of the Five Percenters. My plan was to track down every surviving scrap of information on Allah from the 1960s, recover what I could from the memories of those who knew him, and examine the culture's development up to the present. I drove across the northeastern United States going to parliaments, interviewing elders, collecting old Five Percenter newspapers, digging through files from Matteawan State Hospital for the Criminally Insane, and hanging around the Allah School, asking questions and taking notes, slowly becoming a known fixture in the community.

I also spent a great deal of time with Allah's death angel, Azreal; at one point we lived in my car for a week. Azreal eventually named me Azreal Wisdom (meaning "Azreal 2" in Supreme Mathematics). I accepted the name with full seriousness, knowing what it meant to him. Azreal was my teacher, I was his student, and—as Allah used to say, if you want to keep what you have, you must give it away—Azreal shared with me what Allah had shared with him. Even if I wasn't a Five Percenter, I had become a branch of a historically important Five Percenter's tree, and I had to respect this inheritance.

WHEN RESEARCHING THE Five Percent, I faced a problem of sources: what exactly did it mean to be a Five Percenter, and whose definition could I trust? To study a culture isn't as simple as sitting in a pew with a notepad, writing down every word exactly as it comes from the unified voice of the choir. There's no unified voice; it's more like shoving your way through a dark and crowded party, catching snippets of conversations as you pass. Traditions are never coherent; they don't hold themselves together as well as their loudest voices want you to think. As with other traditions, the Five Percent has its own dominant orthodoxies and marginalized heresies, major figures and minor figures. While most Five Percenters reject the religion of Islam, there are also self-identified "Muslim gods"; though most would not advocate equal godhood for black women, there are female gods. The community overwhelmingly opposes homosexuality, but I know queer gods; I build with gay men who are Five Percenters. When it comes to my understanding of the culture, these voices are also part of the equation. The challenge for anyone approaching a culture from the outside, whether as detached observer or new convert, is to remember that no one speaks for everyone. I can't choose between the various schools of thought and speak on what an authentic "Five Percenterism" would teach, but only on which ideas appear to be more popular than others.

To investigate the Five Percent could have been politically complicated, as I come from more than one place of privilege with respect to the black god: a white man in America and a Muslim from the mainstream mosque (in terms of privilege, Sunnīs are like the "white people" of Islam). Asking questions like "Can someone be both Five Percenter and Muslim?" or "Are white people really devils?" touched upon a serious danger: that an outsider writing on a culture could re-create that culture in her or his own image, offering a portrayal that's only an act of ventriloquism.

I found my way through these concerns, and my research became a book, *The Five Percenters: Islam, Hip-Hop, and the Gods of New York.* After receiving my author copies from the publisher, I walked to the Allah School and gave one to its executive director, Allah B, thanking him for all that he had done to help the project, and I assumed that it was the last time that I'd have anything to do with the Five Percenters.

It didn't work out that way. As my book circulated throughout the community, and Five Percenters wrote to me to share their thoughts, I became even more immersed in the culture than I had been while doing formal interviews and research. We'd get to talking history and the lessons, and my responses often gave the impression that I had crossed the line between reporter and convert. Our dialogues would eventually turn from my writing project to my personal views. *Based on your study of the lessons, how do you see yourself?* I've been asked more than once. *Are you the Devil? God? A Muslim?* It hit me that I didn't know the answer, and also that I cared.

ANTHROPOLOGIST SUSAN FRIEND HARDING describes conversion as a "process of acquiring a specific religious language or dialect."[5] Recounting her fieldwork among Christian fundamentalists, she writes of one pastor's "witnessing" to her as "so intense and strange, yet deceptively plain and familiar, full of complex nuances and pushes and pulls, that I had no time, no spare inner speech, to interpret him consciously, to rework what he said into my own words as he talked."[6] She also reports that growing comfortable with the fundamentalists' unique parlance only made it more difficult for her to maintain outsider status. Intending to remain a noncommitted observer, simply researching the culture and collecting information, she instead found herself personally transformed: "I began to acquire the knowledge and vision and sensibilities, to share the experience, of a believer."[7] Though not a believing Christian, Harding gradually reached a "state of unconscious belief" in which she would "respond to, interpret, and act in the world" as though she were.[8] Harding's entry into the mind of Christian fundamentalism became so thorough that when narrowly escaping a car accident, she heard the voice of God speaking to her. To some extent, whether she wanted it or not, she had been born again.

Stepping into the Five Percent cipher, I drowned in specialized language. When I first began attending parliaments, even purchasing food or merchandise was difficult, as I'd pause to figure out how much I owed a vendor who asked for "wisdom cipher" dollars. Over time, I became familiar enough with the codes to converse and even dream in them, and that's when everything changed. With the learning of a new language, I stepped into another reality.

While my encounter with the Five Percenters influenced my thinking about race and religion, something else happened, something deeper than intellectual positions. I found myself contemplating these issues not only with Five Percenter influence, but in Five Percenter terms, using Five Percenter language. The stories and symbols through which the Five Percent gave its argument became as important as the argument itself; I was starting to view myself and society through a Five Percenter lens. It felt completely natural for me to reflect on the day's date using Supreme Mathematics, or analyze the Qur'ān's stories of Moses through his depiction in the lessons. There were even times when I experienced a deeper emotional resonance with narratives of the former Clarence 13X and his teen gods than with those of the Prophet Muḥammad and his companions. As far removed as I could be from the lives of black men in 1960s Harlem, the history in which Five Percenter culture developed was at least more relatable to my world than the unimaginable setting of premodern Arabia. To stand in front of the Hotel Theresa, where Allah had been arrested, or visit Marcus Garvey Park, where Allah held his first parliament, would affect me as no less than a *pilgrimage*, and gazing upon the Five Percenters' emblem, the Universal Flag, I felt a strong pull on my heart. Reflecting on one element in the contested definition of religion crafted by anthropologist Clifford Geertz—"a system of symbols which act to produce powerful, pervasive, and long-lasting moods and motivations"[9]—I could say that my religion came from Master Fard Muhammad's lessons, the Wu-Tang Clan, sacred algebra that I had learned at the Allah School, and my new righteous name, the name of my teacher. I was becoming Azreal Wisdom in a very real way.

My only advice to researchers attempting fieldwork: keep your guard up and keep your distance. You spend that much time with a culture and fail to check yourself, you'll fall in love and become your subject. On some level, even if I hadn't sorted out all of the doctrinal and social complexities, I was a Five Percenter.

Still a Muslim, I began to experiment with the borders between these traditions. One Friday afternoon, I went into Masjid Malcolm Shabazz (named for Malcolm X, who had been the mosque's minister during its days as a Nation of Islam institution) for Sunnī *jum 'aa* prayer wearing a Five Percenter pin with the former Clarence 13X's portrait and bold caption, "ALLAH," on my jacket. A Muslim asked me about it.

"You ever hear of the Five Percenters?" I replied.

"Oh sure," he said, shaking his head. "I know *all* about those guys. You believe that that man's Allah?"

"I don't pray to him," I said. "It's just his name."

My answer didn't do anything for him. As far as he could see, it was impossible for a man to call himself a Muslim while calling another man Allah, and my Allah pin had sullied the mosque with the worst sin, the worship of created things as the Creator.

"*As-salāmu alaikum,*" I said to him on my way out.

"*Wa alaikum,*" he answered, giving the shortened response that was reserved for unbelievers, making it clear that I was not his brother.

Then I walked ten blocks north, to the Allah School, where a middle-aged black man greeted me with "Peace."

"Peace, god!" I replied.

"Are you Michael Muhammad Knight?" he asked. Must not have been too many white boys showing up at the school.

"True indeed, god."

"So how'd you come to our nation?"

"Well," I told him, "I'm Muslim, and—"

"We're *not* Muslims," the god interrupted. "We're not a religion. We deal in facts, not beliefs." Unfortunately, a statement like "We deal in facts, not beliefs" goes beyond mere religion: it's the language of religious fundamentalists.

"That's peace," I answered, a common Five Percenter affirmation.

"Islam is peace," he said. "The word *islām* only means 'peace.' The word *muslim* means 'one of peace.' Islam's not a religion." I sensed a slight tension between the god's simultaneous rejection of Islam ("We're not Muslims") and claim to ownership of Islam's true message ("Islam's not a religion").

Islām is a Form IV *masdar* (verbal noun), signifying the act of submission or surrender; *muslim* is the active participle, meaning someone who submits or surrenders. Converting the word's *s-l-m* root letters into a Form II masdar would give us *sallim*, "making peace," and the performer of *sallim* would be a *musallim*. Hassles over etymology exposed the theological break between Muslims and Five Percenters. One group based everything on belief in an abstract, immaterial Creator to whom we must *submit;* the other denied that such a being existed, reading Islam instead as a life of *peace.* I could somehow nod my head for both arguments, and each side's concept of the divine gave me something through which I justified my embrace of the other. Each side kept the other in check; Five Percenters guarded my life in the mosque against superstition and dogmatism, and Islam's spiritual dimension guarded my Five Percenter thought from arrogance and materialism. It was the antiprayer Five Percenters who gave me a new way to understand my Muslim prayer, and Islam's concept of *tawhīd*—the absolute unity of God—that empowered me to affirm the Five Percent's declaration "There is no mystery god."

Of course, this would leave neither side satisfied. For most Muslims and Five Percenters, the line dividing these systems was clearly drawn, and everyone had to choose a side and stay on it. After my presentation on Five Percenters at the American Academy of Religion conference, I was confronted by Sherman Jackson, a star in Islamic scholarship and advocate of the "intellectual legacy of the classical Sunnī tradition" as the foundation for African-American Islam. In his work, Jackson gives backhanded respect to the Nation of Islam as a "proto-Islamic" move-ment, comparing it to short-lived sects from the early period that, while straying from the Islam that he would see as legitimate, nonetheless paved the way for orthodoxy. In Jackson's view, the Nation of Islam's only *Islamic* value would be that it prepared African Americans to eventually find Sunnism. For thinkers so grounded in what we'd call "mainstream" Islam, Five Percenters pose a continuing nuisance.

"The Five Percenters don't call themselves Muslims?" he asked.

"Most of them don't," I answered, as a circle of onlookers gathered around us. "Some do, but they're the minority."

"If Five Percenters don't want to be called Muslims, why do they wear the star and crescent?"

"They have an historical attachment to the symbol through the Nation of Islam, and they've produced their own meanings for it—"

"But isn't that going to confuse people?"

"I don't think that anyone's going to change what's meaningful for them," I said. "How others read it isn't really their problem."

Jackson huffed and went on his way. I wonder what he would say about those of us who have regressed from what he'd call "real" Islam to mere "proto-Islam;" I've known several former "mainstream" Mus-lims who are now in the Nation and Five Percent, but Jackson never acknowledges the possibility.

While reading scholar Ebrahim Moosa's work on al-Ghazālī, I found a line that read as a personal warning. In a discussion of the philosopher Ibn Sīna (Avicenna) as the son of a prominent Ismāʿīlī, and the fact that this would have been damaging to Ibn Sīna's credentials in Sunnī circles, Moosa writes, "Affiliation with marginal groups and sects of disrepute could savagely stigmatize a person in the medieval world, as it can today."[10] Five Percenters won't be getting respect from the Sherman Jacksons of the Muslim community any time soon. For me to acknowledge the Five Percent as having something to offer—not only as political consciousness, but my understanding of Islam—would be more than a statement of personal belief. It put me on one side of the line.

THE CATHOLIC THEOLOGIAN Raimon Panikkar once wrote, "I left Europe as a Christian, I discovered I was a Hindu, and returned as a Buddhist without ever having ceased to be Christian."[11] I was starting to understand. Traditions like to imagine that their borders are strictly guarded, allowing nothing to be carried from one side to the other— but the border in my case was only flesh and blood, this body standing between the Sunnī mosque and the Allah School, holding elements of both within myself. Considering that it could be possible to live in two systems (or that I did not have to regard the two systems as separate), I saw myself as a Five Percenter while visiting Ṣūfī shrines in Pakistan, musing on what the Punjab's rebel saints such as Bulleh Shah might have said if they met Harlem's Allah. The Five Percent even stayed with me during my most Muslim Muslim act, my trip to Saudi Arabia for the hajj. Walking my seven circuits around the Kaʾba, I built on each lap using Supreme Mathematics or reciting Rakim lyrics; I even performed an *umrah*, the Mecca portion of pilgrimage, in Azreal's name. I was still a Muslim, but the Five Percenters informed my reading of Muslim-ness. It was largely through the Five Percent that I found the power to take charge of my hajj, deciding its meanings for myself. In

Mecca, I performed rites that centered around stories of Abraham and his family, but I am not convinced that Abraham ever physically existed. Inspired by the Five Percent, I could find value in these stories and rituals without getting spooky—I could run circles around my own mental Ka'ba smashing idols, acting by the Prophet's example but with a Five Percenter thought.

If someone calls me a Five Percenter, I cannot deny it, because I use the Five Percenter tradition as something real and legitimate; but I am also *not* Five Percent, because the gods aren't going to Saudi Arabia or fasting during Ramadan. So that's my weird position, and here's my next book, no longer from an outsider's place nor entirely inside. The original Azreal had told me, "Being Azreal is a lonely thing." All I can really do here is show what works for me, how a white man can get into a black-god movement and a Muslim could build with men who call each other Allah, how I read myself into these texts, and what my absorption into the culture has done for me.

Two more notes: First, the citing of Master Fard Muhammad's Supreme Wisdom Lessons. The Five Percenter version of this scripture is commonly referred to as the "120," for its total number of "degrees." When referring to degrees in a particular lesson, the degree number is given and then followed by the total number of degrees in that lesson. For example: Lost-Found Muslim Lesson No. 1 contains 14 degrees, and if I quoted from the sixth degree, I would cite it as 6:14.

Second, a word of caution. When I write about Allah here, I'm usually referring to Allah the Father, the former Clarence 13X, but on many pages, "Allah" can also refer to something else. Unless quoting text by another author, I distinguish between the two with a diacritical mark: a proper transliteration of the Arabic word for God would be Allāh. When discussing the former Clarence 13X, a non-Arabic speaker who interpreted his name as an acronym for "Arm Leg Leg Arm Head," diacritical marks should not be required; his "Allah" is an English word. Context also helps to keep things clear. If I write, "Allah shook hands with Governor Rockefeller," it should be obvious that I'm not referring to the Allāh who is believed by Muslims to have created the heavens and Earth and revealed the Qur'ān to the Prophet Muḥammad. If I write, "The medieval Sūfī master Ibn al-'Arabī viewed the universe as an overflowing of Allāh's Divine Attributes," the Allāh in question is not a man who was born in 1928. Sorry if this ever gets confusing or offensive, but welcome to my Islam.

TWO

KILL ALL THE WHITE MEN

Who is the Colored Man?
The Colored Man is the Caucasian (whiteman), Yakub's
grafted devil of the planet Earth.

—2:10

THIS IS THE DEGREE as it was given to me. Through decades of oral transmission from one memorizer to the next, along with typographical errors in hard copies, the 120 has evolved in numerous versions. Usually, the differences are just a matter of wording. In the above degree, the variation is a little more serious: the original Nation of Islam text additionally describes the white man as "skunk of the planet earth." Among Five Percenters, debate lingers as to who removed "skunk" from their lessons. A prevailing narrative says that Allah himself had changed the degree as part of his reforms, while some gods keep the "skunk," denying that Allah would go so far as to alter the text.

As the second degree in the initiatory Student Enrollment, "Who is the Colored Man?" could be seen as the second most important truth offered by the lessons. Prior to receiving this degree, the new student learned only that the Original Man was the Asiatic Black Man, "the maker, the owner, cream of the planet Earth, father of civilization, god of the universe." When read together, these first and second degrees flip traditional American paradigms upside down: the black man is God, and the white man is "colored." These words, if sufficiently internalized

by a neophyte, transform everything. By memorizing the degrees, pro-
gramming them into his consciousness, and then traveling his terrain
of Harlem or Brooklyn or Detroit or Chicago, standing tall on the corner when cops passed by, knowing what they were and what he was, the
Student's psyche officially became Enrolled.

> *Walk on water? Nah, neither did Jesus*
> *It's a parable to make followers and readers believers*
> —Rakim, "Holy Are You"[1]

When I engage the idea that white people are devils, it does not
mean that I accept uncritically the myth of racial origins offered by
Master Fard Muhammad, in which a megalomaniacal scientist named
Yakub created pale skin through selective breeding on the Greek
island of Patmos approximately six thousand years ago. My entry
into the lessons does not depend on this being serious history, just as
my being a Muslim does not depend on my literal belief in the Devil
as a fallen angel or jinn. There are Muslims who find genuine value
in stories of the *Shayṭān,* despite choosing to interpret this entity as
a representation of their "lower selves," ego, base desires, and so on,
rather than as a supernatural character. Of course, allegorical readings aren't going to satisfy everyone. When I arrived in Saudi Arabia
for the hajj, government officials at the airport were handing out
booklets that demanded recognition of the Devil as a real creature of
the unseen—what the Five Percent would call a "mystery devil"—on
the threat of our pilgrimage being invalidated. In my personal experience of hajj, this article of faith was not crucial. Stoning the Devil on
my own terms, I did what I could to make the Qur'ān's stories work
for me.

Just as thinkers within the Islamic tradition have read their mythologies in all kinds of ways, you'll find a diversity of Five Percenter
opinions on how to read the lessons; there's not a consensus on the

importance of Yakub's historicity. Some Five Percenters perform ardu-ous research to support the 120's account of racial difference as literal or semiliteral, while others regard the exile of Yakub and his 59,999 fol-lowers to the Aegean Sea as a parable based on the first migration out of Africa, or possibly an allegory for the divisive ideology of white supremacy.

Before finding my own meaning for the Yakub story, I had to define my terms. Pulling apart the concept of "white people," reflecting on where it came from and what it does, I could make sense of Fard's "white devil" without resorting to pseudoscience. While debunking any genetic basis for the white devil, I found a more challenging truth. Even if there was no Yakub, and even if race is not the key to understand-ing every injustice throughout the whole of human history, recognizing whiteness as Satanic gave me something that I could use. The Student Enrollment's second degree tells me something real about my world and how I should respond to it.

FIRST, HERE'S THE non-Yakub explanation for differences in human skin color: the sun builds and destroys. We need enough ultravio-let radiation to produce vitamin D, but not so much that we get skin cancer and die. The balance is achieved by our skin's adaptation. Our prehuman ancestors had light skin, which would have increased their vulnerability to the African sun; their protection was thick body hair, which also provided insulation that actually reduced heat gain. In late Pliocene and early Pleistocene Africa, the appearance of larger bod-ies and longer legs would come with higher activity levels, requiring a more efficient system for heat management: this led to increased density of eccrine sweat glands and the loss of most body hair.[2] The resulting exposure of naked skin to ultraviolet waves forced another adaptation: melanization, the darkening of skin.

It was not only larger torsos and limbs that increased activity but also growing *brains.* Pigmentation was therefore related to the birth of consciousness; becoming black was part of becoming human. "The early members of the genus *Homo,*" writes paleoanthropologist Nina Jablonski, "the ancestral stock from which all humans evolved, were, thus, darkly pigmented."[3] The original members of the human race, the first to conceptualize things like "God" and "ethical responsibility," were black.

Between fifty and one hundred thousand years ago, humans migrated out of eastern Africa, and would eventually cover the globe. Finding themselves in a variety of strange new settings—deserts, rain forests, tropical islands, frozen steppes, and mountain ranges—their bodies adapted. Each new environment favored some genetic traits over others, enabling certain mutations to spread through natural selection. In the high altitudes of Tibet, for example, humans adapted to the thinner air by producing more red blood cells. With the advent of dairy farming in East Africa, the Middle East, and Europe, the lactase gene evolved to assist human digestion of cattle milk.

In colder, darker Europe, humans received less UV radiation than in Africa, and thus synthesized less vitamin D. As opposed to Africans, for whom dark skin offered protection from the sun, Europeans required *more* exposure. As a consequence, the mutation of light skin became advantaged. Anywhere from six to twelve thousand years ago, Europeans lost their pigmentation.

The first light-skinned people did come from dark-skinned people; but in response to the sun, skin can adapt both ways. In the farthest north, where direct solar irradiation and sunlight reflection from the snow caused greater ultraviolet threats, and a fish-heavy diet rich in vitamin D reduced the pressure for depigmentation, the Eskimo-Aleuts evolved darker skin.[4] The skin of unpigmented peoples may undergo further change as global warming introduces a new crisis in UV radiation.[5] By itself, none of this really translates into "god" and "devil." We're getting to that part.

I'm goin' out of my fucking mind, everytime I get around
devils

—Ol' Dirty Bastard, "Rawhide"[6]

BY "DEVILS," I'm speculating that Ol' Dirty Bastard (aka Unique Ason Allah) could mean white people. There are times when being around them also puts me out of my fucking mind.

But what exactly are white people?

From a purely biological perspective, there is no such thing. As the study of population genetics advances, the concept of "race" slowly dies (at least for the scientific community).[7] In the face of our advancing knowledge, race emerges less as a scientific reality and more as a cultural construct, described by Jablonski as "devoid of explanatory power and destructive of human and social relations."[8] That's where "devil" starts to come in.

Going by popular understandings of race, I would be categorized as a white person; but there is no defining genetic trait that I share with all other white people, and no characteristics of white people that cannot be found among nonwhite people.[9] There are people with dark skin and blue eyes, such as Sharbat Gula, the Pashtun refugee in that famous *National Geographic* photo. In the South Pacific, people sometimes have dark skin and blond hair. Some Greeks may have darker skin than some Arabs, but Greeks are universally labeled as "white" today, and Arabs are not as universally "white," though both are classified as "Caucasians." We are not consistent in our terms.

There could perhaps be such things as races if we compared the populations of Norway and Nigeria; but if someone were to walk from Norway to Nigeria, or from France to Mongolia, there's no clear dividing line at which one race ends and another begins. This does not mean that there are no differences between groups of people, but only that our standard definitions of races are, in the words of population geneticist Luigi Luca Cavalli-Sforza, based on "very narrow, essentially incorrect criteria."[10] Populations are real, but races are made up.[11] Within what we consider to be monolithic races exists extraordinary genetic diversity (by far, the greatest diversity is found in Africa, providing more evidence for Africa as the birthplace of humankind). In an area as relatively local as Italy, the map can be broken down according to multiple ancestries: Celtic descent in the north, Greek descent in the south. In the Apennines, we find genetic remnants of ancient populations such as the Etruscans and Ligurians. The eastern half of Sicily still bears genetic witness to Greek colonization, while the western half—which the Greeks had not colonized—hosts descent from Phoenicians, Carthaginians, and other groups. Arabs and sub-Saharan Africans have also contributed DNA. It becomes difficult to imagine a biologically unified "white race" when even a term as specific as "Italian" can be picked apart.[12] According to Cavalli-Sforza, to look at race from a purely genetic perspective could lead to us arranging humans into one million unique categories.[13]

Genetics may explain why the Kalenjin tribe, which comprises only 11 percent of Kenya's population, produces 75 percent of Kenya's elite runners—or why, while East Africans dominate endurance races, runners from West Africa fare better in short-distance races; but it does not give us an answer as simple as "Black people run fast." To betray human diversity by grouping us all into a mere three to five categories, based primarily on traits that are most obvious to the naked eye, just doesn't hold up. The "tree" or "candelabra" model of human diversity, in which distinct races clearly branch off from one another and evolve separately, is not supported by modern science.[14] Science journalist Steve Olson suggests an alternative model: viewing human groups as "more like clouds forming, merging, and dissipating on a hot summer day."[15] With human migrations occurring in numerous waves and directions, there is not, nor has there ever been, a pure race.

Because skin color is an adaptation influenced by environment, it cannot consistently signify relationships between populations.[16] If two indigenous populations share a similar skin color, it tells us that they developed in similar climates; it does not allow us to assume a closely related ancestry. Europeans are genetically closer to Africans and Melanesians than Africans and Melanesians are to each other, despite the fact that Africans and Melanesians share dark skin.[17] Instead of skin color, we could just as easily base our racial classifications on vulnerability to sickle cell anemia. Many Americans regard sickle cell anemia as a disease of black people, though it has nothing to do with complexion. Sickle cell is a risk for those with ancestry from western and central Africa—but not the rest of the continent—and also some non-African populations. Americans only perceive sickle cell as a "black disease" because America's slaves were taken from West Africa. The determining factor is descent from regions in which people evolved certain traits as defenses against malaria.[18] If the likelihood of sickle cell was used to define a "race" this race would include not only western and central Africans but also Greeks, Italians, Turks, and Indians.[19]

So race does not exist, and the term "white people" doesn't hold much currency for scientists. But I still say that there are white people, and I say that white people are devils. Looking back at exactly how, when, and *why* white people arrived, it's not hard to see why they should be taken off the planet.

WHILE RACE AND RACISM are understood to be inventions of modern Europe, what has been called "proto-racism" existed in the ancient world.[20] Before race existed as a biological concept, alterity was understood through a dichotomy of "civilized" and "barbarian" communities.[21] In ancient Mesopotomia, this dualism contrasted sedentary urban life with pastoral nomadism; civilization was equated with the city and its social order, the stability of which was under constant threat from the wandering, unsettled peoples beyond its outer limits.[22] Local nomads, having never been taught to properly worship gods or perform rituals, were seen as far more "alien" than civilized urban dwellers from far-off lands.[23] Among the nomads were Amorites, the subjects of unflattering descriptions in Babylonian texts:

> He eats raw meat,
>> Lives his life without a home,
>>> And, when he dies, he is not buried according to proper ritual.[24]

The region was known as the "Land of the Black-Headed People," though neither its urban nor its pastoral peoples have been identified with exclusive ethnic or linguistic groups.[25] It has not been demonstrated that the Amorites were bound by common religion, language, or physical traits; some have argued that the name, deriving from a word meaning "western," was simply a blanket term for "other."[26] In modern times, the identification of ancient Amorites with white people would persist in various Afrocentric discourses, most famously the Ansaru Allah Community/Nubian Islamic Hebrews that had a strong presence in mid-1980s Brooklyn. This may help with comprehension of 1990's "The Originators," in which a young Jay-Z says, "Amorites just can't understand the groove we're in."[27]

THE APPEARANCE OF systematic abstract thought in Greek civilization is said to have been accompanied by the world's first systematized notions of supremacy over other groups.[28] Greek proto-racism developed from belief that a people's shared characteristics—not only physical but mental and spiritual—were determined by environment. For someone to have physical traits associated with people from a certain geographical region would lead to the assumption that s/he also possessed corresponding psychological traits—even if s/he had not come

from that region. Historian Benjamin Isaac provides an example: if
Egyptians were assumed to have tightly curled hair and be "cunning"
in nature, a Greek person who happened to have tightly curled hair was
also presumed to be cunning.[29] The importance given to environment
in a people's national character led Greeks and Romans to believe that
certain regions—naturally, their own—were better than others at producing rulers. Likewise, they regarded some peoples, such as the Persians, to be natural slaves. And with that, we find a logic for conquest.[30]

  With the soul of a nation held to be connected to its local geography,
admixture with peoples from other regions was regarded as destructive. The Celts were viewed as a degenerated people for having migrated
from their original home and mixed with others. The Athenians, imag-
ining themselves to possess an unmixed, uncorrupted lineage, viewed
their position as superior to peoples of impure descent, even other
Greeks. Their self-image came close to what we would consider a race
today, and would influence later European thought on human divisions.[31]

  It has been suggested that the word "race" derives from the Latin
generatio ("generation" or "begetting"), or perhaps from the French
haras, meaning "stud farm."[32] The earliest known attempt at modern
racial science, published in 1684 by a French physician to a Mughal
emperor, divided humanity into four categories. The first race included
Europeans, North Africans, some Southeast Asians, and Native Americans. The second category consisted of black Africans. His third race
included the Chinese, Semitic peoples of the Fertile Crescent and Levant,
inhabitants of the Caucasus region and central Asia, and "Muscovy," the
area surrounding Moscow; this category was described as "truly white,"
but differed from the first through other characteristics. The fourth race
was reserved for the ambiguous Sami/Lapps.[33]

  The biblically rooted account of human diversity—that Noah's three
sons each fathered a race after the flood—would influence science to
adopt a three-race model, dividing humanity between Caucasians,
Negroids, and Mongoloids. Racial science eventually provided its

own opportunities for transcendent origins, as European Orientalists projected their own prejudices upon "soft facts" in the Rig Veda
to imagine ancient Aryans as their ethnogenesis.[34] According to one
theory, the Aryans had originated in the Caucasus region before split-
ting off into two separate subgroups: the "Hindus" and a second branch
from which peoples such as the Celts, Teutons, Italians, Greeks, and
Persians would emerge. Another argument supposed that the Aryans
had first appeared in the Himalayas and followed a westward migration that would lead to the founding of civilizations in India, Egypt,
and Europe.[35] "These scholars lived at a time when European imperialism dominated the world," writes historian Burjor Avari, and they
became consumed with understanding what they viewed as their own
superiority.[36]

Interpreting language as the mark of racial difference, Orientalists
depicted members of the Indo-Aryan language family as light-skinned
bearers of civilization who triumphed in a race war with dark-skinned
and "savage" Dravidians. As these myths developed in nineteenth-
century Germany (alongside ideas that Jews were a distinct and inferior non-Aryan race[37]) and found a political value in racially segregated
America, it was believed that Aryan invaders had established India's
caste system as a guard against race mixing.[38] Such theories falsely
assumed that both ancient Aryans and modern high-caste Indians were
light-complexioned and thus easily distinguished from non-Aryans.[39]
The study of linguistics does provide evidence of ancient migrations,
but the idea of a blond-haired, blue-eyed Aryan "race" ruling India has
been dismissed as the fantasy of nineteenth-century Europeans.[40] Avari
describes the Aryans as neither white supremacists nor the founders of
Indian civilization, but merely "nomadic and pastoral migrants from
Afghanistan, some with an inflated sense of self-esteem."[41]

According to Benjamin Franklin, "The number of purely white people in the world is proportionately very small." It was even smaller in
his time than in ours, as he considered the vast majority of Europeans

too "swarthy" to make the cut.[42] Disqualified from Franklin's white race were Spanish, Italian, French, Russian, Swedish, and German (except for Saxon) peoples. Only the Saxons and English comprised "the principal Body of the White People on the Face of the Earth. I could wish their numbers were increased."[43]

Unfortunately for Franklin, a substantial number of the undesirables shipped to America were Irish Catholics.[44] In the first century of America's independence, the Anglo-Saxon power would be swimming in swarth, receiving millions of immigrants; most came from famine-stricken Ireland and Germany. These Europeans arrived at a time when America was working to define its whiteness. As the young republic held slaves, fought a war against itself over slaves, denied social equality to its freed slaves, annihilated indigenous peoples in the name of "Manifest Destiny," and waged war in Mexico, it also faced the issue of what to do with people who were—in the view of that time—*kind of white*. Europe was still seen as home to numerous races, with some privileged over others. In the second half of the 1800s, when people talked about the "English race" and "Anglo-Saxon race," the Irish were mentioned along with "cross-bred" Germans and French as "the most degenerate races of olden day Europe . . . human flotsam."[45] Italians were of "even more doubtful stock."[46]

In the Civil War years, America's leading advocates for a unified "white race" were pro-slavery Northerners who looked to Irish immigrants for support, claiming that liberation movements for black slaves had been funded on the backs of Irish toil and suffering.[47] Irish immigrants picked up the banner of white supremacy on both sides of the Mason-Dixon Line, as the Irish community in the South widely supported slavery and the Confederacy.[48] In California, Irish Americans also joined in white attacks against Chinese immigrants. These agitations culminated in a race-based immigration law, 1882's Chinese Exclusion Act, but mob expulsions of Chinese immigrants from their homes and jobs continued even after the law was passed.[49] With the promise of entry into white power, the white ruling class persuaded the Irish underclass to do much of its dirty work.

At the turn of the twentieth century, various European groups were still excluded from American whiteness. In 1891, eleven Italians were lynched in New Orleans. In a letter to the *Washington Post*, a resident of Brazos County, Texas, insisted that whites and blacks in the area got along so well, the county's black people remained confident that white landlords would never "supplant them with other races"—a reference to the Italians, whose racial identity remained unclear, especially in the South.[50] The Democratic Party in Brazos County limited its 1904 primary to white men, specifying that "white" excluded not only black people but also Mexicans and Italians.[51] Consequently, Italian anarchists and socialists identified more with African Americans. "Who do they think they are, these arrogant whites?" asked *Il Proletario*, official newspaper of the Italian Socialist Federation, in 1909. "From where do they think they come?" For working-class Italian revolutionaries, the key to justice was "not race struggle but class struggle," a uniting of oppressed peoples of all colors against the ruling class.[52]

Ultimately, in a society divided into two classes—lynchers and lynched—European immigrants found it more desirable to side with the unjust power than the resistance against it. By participating in the subjugation of non-Europeans, questionable European groups were able to become white. In *Lynching to Belong*, an examination of Brazos County during this period, historian Cynthia Skove Nevels provides evidence that Italian, Irish, and Czech immigrants achieved assimilation into whiteness in part by joining organized white violence against black people.

SINCE 1790, the United States had allowed only "free white persons" to become citizens; in the twentieth century, as non-European immigrants applied for citizenship, it became the responsibility of the courts to set limits upon whiteness. George Dow, a Syrian immigrant, was denied eligibility for citizenship on the basis that geography defined race: to be white was to be European. Dow managed to win an appeal, demonstrating that Syrians were indeed members of the white race.[53] In 1922, a Japanese immigrant named Takao Ozawa argued that he should be considered a white person because his skin was literally white, asserting that many Japanese people were "whiter than the average Italian, Spaniard or Portuguese."[54] His case would go all the way to the Supreme Court, which rejected his claim to citizenship and the idea that race could be determined by skin tone: "To adopt the color test alone would result in a confused overlapping of races and a gradual merging of one into the other, without any practical line of separation."[55] Turning to the science of the day, the Court ruled that "the words 'white person' are synonymous with the words 'a person of the Caucasian race.'" Since Ozawa was not a Caucasian, he could not be white.[56]

Only three months later, in the case of an Indian immigrant named Bhagat Singh Thind, the Supreme Court betrayed its *Ozawa* ruling and declared that while all whites were Caucasian, not all Caucasians were white. Scientists classified Thind as undeniably Caucasian, but the Court insisted that "white" must mean something more: "It may be true that the blond Scandinavian and the brown Hindu have a common ancestor in the dim reaches of antiquity, but the average man knows perfectly well that there are unmistakable and profound differences between them today."[57] To prove his purity, Thind invoked the Aryanist myth of ancient white conquerors setting up the caste system to preserve their race. "The high-class Hindu," he argued, "regards the aboriginal Indian Mongoloid in the same manner as the American regards the negro."[58] Regardless, the man they called "Hindoo Thind" (who was actually a Sikh) was denied citizenship. Within the category of "Caucasian," the Court noted, one could find a wide range of peoples, including South Asians, Polynesians, and even "the Hamites of Africa, upon the ground of their Caucasic cast of features, though in color they range from brown to black."[59] For reasons not clearly articulated, the Court decided that Thind was not white, and therefore not eligible for acceptance by the white empire. In the wake of the ruling, many Indian immigrants were stripped of their U.S. citizenship, while the *San Francisco Chronicle* applauded the end of "the menacing spread of Hindus holding our lands."[60]

That the Supreme Court could reject a white-skinned Japanese man because he was not Caucasian, and a brown-skinned Caucasian because he was not white, reveals what race has always been: an unscientific and inconsistent means of enforcing social inequality in the name of an impossible purity. In the *Thind* ruling, the Court said so itself: "What we now hold is that the words 'free white persons' are words of common speech, to be interpreted in accordance with the understanding of the common man, synonymous with the word 'Caucasian' only as that word is popularly understood."[61] In other words, whiteness was whatever white people said it was, and nothing more. White people were a figment of their own imagination.

The half century or so between the American Civil War and the White Civil War (World War I) also saw the rise of eugenics, represented in America by groups like the American Breeder's Association and the Immigration Restriction League. Eugenics had even received support from Theodore Roosevelt, who proclaimed the duty of the "good citizen of the right type" to pass on his or her genes. In 1924, the passing of the Johnson-Reed Act, which reformed immigration quotas based on theories of "racial hygiene" to privilege Anglo-Saxons and completely prohibit Asian and Indian immigration, helped to further the idea of "monolithic whiteness."[62] In support of the Johnson-Reed Act, one eugenicist would insist before Congress that the American people, "if they are to remain American," should assimilate "many thousands of Northwestern European immigrants.... But we can assimilate only a small fraction of this number of other white races; and of the colored races practically none."[63] Eugenics found favor with the scientific establishment of its time, as medical journals published articles such as "Eugenics in Ancient Greece," describing Sparta's systematized infanticide as an "advance towards civilization."[64] By 1928, eugenics was endorsed in high school textbooks and nearly four hundred college courses across the United States.

It was upon this America that Master Fard Muhammad would arrive. The United States was a breeding experiment guided by bad science; with his Yakub narrative, Fard would only flip the bad science and its discourses upside down to speak for the oppressed rather than the oppressor. In Fard's mirror of eugenics mythology, selective breeding in ancient Greece produced not a noble race, but only savage beasts who would conquer and enslave the Earth. Yakub's Patmos is America itself, the strange island of exile that created white people as we now know them.

Like Bhagat Singh Thind, Fard was among the roughly 6,400 South Asian immigrants to arrive in the United States by 1920.[65] There is reason to believe that he was born near the present Afghanistan-Pakistan border. He could have come in the early waves of men sent by their families to find jobs in America, many of whom married Mexican women, creating a unique hybrid culture in southern California. As the Thind case demonstrates, Fard's racial identity was not easily defined. In his liminal position, Fard could travel among all spheres of American life, changing his name at least fifty times, presenting himself at one point as a native of New Zealand, and shifting between white and black. After experiencing life in America's racial hierarchy, which included a stint at San Quentin as a convicted drug dealer, he journeyed to Detroit with a mission to destroy the white race as it was "popularly understood."

Several years before Fard's appearance in Detroit, a religio-political movement led by a South Carolina migrant had taken root in Chicago. The movement's founder, a slave's son calling himself Noble Drew Ali, proclaimed that he was a prophet sent to restore African Americans to their lost "Moorish" citizenship—which would be accompanied by a spiritual birth in their natural religion, "Islamism." Legend depicts Noble Drew Ali and Woodrow Wilson in the basement of the White House, retrieving old banners from a safe until finding the flag of Morocco, upon which the prophet exclaimed to the president, "That's our flag!" The Moorish Science Temple's distribution of "national names" and "passports" to members may reveal how its prophet had considered the increasing success of European immigrants. White people were Italians, Germans, Czechs, Poles, and Hungarians, each group boasting its own banner and language; even if these groups had not yet fully assimilated into American whiteness, the racial hierarchy still placed them above black people, who were viewed simply as nationless "Negroes." For Noble Drew Ali, the answer was to uplift African Americans with their own nationality, to provide a flag that would make them not merely "black" but properly ethnic. He might have misjudged the situation: what would help European immigrants was not their distinctive nationalities, but the ability to shed their distinctiveness and blend into the white race. Despite the eugenicists' best efforts to keep white power properly Nordic, a drastic transformation was taking place in America: Anglo-Saxon supremacy was fading fast, to be replaced by pan-white supremacy.[66] Racial science came to endorse "probationary white groups" such as Celts, Slavs, Greeks, and Hebrews as full-fledged members of whiteness.[67]

The merging of probationary groups into full whiteness was largely influenced by the mass migration of African Americans from Southern states into the North. The migrants included not only Noble Drew Ali but also the future Elijah Muhammad, his wife, Clara, and their children, who arrived in Detroit from rural Georgia in 1923. These shifting demographics and the rise of black Civil Rights movements led Europeans to come together on the basis of what they were not, that is, the descendents of African slaves. Aryanism's horrific climax in Nazi Germany wasn't enough to make white Americans discard racism altogether, but it at least inspired them to rethink ethnic prejudice.[68]

Denouncing the idea of an Aryan "master race," white people saw themselves as "equally superior." The amalgamation of European peoples into a single American whiteness would prove so successful that in 1960, Benjamin Franklin's nightmare materialized with the election of a Celtic president. While John F. Kennedy's Catholicism became a point of controversy, no one doubted his good standing in the white race.

"CAUCASIAN" REMAINS A WORD of choice when people want their theories on race to sound scientific and intellectually mature, perhaps because its historical ugliness doesn't fully match that of "Aryan." The term originated in 1795 with Johann Friedrich Blumenbach, who argued that the area around Mount Caucasus produced "the most beautiful race of men."[69] Basing his racial categories on aesthetics, Blumenbach held the Caucasian race to be physically identifiable by "that kind of appearance which . . . we consider most handsome and becoming."[70] His vision of the Caucasians expanded beyond the Caucasus region to include "the inhabitants of Europe (except the Sami/Lapps and the remaining descendents of the Finns) and those of Eastern Asia, as far as the river Obi, the Caspian Sea and the Ganges; and lastly, those of Northern Africa."[71]

The 120 describes white devils as Caucasian, though virtually all of the theories assigned to Master Fard's identity—Indian, Arab, Turkish, Persian—could be used to qualify the Master as Caucasian himself. Elijah Muhammad depicted Fard as half-Caucasian, the son of a black man and white woman from the Caucasus Mountains. Fard's mother, the Apostle claimed, had undergone a spiritual purification prior to his conception. By the 1930s, when Fard and his student compiled the lessons, "Caucasian" was growing in acceptance as a scientific term; in using this word to answer Fard's question "Who is the Colored Man?" Elijah Muhammad was only using the language of his day.

While there is no such thing as a Caucasian race, there are Caucasian peoples—approximately fifty distinct ethnic groups—so named
for where they live. The 170,000-square-mile Caucasus region, which
includes the Caucasus Mountains, Chechnya, Dagestan, Georgia, Azerbaijan, and Armenia, has for centuries been a borderland between identities: East and West, Asia and Europe, Islam and Christianity. Though
the Caucasians were once seen as paragons of racial purity, their blood
is a place of intersection, hosting the genetic legacies of Mongols, Huns,
Arabs, Turks, and Persians.[72] At one time a battlefield between Muslim
empires, the Caucasus would experience increasing Russian presence
and influence from the sixteenth century onward. Around the time
that Blumenbach coined his term, the North Caucasus was culturally
fragmented, and the Russians made their military advances.[73] Mansur
Ushurma, a Sūfī *shaykh* from Chechnya, managed to bring the region's
diverse groups together in a "holy war against the Russians."[74] Despite
the eventual Russian takeover, Islam would survive as a form of resistance.[75] Islamic revolts against Russian power continued into the Soviet
era, resisting the USSR's efforts to whiten the Caucasus through Russian
settlements, mass deportation, and attempts to undermine Islam.[76]

As it always turns out with race, the Caucasians' whiteness depended
upon the political position from which one viewed them. In the early
to mid-twentieth century, as the concept of a "Caucasian race" gained
ground in Europe and America, Soviet scientists chose to categorize
Caucasians—the *actual* Caucasians, as in people from the Caucasus—
as a racial group distinct from Slavic Russians, who joined other "true"
white people in what they preferred to call the "Europeoid" race.[77] In
the later twentieth century, the perceived racial difference between
Caucasians and "white" Russians would factor into the country's new
identity crisis: the fact that if we judge by the map alone, Russia is obviously an Asian country, spanning from the edge of Europe to Mongolia
and Japan.

During the Cold War, Russia's geography was used against it in propaganda designed to "Asianize" communism.[78] Eastern Europeans under Soviet rule commonly depicted the USSR as an alien, Asiatic oppressor; in 1989, Estonian politician Tiit Made suggested that the psychological essence of the Soviet Union was rooted in Mongol invasions from centuries earlier, during which Asian men raped countless Russian women.[79] Pulling the empire westward, Mikhail Gorbachev complained of attempts to exclude the USSR from "Europe, our common home."[80] After the Soviet Union's collapse, the foreign minister of the newly independent Ukraine compared his own "wholly European country" to the "Eurasian" Russia.[81]

As Russia struggled to define itself in the post–Cold War years, people from the Caucasus were increasingly referred to as "black." The term had already been in use for generations to describe Russians with dark skin, and was said to originally carry no negative racial connotation.[82] In the 1990s, however, amidst "changing ideas about Europe's boundaries, and Russia's debates and anxieties concerning its 'Europeanness,'" Slavic Russians were able to understand themselves as fully white through opposition to the "black" and "Asiatic" Chechens, Georgians, Armenians, and Dagestanis.[83] "When these blacks rape your daughters," exclaimed a Russian police officer in 1994, after an incident of paratrooper brutality upon dark-skinned Caucasians, "you'll be complaining. Let these guys sort them out."[84] American history, anyone?

During the chaos of post–Soviet Russia, Chechens rose up against their occupiers and declared independence. Russia did its best to squash the liberation of its occupied peoples, but the war has never really ended. The Caucasus region, home of the Asiatic White Man, tells a long tale of invasion, colonialism, assimilation, marginalization, exile, and revolt. As a place of linguistic and religious mash-ups, it makes a fitting origin for Fard's mother. Though full of bloodshed, the history of the Caucasus reads like a satire, pointing to the absurdity of our divisions. In one of racism's more astounding mindfucks, the only people in the world who can rightfully be called "Caucasians" are not considered "white" by their neighbors.

THERE'S STILL ONE BETTER: the case of Sandra Laing, who was born in 1950s South Africa to parents who were not only white but apartheid supporters in the National Party. She had two brothers, one older and one younger, both of whom looked "white." Sandra, however, looked "black"; apparently, one of her parents carried the genetic heritage of a distant African ancestor. So what was Sandra's natural race—that of her immediate family or this long-lost contributor to her DNA? Apartheid answered the question, as the South African government classified her as "Colored." In racism's all-time astounding mindfuck, Sandra Laing was found to be of a different race than her biological parents.

This brings us back to the problem of definitions; if not the Caucasians or the daughter of two apartheid supporters, who's really white? Noel Ignatiev, editor of the famed *Race Traitor* journal, defined white people as "those who partake of the privileges of white skin in this society."[85] With recognition of race as an artificial and unstable construction, Ignatiev argues that people are not privileged because of whiteness, but rather marked as white because they are privileged.[86] Sandra Laing was white in one sense, because her parents were white; but she was also not white, because she did not derive social, political, or economic benefit from her whiteness.

With whiteness defined by access to privilege, the story of Yakub may find new meanings as social contexts change. Shifting economic and political conditions periodically open and close the gates of the devil's kingdom, inviting people into whiteness or forcing them out. Ignatiev's book on this dynamic, *How the Irish Became White*, has influenced similarly titled works such as *How the Jews Became White Folks* and *Are the Italians White?* As race relations in America continue to evolve, and immigration causes the intersection of race and class to grow even more complicated, racism doesn't die; it adapts, as it has always done. As Walter Benn Michaels suggests, the time will soon come for *How the Asians Became White*. Though the political climate damages the immigrant Muslim community's prospects for full whiteness, it also has higher economic and educational attainments than the national average. I've had dinner conversations with wealthy South Asian Americans who, though still brown enough to taste the injustices in U.S. foreign policy, FBI mistreatment of Muslims, Islamophobic media hysteria, and reports of anti-Islamic hate crimes, transform instantly into arch-conservatives when discussion turns to issues such as health care, economic reform, or black people; perhaps *How the Desis Became White* is next.

What the white race truly marks is separation from humanity. White people do not exist, and white culture does not exist. We could speak of French culture or Appalachian culture, London culture or Boston culture, but where is *white* culture? Taking white people from rural Kentucky and depositing them in Berlin, I don't imagine a seamless assimilation. Nor can I see white Mormons in Utah and white secular humanists in Sweden, or poor white people and rich white people anywhere, as occupying the same culture. I am a white man, but is my culture white? On my father's side, descended from the Pennsylvania Dutch, I'm white; my mother's side, predominantly Irish Catholic, has been white for nearly a century; but I'm not sure what aspects of "white culture" I could pass down to my heirs. If my wife and I had children, I would not be qualified to teach them about kilts, Anabaptists, Irish beer, Vienna sausage, Vatican II, Mozart, Bono, NASCAR or whatever my heritage is supposed to be. I do know a great deal about professional wrestling, so perhaps that counts.

If your culture's preservation requires conscious effort, it has nothing to do with your biology; culture itself cannot be white or black. "We don't worry," writes Walter Benn Michaels, "that a child whose genetic heritage has destined him to be tall will, surrounded by short people, be assimilated into shortness."[87] When racial separatists talk about white culture, they mean white power. The preservation of white culture only means the maintenance of a social order in which white people rule over nonwhite people, whatever those terms mean in a particular setting.

For about as long as whiteness has ruled America, white people have been speculating on a future racial apocalypse: the day that they are no longer the majority. Efforts to push back this future have directed legislation, religion, immigration, and sex, but the final hour belongs to God. The end of the world as white people know it has now drawn near enough that devils can officially start freaking out, and they have. In 2008, the defenders of whiteness began to lose their minds with the growing recognition that a black family could move into the White House. Election-time ugliness about Barack Obama's birth certificate and alleged secret Islam—the same old racism, now sanitized in talk of citizenship and religion—would persist into his presidency, while New Yorkers protested against the so-called Ground Zero Mosque, a Florida pastor planned a "Burn the Qur'ān Day," and Arizona passed legislation that essentially required all brown people to carry identification. White America has started to look like a wounded and rabid animal, foaming at the mouth, half-blind and diseased in the brain, backed into a corner and gnashing its sharp teeth at whatever comes close. That sick dog will only get meaner and crazier until it's finally put down.

Do you need me to ask who the devil is?
—Jeru the Damaja, "Scientifical Madness"[88]

UNDERSTANDING WHAT MAKES a white person a devil is easier than understanding what makes a white person a white person. If the "white race" is only a social construct developed by power relations, designed to create and enforce inequality and undeserved privilege, what do you call someone who lives in that privilege? A god named C'BS ALife Allah once remarked that while much attention has been paid to slavery's psychological impact on the descendents of slaves, we haven't really considered its effect on the descendents of slave*owners*. This is what we call "white privilege." Not only do white people benefit from whiteness in every aspect of life; they are taught from birth that this is the normal, natural condition. Five Percenters commonly refer to such culturations as "pins and needles," referencing Yakub's nurses who murdered black babies by stabbing them in the brains. White supremacy plants its pins and needles deep into a child's head, writing every script for how that child will deal with the world. The "bad faith of whiteness," in the words of philosopher Robert E. Birt, is the "self-deception of the privileged."[89]

"Ask a fish what water is," writes antiracist activist Tim Wise, "and you'll get no answer.... When water surrounds you every minute of the day, explaining what it is becomes impossible."[90] Perhaps if a fish spent thirty-five to fifty years on the project, such advanced mindfulness could be attained. The shit's in white people so deep, a white person who vehemently despises white supremacy may still be acting it out. We don't even know what we're doing when we do it. Maybe I'm being a devil right now.

I can find accidental traces of white privilege in my work. In my travelogue, *Blue-Eyed Devil: A Road Odyssey Through Islamic America*, I recount an episode in which I was wandering through Chicago's South Side, having just visited a historically significant Ahmadiyya mosque. A fire truck pulled over, and its driver—whom I described in the book as an "archetypal old Irish fireman"—called out to me.

"Where are you coming from?" he asked.

"Buffalo, New York," I answered. The driver immediately told me to get in the truck. He assured me that this was the worst section of Chicago, and I wouldn't have lasted much longer.

"We'd rather pick you up now," he said, "than ten minutes from now."[91]

He dropped me off safely in Chinatown. That afternoon, I only attributed my rescue to the mystery god; but reading the passage today, I can see what happened. Though I was scruffy, unwashed, and dressed shabbily, *something* told this firefighter that I did not belong in the bad part of town. That's white privilege: I don't have to present myself as a member of the ruling class to be treated like one.

I wasn't a devil by conscious choice, just the opposite: I had failed to be conscious, even when writing a book that was largely about race, even with *Blue-Eyed Devil* for a title. What was "devil" about the situation was that it would take me nearly five years to realize that perhaps the firefighter's kindness had something to do with my whiteness. "Being white," said James Baldwin, "means never having to think about it."[92]

Can you reform him devil?

No. All the prophets have tried to reform him but were unable. So they have agreed that it cannot be done unless we graft him back into the original man which takes six hundred years. So instead of losing time grafting him back, they have decided to take him off the planet—who numbers only one to every eleven original people.

—34:40

FOR NERVOUS WHITE PEOPLE, the 120 reads as a manifesto for race war. I've heard Five Percenters read the lessons as simply pointing to self-sufficiency: rather than waste time trying to enlighten white people, black people should focus on making positive change in their own communities. In my personal dialogue with 34:40, I remember that I am not the addressee of the question "Can you reform him devil?" The degree was not meant for my eyes; Master Fard asks the black man whether I'm worth his time, and the answer is no. Responsibility for my salvation falls upon me alone.

Ignatiev brought on a firestorm of controversy in the 1990s when he issued a proclamation that sounds like 34:40: "The key to solving the social problems of our age is to abolish the white race."[93] For those who thought of race as something that occurs in nature, he appeared to be calling for physical genocide. The white race, however, is more like a political party, based on a fiction that becomes real when enough people believe in it: "the white race must have the support of all those it has designated as its constituency, or it ceases to exist."[94] Because race is not scientific but ideological, the destruction of a race could be achieved in part by a transformation of its members' consciousness. What if legions of white people followed Tim Wise in declaring, "It's time to revoke the privileges of whiteness," and actually carried out that revocation in their personal and political lives?[95] How long would whiteness or white people continue to exist?

As a white reader of 34:40, informed by Ignatiev and Wise, I interpret the degree for use in my cipher: the part of myself that is called "white" cannot be redeemed. To affiliate with whiteness is to claim unjust privilege. Other than recognition of the fact that I have benefited from this inequality—that the social effects of racism are real even if race itself is not—I can derive no moral good from the word. In the words of Ignatiev, "Treason against whiteness is loyalty to humanity."

I was forced to confront 34:40 when my father passed away; my father had not only identified himself as a white man, but treasured whiteness as the essence of his being. His primary sources of information on race were his Appalachian upbringing, his military service, and his travels through the culture of outlaw motorcycle clubs, in which white supremacy runs wild. Meeting my father at fifteen, I heard the word "nigger" out of his mouth within the first hour that I knew him.

My father had made his own path in the world, and I made mine.

When he died, his path of whiteness came to an end, because his son chose not to continue it. My father personified the devil in more than one sense, but he has no one to claim that inheritance, so the devil is taken off the planet. The reward for his destruction, according to the 120: "peace and happiness."

During one of my visits to the Allah School, I told Allah B about my family history—not only my racist father, but an ancestry of Confederate captains and likely slaveowners. I told Allah B that I understood what it meant to be born a devil, and asked him what "knowledge of self" would mean for me. Allah B looked me in the eyes and told me that if I turned my back on white supremacy and lived in righteousness, I could not be called a devil.

When Allah marched with John Lindsay after Martin Luther King, Jr.'s assassination, he is said to have announced that the devil is taken off the planet when he chooses to walk hand in hand with God. That's how I made sense of the Yakub story. It's not about a mad scientist from six thousand years ago; proving or disproving that white people were created by selective breeding proves nothing. White people are devils not because of their origin or skin color but because of the meaning that they have given to whiteness and what this meaning has achieved in the world. When I discussed Yakub with Dorothy Blake Fardan, a seventy-one-year-old white woman who identifies as a follower of Elijah Muhammad, she told me: "I'm okay with the story of Yakub being true, and I'm okay with it being not true. The results are the same."

Trying to make sense of our American disease, I found Yakub to work as well as anything. As a mythical rationale for human evil, the story of a eugenics regime on Patmos was clearly an oversimplification; but oversimplifications could allow us to do our own work toward producing a myth's substance. The myth becomes more true when we have to add on, filling in the gaps ourselves. When Master Fard Muhammad told Elijah that white people were devils, it wasn't really new information for him; at just ten years old, Elijah had witnessed the lynching of a friend by whites. Rather, Fard used Yakub to trigger Elijah's more profound understandings of what Elijah already knew. "Real" or not, the Yakub narrative would do the same for countless gods, including a convict at Charlestown State Prison named Malcolm Little—who, after first hearing that white people were devils, imagined all of the white people that he had ever known: white social workers, white teachers, white cops, white judges, white women and men looking for "exotic" black sex, white prison guards, and the faceless white people who killed his father and institutionalized his mother. The myth of Yakub would also speak to some devils for whom this world has forced our signatures upon Fard's lessons.

THREE

WONDERBREAD GODS

*I know when I said I was Allah, the Mus—the whole
world was what? Against me. I don't care. And now
they really against me because I'm not anti-white nor
pro-black. They really against me because everybody
is against the white. Well, let me show you something.
Who is man if he ain't man? Tell me. So this is up to
you to make your country what? God. It's up to you
and if you don't teach the young right, you not hurting
me, you hurting yourself. . . . Anybody can be a Five
Percenter, white, I don't care who they are, can be a
Five Percenter. Because a Five Percenter is one that is
civilized.*

—Allah[1]

I'M NOT THE FIRST white person to have a relationship with the Five Percenters; there's no telling how many came before me. As far back as 1967,
while Allah was teaching Azreal at Matteawan State Hospital for the Criminally Insane, white kids on the streets of New York were encountering the
120 through black friends. In the Bronx, Hakiem (the future Allah B) had a
white student named Barkim. After his release, Allah said that he regarded
Barry Gottehrer and Sid Davidoff, two white City Hall officials who had
worked with him on behalf of Mayor Lindsay, as Five Percenters. In the
years since Allah's assassination, there have been occasional appearances

of white participants, referred to as "Muslim Sons and Daughters," "death angels," or "culture seeds," and it's generally a tense position. Allah said that whites could be Five Percenters, but did not define what exactly this meant for them—at least not in a recorded statement that has survived to our time. We have been left to figure it out for ourselves.

By recognizing that white people are devils, the white Five Percenter can be less of a devil than other whites, and for many black gods, not a devil at all. Near the end of his life, Elijah Muhammad even said, "You do not disrespect people that are trying to respect you. . . . It's time for us to stop calling white folks the devil."[2] It's a reasonable next step to then ask, "If I'm not a devil, what am I?" which inevitably leads to the white Five Percenter's confrontation of black godhood and another question: Can the children of devils come in Allah's Name?

INTERPRETING THE WHITE DEVIL as a cultural product worked for my own knowledge of self; but for many Five Percenters, the truth of gods and devils is found in genetics. Rather than critically examining the social invention of "race," they build on the assumptions of America's lingering miscegenation drama—the "one drop" view that a person can only have one racial identity, and that a person who does not appear entirely white must be marked as entirely nonwhite. Originating in slaveowner ideology, these assumptions persist today, and have been reread by Five Percenters to value blackness as biologically superior and inherently divine: the black man is God because weak white people came from dominant black people, but a black person cannot come from white parents.

> White man, black woman: black baby
> Black man, white woman: black baby
> —Public Enemy, "Fear of a Black Planet"[3]

THERE'S NO MEANS by which one can scientifically test this, because terms like "black" and "white" are not scientific to begin with. As skin color, eye color, hair texture, and facial features don't add up to equal racial difference until society interprets them as such, they lose their power to represent "god" or "devil" in any sense that could be more real than the symbolic power assigned to them by social forces. However, I say this with recognition that the social forces do matter. "Interbreeding between light and dark skin color phenotypes produces offspring of intermediate pigmentation," writes Jablonski;[4] but if society defines this intermediate pigmentation as "black," then it's black. The notion that my child is less "me" if s/he does not share my complexion is only true if I personally believe it to be true; but white people have in fact believed it, to the extent that slaveowners could make new products to sell simply by raping their slaves into pregnancy.

While dividing humanity into only three to five races can get messy enough, it gets messier. The 120 parts the entire species into two categories, "Original" and "Colored": the Colored people are whites, and the Original people are everyone else. Yakub's eugenics laws had spawned the lighter shades, but did not produce devils until creating white people. The rest of the human race, therefore, can claim godhood.

> "Well, these books are all scientific," insisted Tom, glancing at her impatiently. "This fellow has worked out the whole thing. It's up to us, who are the dominant race, to watch out or these other races will have control of things."
>
> —F. Scott Fitzgerald, *The Great Gatsby*[5]

Master Fard Muhammad's racial dualism of Original/Colored envisioned the colonized rising up collectively against their colonizers.

Fard had affiliated with pro-Japanese subversives who advocated unity among peoples of color against white power.[6]

Whiteness continues to name the terms, functioning as the basis against which all populations are measured. It is only because of "Non-Original" people that a concept of "Original" can exist; West African, East African, Chinese, Japanese, Indian, Afghan, Persian, Native American, Mongolian, and Indonesian people are all grouped together into a category that means nothing other than "non-European." As one should expect, the paradigm breaks down at places; I have observed discussions among Five Percenters as to whether Mexicans should be considered Original and Sicilians could be "Half-Original." When debates hinge on genetics and ignore politics, gods may be missing the point: traces of European ancestry do not help a Mexican immigrant in Arizona, and having distant Arab ancestors does not cause Sicilians to be accused of ties to al-Qaeda. Because genetic difference is increased with geographic distance, Africans are more closely related to Europeans than they are to Native Americans, but these relations cannot be shown to have any political consequences.

In the 1950s, Elijah Muhammad wrote that the Prophet Muḥammad, "an Arab, was a member of the black nation."[7] While he expressed disagreement with Arab attempts to bring Islam to white people, Elijah claimed the Nation of Islam to be part of the worldwide Muslim community, the *ummah*, and assured both followers and critics that an NOI Muslim would be "welcomed with sincere and open arms and recognized by his light-skinned or copper-colored Arab brother."[8] Years later, when it became clear that this wasn't going to happen, and Elijah himself lost interest in being accepted by Arab Muslims, his views on their race changed: "We have a New Islam coming up. The Old Islam was led by white people, white Muslims, but this one will not be. This Islam will be established and led by Black Muslims only."[9] Elijah proclaimed himself to be the true "Muhammad of the Qur'ān," as opposed to the Muḥammad of seventh-century Arabia. His views of the Prophet's race changed: "The Muhammad that was here 1,400 years ago," he explained,

"was a white man," and therefore not the "real Muhammad." The sign
of the real Muhammad who would come later was the Black Stone in
Mecca: "So I was there kissing the sign of myself and I was afraid to tell
them that this is me you're talking about here."[10]

THOUGH I HAD no interest in entertaining "race" as biological essentialism, I still participated in a culture that held "blackness" to be divine.
As with the white devil, I would look to the meaning of the black god
within the history that produced it.

In 1983, during an episode of *Monday Night Football*, broadcaster
Howard Cosell remarked of Alvin Garrett, wide receiver for the Washington Redskins, "That little monkey gets loose, doesn't he?" Amidst
the controversy that followed, Cosell refused to apologize, insisting
that he had also referred to white athletes as monkeys, and even used
"little monkey" as a term of endearment for his grandson. It's fully plau-
sible that Cosell had no hateful intentions when he said "little monkey"; he was at least cool enough to support Muhammad Ali when they
took the title from him. But it doesn't really matter; whatever the word
meant to him personally, Cosell should have recognized that "monkey"
changes its meaning when said by a white person about a black person.

I never understood how this could be a difficult thing for some white
people to grasp; there will always be a white person who claims that for
words to transform according to when, where, by whom, and about
whom they're said equals "reverse racism." It's the worst with white guys
who complain that they're not allowed to say "nigger." "Why is it okay
for black guys to say it?" they plead in complete earnest, on the verge of
tears—as though the greatest injustice of our time is that people born
into a legacy of oppressive privilege are discouraged from using a word
that, more than any other, expressed the ideology of their oppressive
privilege. As with Cosell, their argument isn't exactly irrational—I can
see the logic—but it's still embarassing.

Some words are too loaded with history. Even if the ideal would be to force collective amnesia and reboot the language, it's more practical to respect the weight that comes with these terms. The violence in words like "monkey" and "nigger" shouldn't require explanation, and most white people seem to recognize that the words' meanings change depending on who says them. What most Americans don't realize is that "God" is also such a word. As much as ape imagery and the n-word, the Name has been a weapon in America's long race war, a semiotic shrapnel bomb bringing unspeakable carnage and suffering upon the masses.

IN AMERICAN SLAVERY, African language and religion were feared as the potential ingredients for uniting and rallying slaves against their masters. Despite efforts to wipe out all traces of African culture, however, there was not widespread initiative to Christianize slaves in the early colonial period.[11] Concepts of racial hierarchy were entangled with religious difference; European settlers in America saw themselves as superior on the basis of their salvation in Christ.[12] The earliest colonial legislation against interracial sex, passed in Antigua in 1644, was titled "An Act against Carnal Copulation between Christian and Heathen."[13] Slave codes in Barbados and Jamaica in 1661 and 1664 named punishments for slaves who "shall offer any violence to any Christian."[14] It was understood that "Christian" signified European.

Because of this relationship between Christianity and the ruling class, many African slaves came to the conclusion that they could win their freedom simply by getting baptized. Destabilizing the racial-religious hierarchy, these African Christians caused a brief crisis for America's developing slavocracy. Lawmakers responded by explicitly rejecting any connection between religion and free/slave status; becoming Christian would not remove the chains. With religious differences no longer marking America's castes, slavery could thus be seen as inherent to Africans, and the concept of indentured white servitude would fade.[15]

The Christian/heathen distinction was phased out of colonial laws in favor of explicit references to skin color.[16] By 1680, categories were sufficiently defined that "Negro" and "slave" could be used as synonyms.[17] For religion to have no effect on the legal status of black people was actually favored by Christian missionaries, who feared that if slaves could free themselves by accepting Jesus, slaveowners would block them from hearing the Gospel. Rather than do anything to improve conditions for the slaves, missionaries gave priority to the fates of their eternal souls, while also submitting to the economic interests of the slaveholding ruling class. This would prove to be, in the words of religion scholar Theophus H. Smith, "disasterous for the theological integrity of American Christianity."[18] And here we can find the first rationale for a Five Percenter critique of religion.

Even after legislature politically disarmed baptism, slaveowners remained uneasy about their slaves becoming Christians. They feared that Christian slaves might use religion to their advantage—if not as a basis for freedom, at least for better conditions. How do you whip a fellow Christian? At the very least, becoming Christian (and thus equal to the slaveowners, at least in God's eyes) threatened to make slaves arrogant and rebellious.

In response to slaveowner concerns, evangelists promised that Christianity would only make the slaves more obedient and better servants to their masters. The Bible, they argued, "far from making any Alteration in Civil Rights, expressly directs, that *every Man abide in the Condition wherein he is called, with great Indifference of Mind* concerning outward circumstances."[19] Despite these assurances, the slaveowners' worst nightmares were realized with preacher-led slave revolts in 1800 and 1831. For terrified white power, Nat Turner's slave army became proof that a Bible in black hands could become a weapon against the plantation order. Evangelists pleaded that such radical preachers had only poisoned good Christian slaves with religious fanaticism. Their answer was not to prohibit slaves from accepting Christ; rather, slaveowners needed to take proactive steps to dictate their slaves' religion, to supervise their instruction at every step. Plantation owners asserted increasing control over black Christianity. One planter decreed that slaves should not become "acquainted with the whole Bible," but only "the prominent portions of Scripture which shew the duties of servants and the rights of masters."[20] Hundreds of laws placed restriction on the spiritual lives of slaves, banning Africans from assembling for religious instruction without a white minister or "responsible" white person present; in some places, black preachers were forbidden altogether. In South Carolina, it was illegal for black people—with or without a white chaperone—to assemble after dark "for the purpose of mental instruction or religious worship."[21] Even drums were forbidden, for fear that Africans would use them as code to "give sign or notice to one another of their wicked designs and purposes."[22] Near the end of the twentieth century, South Carolina's Department of Corrections would make similar efforts to prevent the spread of Five Percenter doctrine in its state prisons, placing gods in solitary confinement until they renounced their affiliation.

One special danger posed by slaves converting to a scripture-based religion was the chance that they might want to learn to read. Missionaries feared that abolitionist literature, which often used theological arguments, might reach the slaves and threaten the slaveowners' delicate support for evangelism. To protect plantation control of slave religion, laws were passed against black people learning to read and white people teaching them. For an insecure slavocracy, delivering the good news of Christ to slaves depended on there being no way that Christ could actually help them in this lifetime.

Some slaves, dissatisfied with their plantation-approved Christianity ("All that preacher talked about was for us slaves to obey our masters," a former slave recounted[23]), broke the law for the right to their own conscience, sneaking off to secret congregations at the risk of whippings. At these illegal prayer meetings, slaves learned that the stories of the Israelites in bondage actually told *their* story, and that some day the present Pharaoh's world would be destroyed. Many believed that with God's mercy, social hierarchies would someday be reversed, and black people would own white slaves.[24] Some slaves considered that the Bible they were given, the *master's* Bible, was not God's real book, but a corrupted version meant to enforce their subjugation.[25] In addition to these transformations of the slave master's religion into the slave's resistance, there were slaves who rejected Christianity altogether. They insisted that if God was truly just and full of love, he would never have allowed white people to torture black people in such ways.[26]

"Can the Americans escape God Almighty?" asked abolitionist David Walker in 1830; by "Americans" he meant whites. "If they do, can he be to us a God of Justice?"[27] The mystery god and his advocates had not shown themselves to be friends of black people. Frederick Douglass attacked those who claim to "love God whom they have not seen, whilst they hate their brother whom they have seen,"[28] and confessed that American "sham religion" led to his certainty that "prayers were unavailing and delusive."[29] In his autobiography, Douglass revealed that while teaching at an illegal Sabbath school for slaves, he would become overwhelmed with emotion and hold back from crying, "Does a righteous God govern the universe? And for what does he hold the thunders in his right hand, if not to smite the oppressor, and deliver the spoiled out of the hand of the spoiler?"[30] During a public address in 1870, Douglass expressed a humanistic vision of the divine that might qualify him for Allah's Five Percent: "I want to express my love to God and gratitude to God, by thanking those faithful men and women, who have devoted the great energies of their souls to the welfare of mankind. It is only through such men and such women that I can get any glimpse of God anywhere."[31]

IN THE 120, the devil is described as manipulating Jesus to "shield his dirty religion. . . . Jesus' teaching was not Christianity. It was Freedom, Justice, and Equality" (5:14). Elijah Muhammad here echoes the words of Frederick Douglass, who had drawn a brutally sharp contrast between the "pure, peaceable, and impartial Christianity of Christ" and the "corrupt, slaveholding, women-whipping, cradle-plundering, partial and hypocritical Christianity of this land."[32]

He who sells my sister, for purposes of prostitution, stands forth as the pious advocate of purity. . . . We see the thief preaching against theft and the adulterer against adultery. We have men sold to build churches, women sold to support the gospel, and babes sold to purchase Bibles for the POOR HEATHEN! . . . The slave auctioneer's bell and the church-going bell chime in with each other, and the bitter cries of the heart-broken slave are drowned in the religious shouts of his pious master. . . . The dealer [in slaves] gives his blood-stained gold to support the pulpit, and the pulpit, in return, covers his infernal business with the garb of Christianity. Here we have religion and robbery the allies of each other—devils dressed in angels' robes, and hell presenting the semblance of paradise.[33]

After emancipation, Christianity was still seen by many as a device of white rule. Central to this criticism was the depiction of Jesus Christ as a white man. W.E.B. Du Bois saw the whitening of Christ's "Mongoloid and Negroid elements" as an attempt at justification for the oppression of nonwhite peoples: "Nordics who have never accepted his doctrine of submission to evil, repudiation of riches, and love for mankind, have usually limned him as Caucasoid."[34] Christ, he pointed out, was born in the "Egypto-Syrian area" and may have "inherited Ethiopian blood."[35] In poems and short stories, Du Bois portrayed Christ as black, sometimes appearing in the United States. A man of the people, this Christ would affiliate with "the Negroes and Italians and working people," white prostitutes, and Communists, but is usually unrecognized and rejected by whites. In the story "Jesus Christ in Texas," white people hang Christ from a tree.[36]

In the first decades of the twentieth century, Africans in the western hemisphere sought not only legal equality, political agency, and economic justice but a healing and reclaiming of their inner selves through religious, cultural, and symbolic power. In this project, the white Jesus had to go. Marcus Garvey encouraged depictions of Jesus and Mary as black, while white media denounced his call to "paint God black" as "revolting even to the Negro."[37] Garvey proclaimed the need for a whole new black religion, and prophesied that someone would come to deliver it.

Considering the full evil of the slavery and oppression that preceded Master Fard Muhammad's arrival, I can say that Allāh appeared in his person—but not in any spooky thought of incarnation, as neither traditional Muslims nor Five Percenters wish to make idols of human beings. Allāh appeared in Fard the way that Allāh "appears" in rains of fire and brimstone upon the wicked, or the parting of a sea for the righteous; Fard's emergence in Detroit on the Fourth of July was an intervention of divine attributes. America deserved Master Fard Muhammad, all of the love and wrath that he brought. American history made him not only possible, but completely appropriate.

In 1930, when Master Fard first went from door to door across Detroit's ghettos, peddling silks, he enthralled potential customers with tales from his travels through Africa. If Fard was invited to stay for dinner, he would eat whatever he was offered—but later informed his hosts that black people in Africa did not eat such food. The reason that black people in America were more prone to diseases and ailments, he told them, was because they had lost touch with their natural way of life. He brings attention to this in the 120's "English Lesson C-1":

6. He likes the Devil because the Devil gives him nothing.

7. Why does he like the Devil?

8. Because the Devil put fear in him when he was a little boy.

9. Why does he fear now, since he is a big man?

10. Because the Devil taught him to eat the wrong food.

11. Does that have anything to do with the above question, No. 10?

12. Yes, sir! That makes him other than his own self.

13. What is his own self?

14. His own self is a righteous Muslim.

The "wrong food" was not only pork, but the *mental* swine that Africans had been fed by devils in America: the idea that God was white, white was God, and black was inherently *not* God. "The only thing that will hold the Negro," taught Elijah Muhammad, "is his belief in whites as a people of divinity."[38] To be less godlike was to be less human, but Master Fard Muhammad brought justice to America by reversing its terms. Bestowing divinity upon a trampled people, Fard revealed the control that African Americans could have over their own lives and communities, the power to remake their world.

Master Fard Muhammad, and Elijah Muhammad in his four decades of elaboration on Fard's message, shifted the locus of divine power from white Jesus or an invisible spirit to black people themselves. The mystery god to whom physical and mental slaves had been praying for generations, hoping for changes in their condition, had not helped them and could not help them. The answer was to be god for self. The Qur'ān tells us that God creates from nothing by merely saying, "Be;" Louis Farrakhan explains that God came to America to visit a "destroyed people" that had been reduced to "nothing" and make a new creation from them. God's new creation would be a perfect reflection of himself: "a nation of gods that have the intelligence, the skill, to say, 'Be'—organize their gifts, skills, and talents and resources with a plan and bring what they envision into existence."[39]

Elijah Muhammad's doctrine of the Mothership/Motherplane, a technological marvel designed and built by black men, shifted popular millenarian dreams away from the supernatural return of Christ, and placed the focus on what real human beings can do with determined and disciplined minds. The only divine will was their own; if they could realize this, their potential was unlimited. Some of the wilder points of NOI mythology serve this purpose, such as Elijah's claim that the moon had been "deported" from the Earth by a scientist trillions of years ago. "Man is easily made," wrote Elijah in appropriation of a Qur'anic verse, "but the sun, moon and stars are much harder to make. Yet we are the makers of them."[40] After describing the moon's effect on the tides, Malcolm X added, "All of this was done by man himself, not some mystery god. A black man set this up. And you and I have been running around in the trap that the white man put in us, thinking that the only one who does anything is a mystery god and what the mystery god doesn't do, the white man does."[41] In the 1960s, as the United States and Soviet Union raced each other to the moon, Elijah mocked the puny white men in their puny rockets, struggling to reach what the black man had made; of course, even the white men themselves had been made by the black man.

In 1975, the year of Elijah's passing, an NOI offshoot known as the Nation of Tu'lam attempted to build excitement for a spacecraft called the Fathership. The Fathership was said to have been designed by a scientist named Liyyum Lijab Muhammad, who had also designed the largest portion of the Mothership. At only six years old, the same age that Yakub had discovered magnetic attraction, Liyyum Lijab Muhammad discovered "Carogen," a liquid in the brains of black men that was the cause of the sun's creation.[42] The Nation of Tu'lam appears to have come and gone without leaving any meaningful impact, but its Carogen narrative touches on the same core idea: that the ultimate power in existence rests within one's own head.

Five Percenter culture offers its own progression on NOI mythology, having stripped away many of the explicitly transcendent elements. For Five Percenters, there's no UFO coming down to save the day, no Great Mahdi, no holy redeemer outside the self. "The Mothership is the mother's hip," said Allah, and the Mothership has already launched its bomber planes to destroy the devil's kingdom. It's you, the Mahdi of your own universe, with no one above you. This tenet's full significance was broken down for me by a god named I Majestic Allah at a parliament in Pittsburgh. He told me that to be God, as opposed to what you might expect—the claim to be a "supernatural being"—simply means that you alone are responsible for uplifting yourself, your family, and your community. That's it. You can't save anyone in a church or mosque, praying for the Man in the Clouds to do your work; you have to hit the streets and build. It's true with or without a Yakub at the beginning. Make money, teach kids. That's a god performing his duty, no spaceships required.

This is the genealogy of the black god, a counterimagining of blackness in which the dominant culture loses its hold on meaning. As Farrakhan teaches, "If people of this world can impose on you a limited vision for yourself, then they have already limited your ability to think past their ceiling that they have applied to you."[43] "We were seen as dogs," Lord Jamar told me in one of our interviews. "To go from dog to god is a big leap, you understand?"[44] For white Five Percenters trying to find their place, it is crucial to stay mindful of this legacy. Imagine now, after all of the psychological warfare of white supremacist religion, a culture of black men who undo the devil's work by calling each other God—and a white man showing up in their cipher, demanding that they call *him* God too. It's a bit of a problem.

"WE NEVER HAD any colored gods," wrote Elijah Muhammad in his later years, "until the Black god Yakub made a colored god."[45] The first day that I met Azreal, he told me that white Five Percenters had the potential to be gods. Some black gods do allow for white gods, but this remains a fringe position that will get bombed quick at most parliaments; an even smaller number suggest that white gods can also use the name Allah.

In 2005, word began to spread of Five Percenters in Milwaukee who taught a nonracial interpretation of the lessons, in which ancestry had no bearing on divinity. In their interpretation, the treatment of race as a genuine means of dividing people kept everyone, black and white, "trapped in 6" and unable to reach 7 (God). Azreal and I embarked on a road adventure from Harlem to Milwaukee to see it for ourselves.

Devil's confession time: during our long drive to Milwaukee, I wondered what their parliaments could be like, and it felt really, really good—deep down, at a secret place in my gut that I had hoped did not exist—to imagine white gods. As much as I embraced "white devil" symbology, as much as I wanted a language and text that could attack white supremacy, the presence of white gods also answered my desire. It would mean that at least within its own cipher, the Five Percent's apparent racial hierarchy had actually brought balance to the universe and destroyed racism: the Devil would truly be taken off the planet, with all human families absorbed back into the Original Asiatic Black Man. If there was no scientific basis for race, could this be a reasonable goal? It also made things less complicated as I considered possible relationships between Five Percenter thought and Ṣūfism. I needed Milwaukee.

EVERYTHING THAT we had heard turned out to be true, and the parliament was exactly what I hoped it would be. Azreal and I were welcomed with "Peace, gods!" and we all built in the cipher, black and white gods together. The cipher's main white god was excited to meet such an important historical figure as Azreal, and the three of us would have our picture taken together for the Milwaukee gods' newsletter. This was also the first parliament at which I would be invited to step into the cipher and build. "Peace," I said. "I come in the righteous name of Azreal Wisdom." It felt like a ritual washing away of my whiteness, our shared destruction of a living devil.

The teachings could be reformed, I knew; it had already happened once. In 1975, after the death of Elijah Muhammad, his son Wallace D. Muhammad took over as spiritual head of the Nation of Islam. Less than six months after his father's passing, Wallace was writing about the devil strictly as a "grafted mentality" and without specific reference to white people:

> When we speak of a devil, we are not talking about something physical. We are talking about the person within the physical body. You can destroy a devil by destroying the mind that the person has grown within them. If you can destroy that mind, you can destroy that devil. . . . The Bible never told you that the devil was going to be killed by any kind of physical destruction.[46]

The Nation of Islam was destroying devils "without hands," the new leader promised, "by casting him into our Lake of Fire," which symbolized "Divine Truth and Knowledge." In his first official interview, Wallace was asked if the white man could be Muslim: "Yes, I do," he answered. "But, when he becomes a Muslim, he will no longer be white—he will just simply be Muslim."[47] When asked whether white Muslims could enter NOI mosques, however, he replied, "As for admission into the membership, this is still a 'baby Nation.'"[48] This suggestion of an eventually integrated NOI was confirmed by the end of 1976, when my friend Dorothy Blake Fardan was accepted. Though she didn't exactly have a "slave name" to drop, she became Dorothy 13X. Wallace also changed his own name, becoming Warith Deen Mohammed— spelling his last name differently from his father, and proclaiming himself "Inheritor of the Religion" (*warith ud-dīn*).

The transformation of devils included a redefining of divinity. When "The Honorable Elijah Muhammad said you are the god," taught Warith Deen, "He did not mean that you are God the Creator with a capital 'G'—He meant that you are a god on your own plane of activity."[49] The brilliance of Warith Deen's reforms was that he pulled it off without ever flatly disowning his father; he worked the old Nation of Islam's teachings into the post-Nation community, rereading them to perform a new function. Not only did he insist that his father would have approved of the changes; he even alleged that this had been the plan of his father's teacher, Master Fard Muhammad, all along. In the Nation's history as Warith Deen reimagined it, Master Fard had understood that a foreign religion could not just instantly impose itself on a new environment. Fard developed a scheme through which the Qur'ān would ease its way into American consciousness slowly, over the course of decades, until people were ready to fully embrace Islam. With this renewing of the sacred, Warith Deen Mohammed allowed his community to have the best of both Islams; they could continue to revere their past and its cultural heroes, while leaving behind the more divisive elements of their tradition.

For many of the white people who show up in Warith Deen's later career—folks like Bill Clinton and the Pope—his sweeping reform of the Nation of Islam was simply a move away from "hate" and into full participation as American citizens, loving children of God, and so on. Sunnī Muslims would typically give a grudging respect to Elijah Muhammad's social and political significance, but fail to recognize any meaningful spirituality—or serious and sincere *Islam*—in his teachings. Concerned primarily with authentic religion, Sunnī narratives depicted Warith Deen only as guiding the followers of his father from a quasi-Islamic cult into "real" Islam. These various interpreters forgot one thing: that Warith Deen Mohammed was an actual human being, whose personal trajectory—like those of Muslims who looked to him as their imām—took place not only in political rhetoric and religious doctrines, but in real life. To truly comprehend what had happened, we need to see a fuller picture of the Nation at that moment.

Examining Warith Deen's reforms, scholar Lawrence H. Mamiya suggests a "quasi-Weberian" analysis emphasizing social and economic factors over pure theology.[50] In the forty-five years following its birth in Depression-era Detroit, the Nation of Islam promoted an ideal of rigorous self-improvement that emphasized healthy diet, complete sobriety, strict discipline, stable and loving family structures, the pursuit of education, frugal living, and economic self-sufficiency. Elijah Muhammad's teachings and Malcolm X's outreach to college students and professionals, along with whatever social progress had been achieved in America from 1930 to 1975, resulted in a significant middle class within the Nation of Islam.[51] These middle-class Muslims were ready for the religion to catch up to their changing position in American life. Warith Deen gave it to them, making the message less revolutionary, less antagonistic to the white and black mainstreams, and more relatable to America's growing immigrant Sunnī community. In transforming his father's teachings, Mattias Gardell writes, Warith Deen provided a "bridge to a new context."[52] The United States flag, which Elijah had associated with "Slavery, Suffering, and Death," would now grace the front page of his son's newspaper. In 1979, Warith Deen's organization even received a $22 million award from the U.S. Department of Commerce, and worked with American Pouch Foods Company to produce precooked combat rations for the U.S. military. Warith Deen also built a relationship with Egyptian president Anwar Sadat. Warith Deen suggested that the Muslim world should learn from Sadat's openness to Israel, and Sadat's government awarded scholarships to members of Warith Deen's community to study at Egyptian universities.[53] In both the American and Islamic contexts, Warith Deen worked to bring his followers in from the margins and closer to the centers of power.

Not everyone in the Nation of Islam was capable of (or interested in) assimilation. For many in the Nation, the most accurate expression of their daily reality would still be to call the black man God and the white man the devil, and the reasonable solution was still a separate state for black people. Warith Deen's reforms sparked mass defections, creating an opportunity for Nation revivalists to redirect the message back to the black underclass.[54] These Muslims also found their voice in a leader; in 1978, after Warith Deen had buried the old Nation of Islam, one of his ministers, Louis Farrakhan, brought it back to life with his own version that stressed a more traditional faithfulness to Elijah's teachings. As with the original Muslims after Prophet Muḥammad's death, and also the Nation of Islam after Master Fard's disappearance, the community of Elijah Muhammad was split between rival camps. While Warith Deen's work brought Islam closer to acceptance as a fully American religion, Farrakhan remained the angry holy man in the desert, promising God's Wrath upon the wicked ones in the marketplace.

Economics cannot entirely explain Warith Deen's motive—he had disputed with his father for years over religious matters, and supported Malcolm X's embrace of Sunnī Islam—but it could help to explain his success, and would also prove relevant during my trip to Milwaukee. Hanging out on the gods' front porch, making small talk, I came upon a bit of information that would later be repeated to me whenever I mentioned Milwaukee to black gods elsewhere: the mother of the Milwaukee cipher's first white god was apparently the owner or manager of a hotel, and this had somehow become a valuable resource for the gods, perhaps through the use of its banquet hall or other facilities. According to Five Percenters who opposed the white-god movement, access to the hotel had been the true motivation for the cipher's acceptance of him as a god.

I could never get the full picture of what was going on with the Milwaukee cipher, in part because their local elder was a bit of a crackpot who'd come at me with weird rants and paranoid accusations. Regardless, Warith Deen Mohammed and the Five Percenters of Milwaukee reminded me that theology is never just theology. In some places, the idea of white gods could be right; in other places, it could be right for the wrong reasons, or wrong for the right reasons. Or it's just wrong, terribly wrong.

The whites have always been an unjust, jealous, unmerciful, avaricious and blood-thirsty set of beings, always seeking after power and authority.... While they were heathens, they were too ignorant for such barbarity. But being Christians, enlightened and sensible, they are completely prepared for such hellish cruelties. Now suppose God were to give them more sense, what would they do? If it were possible, would they not *dethrone* Jehovah and seat themselves upon his throne? I, therefore . . . advance my suspicion of them, whether they are *as good by nature* as we are or not. Their actions, since they were known as a people, have been the reverse, I do indeed suspect them, but this, as I before observed, is shut up with the Lord, we cannot exactly tell, it will be proved in succeeding generations.

—David Walker, *Appeal to the Coloured Citizens of
the World, but in Particular, and Very Expressly, to
Those of the United States of America* (1830)[55]

The greatest trick the devil ever pulled off was convincing the world that he didn't exist.

—*The Usual Suspects*[56]

For devils to walk with God means more than becoming "colorblind" and going on with their lives as though white supremacy had never happened. Even if we break down the antiscientific conceptions of race, showing there to be no "devil" gene, white people are still devils in a very real way. Race is real because devils have made it real. To deny race is actually a prime example of white privilege; it's a choice that only white people get to make, because American culture already treats whiteness as generic humanity. If a white person chooses to no longer "identify" as white, nothing changes in his or her life or the privileges that s/he receives.

For legislators, activists, writers, or everyday devils to treat race as a mere fiction would be to deny the kinds of changes required to undo racism's effects. As anthropologist Kamala Visweswaran warns, a flat denial of race could still enforce white supremacy: " 'deracialization' might actually be the sign of a more pernicious racialization."[57] For the beneficiaries of white privilege, rejecting race loyalty is a step toward achieving social equality; for everyone else, race consciousness has provided a means of creating resistance and community in opposition to white supremacy. As Sherman Jackson rightly argues in *Islam and the Blackamerican*, exposing the fallacy of race does not lessen the black man's reality as defined in "sociopolitical and historical circumstances . . . no amount of scientific theorizing will undo him as an ontological-sociohistorical fact."[58] Certainly, if a black man is being assaulted by white police officers, it does not help to tell him, "Don't worry, race is only a social construction."

Azreal seemed to understand these dynamics, and my position is that of my teacher. While privately expressing his right to be God among black gods who would accept him as such, Azreal never challenged Five Percenter orthodoxy in public. He was a righteous man, as Allah had told him, and he knew the mission of the Five Percenters. He also knew that as a white Five Percenter, he was not the maker and owner, but a guest in someone else's house, and he accepted what was offered to him. Azreal makes a special case, the story of an unwell and unloved soul who had only felt valuable when he sang Allah to sleep in Ward 8. That was back in 1967, and Azreal would love that man and his memory for the rest of his life. He regarded Allah as his adoptive father, and Allah appears to have shared the feeling. Some have allowed that while white people couldn't be gods, at least Azreal had a right to his father's name. At any rate, Azreal's devotion to the Five Percent raises the bar high for Wonderbread gods in the cipher. The claim to be God is serious business, and one must show and prove.

The white Five Percenter occupies a strange place, and it doesn't seem that too many stick around; wrestling with lessons that were never meant for them, trying to squeeze themselves in, becomes too much work. With knowledge that I am not the intended audience, there are times when reading the 120 feels like voyeurism, and it can be challenging to bring any scripture into dialogue with new situations.

White Five Percenters aren't expected to pray to the black man to give them food, clothing, and shelter, so they really have no choice but to be the gods of their own ciphers, living out "Arm Leg Leg Arm Head" and "I Self Lord And Master" for themselves. I do not assign any ontological substance to skin color that would make one newborn baby more or less innately divine than another; language, however, has nothing to do with what's innate. Words are just units of culture, invented and reinvented when situations call for them. As much as race is an artificial construction created by politics, it has nothing on "God"— again, only a word, the meaning of which can give power to someone or take it away. The question here is not whether I endorse theories of my own genetic inferiority, but whether I can step into a particular community wearing its family name.

"Caucasians are, in effect, still trapped in a history which they do not understand," wrote James Baldwin, "and until they understand it, they cannot be released from it."[59] At Harlem parliaments, I have been called a civilized man and a righteous death angel; I have also been greeted with "Peace, god" and even "Peace, black man," which I take as an affirmation of my effort to rejoin the human race. As a guest in Allah's house, I accept whatever I am offered, as my teacher instructed me. Recognizing the damage that has been caused by thefts and abuse of the Name, I submit to the need for a place where the Name is not my property and the decision is not mine.

FOUR

ELIJAH MUHAMMAD
VS. MARSHALL MATHERS

You claim to be a Muslim but you're Irish white
—Eminem, featuring D12, "Quitter"[1]

THE ABOVE VERSE, like the entire second half of "Quitter," riffs on "Hit 'Em Up," 2Pac's infamous shot at Notorious B.I.G. Its intended target is Everlast, aka Erik Schrody, aka Whitey Ford, Irish-centric-MC-turned-singer and convert to Islam, with whom Eminem beefed at the turn of the millennium. At the end of the song, Eminem calls Everlast a "black Jesus," "white devil," and "mixed-up cracker"—an attack not only on Everlast's changing musical genres (having "crossed over to country," Eminem claims) but also his apparent religio-racial dissonance. Claiming to be Muslim, one white rapper says to another, makes him less white. When Eminem replaces the "Hit 'Em Up" refrain of "Make money" with "Kill Whitey," it points to much more than Everlast's nickname, mocking his assumed connections to angry black men and their angry black religions— in short, exactly what dominated hip-hop in the early to mid-1990s as Eminem struggled to find his own place in Detroit's underground. These were the years of Spike Lee's seminal retelling of Malcolm X's autobiography, Louis Farrakhan's Million Man March, and rap music saturated with black nationalist, Afrocentric, Kemetic, and Islamic themes from the likes of Public Enemy and Brand Nubian. At least two of the Golden

Age's canonized MCs that Eminem regularly cites as influences, Rakim and Big Daddy Kane, were Five Percenters. Eminem, who would later be described in the *Five Percenter* newspaper as the "Azreal of rap," describes growing up in that era in "Yellow Brick Road"—which, incidentally, he wrote to comment upon racist lyrics that he had recorded as a teenager. "We ain't know what it meant," he says of his youthful embrace of "African symbols and medallions," X-Clan tapes and the "state of red, black, and green," but he at least understood that "crackers is out . . . blackness is in."[2]

This era in hip-hop was also the setting in which I found Islam. Like Eminem, I also had an Africa medallion, and it would forge a path to my first encounter with the Qur'ān.

Religion is always, always, *always* built upon culture. Even puritanical Salafis who strive to live exactly as the Prophet and his companions, condemning all innovations of culture, do not own time machines; their antihistory is only rooted in the fourteen centuries of history that still separate them from the earliest Muslims. The famed Hanbalī jurist Ibn Taymiyya (1263–1328) attacked other Muslims for corrupting Islam with foreign innovations, but also believed that an unnamed figure in the Qur'ān was the mythical personage of Khidr—though Khidr was only a foreign innovation himself, the Islamic recasting of a pagan fertility god. When Muslims today assert that *ḥijāb* "liberates" or "empowers" women, this discourse is not merely "traditional" but in fact completely based in modernity, because such an argument did not exist prior to the twentieth century. It can also be seen as "Western," even if "Western culture" is precisely that from which ḥijāb offers liberation. Whether conservative or progressive, anyone who claims their religion to be entirely within scripture, unaffected by their own culture and history, is running a con.

The aspects of a religion that are considered most crucial by its believers change with the social context. What a religion stands for is often measured by what believers find themselves standing against, and the religion's demands that become emphasized are those that mark it as different from other traditions and communities. In the American context, in which

Muslims are surrounded by a nation of pork eaters, the prohibition of swine can take on special significance, whether among the Nation of Islam or orthodox immigrant communities. I once heard a Muslim adolescent make the staggering claim to his non-Muslim friend that in Islam, "eating pork is as bad as killing someone." Such a thought is only possible when all religions agree that murder is bad, forcing us to move down the ladder of sins to find an appropriate division between believers and infidels.

You don't hear American Muslims stressing the importance of eating beef, because just about everyone eats beef. Cheeseburgers fail to separate Muslims and Christians; at most, Muslims might insist on eating beef that was slaughtered in accordance with Islamic dictates. Throughout India's history, however, we find instances of Muslims emphasizing beef consumption because it marked Islam as distinct from Hinduism, even performing Eid slaughters with cows instead of the traditional goats.

> Is it the pork on your fork, or the swine on your mind
> —Ol' Dirty Bastard, "Harlem World"[3]

America has historically been a nation not only of pork eaters but of savage and bloodthirsty pale beasts wielding shackles, nooses, shotguns, and police batons upon black people. In this environment, Islam evolved a new, unique strain in American culture as resistance to white supremacy. A number of factors made Islam specially qualified for this symbolic choice. The colonial-era linking of whiteness with Christianity would have ramifications throughout the American story.[4] America's social order was established by European Christians, and Islam was regarded as the definitive non-European religion. As opposed to Hinduism and Buddhism, which geography kept at a safe distance, Islam had marched upon Christendom; only Islam could claim that it once had Europe *scared*. It has even been argued that the "idea" of Europe as something more than a geographical distinction took shape largely due to the Islam on its borders. As anthropologist Talal Asad points out, Spain is treated as having existed "outside" Europe during the time that it was ruled by Muslims.[5] Constructions of "Europe" and "Islam" as oppositional "civilizations" thrive today, with both Christians and secularists defining *their* Europe as fundamentally *not* Islamic, while Muslims measure their traditions and cultures against an imaginary realm called "the West."

Adding to the foundation for Islam as a response to whiteness, it is estimated that at least one-tenth of the Africans brought to America as slaves were Muslims. In early American slave society, which mashed together Africans from a variety of tribal, linguistic, and religious identities into one pool of culture, Muslims were seen as especially powerful magicians.[6] Memories of African Islamic heritage would linger throughout the nineteenth century. In the twentieth century, many African Americans would find conversion to Islam to offer a symbolic reclaiming of what had been lost.

In the first decades of the twentieth century, missionaries representing the Ahmadiyya movement—a South Asian Islamic community that has been consistently persecuted and reviled by Sunnīs as a cult of heretical innovators—preached to African Americans with a vision of Islam as fostering the brotherhood that white Christianity had denied them. Only in Islam, the missionaries promised, could human beings of all colors finally join hands as children of God. Despite the appeal of this antiracist Islam, the Ahmadiyyas could not successfully repackage their immigrant faith for the new context. On the Fourth of July, 1930, a superior marketing genius named Master Fard Muhammad arrived in Detroit—the city that would become a microsm of American race mythology in Eminem's semi-autobiographical film, *8 Mile*—with a religion that departed from what the city's Arab American population would have recognized as "Islam." Fard's Islam was custom-designed for his audience, as a Nation of Islam minister explains:

The thing that the Arabs don't understand about Master Fard Muhammad is the love that he had for us, his people . . . what

Master Fard Muhammad did is that he developed a new brand of Islam. The principles are the same, but everything is not the same as the old world of Islam. He developed it in a way that would attract the minds of black people. See, you go to the orthodox Muslim mosque, you sit on the floor. And as black people we're not used to sitting on the floor. And the whole service is in Arabic. Do we speak Arabic? No! We don't speak Arabic, so we're in there sitting on the floor, right, got men with dresses on—so we think, right—and everybody is talking in a language we don't understand. So how are we going to be attracted to a message like that?[7]

In his redesigning of old traditions for the new environment, Fard created the American Islam that would produce Malcolm X, Muhammad Ali, Louis Farrakhan, and a cosmological foundation for Rakim lyrics, and contribute to the view that a white American becoming Muslim made him a "black Jesus" and "mixed-up cracker."

Fast-forward to 1990, when a twelve-year old white boy in rural upstate New York, surrounded by cornfields and trailer parks full of white people, wants to see MC Hammer's concert an hour away in Rochester. His Elvis-loving, John Wayne–loving army veteran stepfather asks him how he'd feel about going to a concert where most of the people were black. The kid doesn't get to see MC Hammer, but he's been given something much more important: the knowledge that black music and black people could irritate and/or intimidate his stepdad. He tosses out his *Please Hammer Don't Hurt 'Em* tape in favor of Public Enemy's *Fear of a Black Planet,* now stomping through the house blasting "Fight the Power" and shouting the part where it calls Elvis a racist and says, "motherfuck him and John Wayne."[8] Better yet was "Black Steel in the Hour of Chaos" from *It Takes a Nation of Millions to Hold Us Back,* which established that the kid had officially switched sides: "I'm a black man, and I could never be a veteran."[9]

"You wouldn't serve your country?" asks the stepdad.

"It's not my country to serve," the kid answers. He stays up late to record *Yo! MTV Raps* and watch Chuck D pumping his fist in front of a giant image of Malcolm X, and the kid has no idea who this Malcolm the Tenth even is, but he looks cool. At fifteen, the kid reads Malcolm's autobiography, which changes everything forever. The Spike Lee movie comes out around the same time that Brand Nubian samples the *adhan*, the Islamic call to prayer, along with clips from a Louis Farrakhan sermon in songs. This kid has never seen the ghetto, but Naughty by Nature's "Ghetto Bastard" provides him with a mantra: "Never knew my dad, motherfuck the fag." He rewinds and replays that single line a thousand times a day, never allowing the song to finish. His grandfather gets pissed when his girl cousin walks around the block with a black guy, so he tells his grandfather that Jesus was black. Then the kid teaches himself Islamic prayers in Arabic and travels to West Virginia for his first meeting with his biological father, who turns out to be a white supremacist biker. The kid's father asks him, "You don't like niggers, do you?" Fast-forward again; now it's 1994 and the kid is seventeen and living in a mosque in Pakistan, contemplating Chechen jihad, of course he is.

Reading *The Autobiography of Malcolm X*, I had found myself drawn to Islam through Malcolm's two Islamic rebirths: first, when the teachings of Elijah Muhammad awakened him to the knowledge of himself and America, followed by his second conversion to Islam, a transracial enlightenment during the pilgrimage to Mecca. In Malcolm's hajj narrative, even "orthodox" Islam is described first and foremost as an antidote to racism. Malcolm tells us that white Muslims in Mecca are different from American whites, because Islam has "removed the 'white' from their *minds,* the 'white' from their *behavior,* and the 'white' from their *attitude.*"[10] His rebirth as a Sunnī was not a calling to give white people a pass. Near the end of his life, when challenged by a heckler who demanded, "Tell us where you're at with them white folks," Malcolm answered:

I haven't changed. I just see things on a broader scale. . . . Now I know it's smarter to say you're going to shoot a man for what he is doing than because he is white. If you attack him because he is white, you give him no out. He can't stop being white. We've got to give the man a chance. He probably won't take it, the snake. But we've got to give him a chance.[11]

Normative Muslims, taking comfort in their own image of Malcolm, employ his post-Mecca reconversion as a foil against the Nation of Islam; but they don't realize that for many American Muslim converts of all racial backgrounds, even if the doctrinal *form* was different, so-called mainstream Islam provided the same social, cultural, and political function. Reading my Qur'ān as a Sunnī, I would interpret Iblis/Satan—who refuses to bow to Adam on the grounds that humans, made from the black earth, are inferior to angels—as the first racist, the founder of white supremacy. In his *Green Book*, Mu'ammar al-Qaddāfī wrote, "Now comes the black race's turn to prevail," and I hung his picture in my locker. I've known white Sunnīs and Shī'īs who, upon their conversions to Islam, chose to rename themselves after Bilāl, the Prophet's Ethiopian companion. Whatever our sects, we sought to undo our whiteness.

I believed in Malcolm's promise that Islam could open a door for me out of the white race; to change my name was to erase my history, to put on a new history. I believed that Islam was the answer to all racism and oppression: by converting to Islam, I was saving the world. This developing personal mythology was reinforced when I met my father; it seems messed up, but I might have gotten off on his being a Nazi. With me already into Malcolm X and Islam, Dad dropping the n-word provided an orgasm of ego fulfillment: *Look at his ignorance and see how awesome you are,* said the voice in my head. My father was proof of something, and *I* was proof of something.

Though my studies did lead me to embrace Islamic monotheism as preferable to my family's Catholic Trinity, the account of my conversion can be given without any mention of God or what we conventionally call "religion." Those Arabic prayers provided me with the right soap to wash myself clean of America, whatever I understood America to be: my father, my stepfather, white Jesus, and all of the ignorant small-town dipshits at my all-white Catholic high school.

I walk with every muscle aching . . . in the Denver colored section, wishing I were a Negro, feeling that the best the white world had offered was not enough ecstasy for me, not enough life, joy, kicks, darkness, music, not enough night . . . I was only myself, Sal Paradise, sad, strolling in this violet dark this unbearably sweet night, wishing I could exchange worlds with the happy, true-hearted, ecstatic Negroes of America.

—Jack Kerouac, *On the Road*[12]

What goes around comes around I figure
Now we got white kids callin' themselves nigger
—KRS-One, "MCs Act Like They Don't Know"[13]

Even when the devil finally gets enlightened and decides to make everything right, he's still prone to act like his devil self and blow it. I failed to realize this at fifteen, but in my conversion to Islam, I was performing an American cliché that frequently emerges from our reservoir of archetypes: a character that I call the "Exceptional Devil."

The phenomenon has been observed at least since Norman Mailer's 1957 article "The White Negro." Critics read the Exceptional Devil myth in films such as *Dances with Wolves* and *Avatar*, in which, as one commenter broke it down, "a white guy manages to get himself accepted into a closed society of people of color and eventually becomes its most awesome member."[14] To find America's all-time Exceptional Devil, I'd go back before Mailer's White Negro, before Kerouac and Elvis, all the way to the nineteenth century and white abolitionists who struggled to bring an end to slavery. It's not John Brown, the white man who fought white men for black freedom and was willing to hang for it—though Brown might have given birth to the *Dances with Wolves/Avatar* archetype, and white people offended by Malcolm's white-devil talk would always ask, "What about John Brown?" The all-time Exceptional Devil, for me at least, would be William Lloyd Garrison.

This isn't a comment on Garrison's sincerity or the value of his contribution; I love Garrison. A true radical in his time, he spoke out for immediate abolition and full racial equality—including intermarriage—thirty years before the Civil War, and he was also a pioneer in the cause of women's rights. He even publicly burned the United States Constitution, calling it an "Agreement with Hell." While a fervent Baptist, he attacked his fellow white Christians for doing "comparatively nothing" to help the slaves, and disagreed with evangelical abolitionists who believed that God would end slavery without human intervention in due time.[15] He had an anticlerical streak and was often hailed as a "prophet"; and more than a century before Ignatiev and Wise would speak on white privilege, he declared, "We are all alike guilty."[16] From where I stand, he comes out looking Five Percent.

To be a "devil" doesn't have to mean that Garrison was burning crosses on someone's lawn; even a good man of good intention can get caught up in whiteness. The Exceptional Devil moment only came when Garrison's protégé, Frederick Douglass, told Garrison that he wanted to start a newspaper. Garrison, fearful that Douglass would draw black readers away from his own paper, and hurt that Douglass would even think of competing against him, discouraged the plan; a white abolitionist in Garrison's camp, Maria Weston Chapman, even doubted that Douglass could have the mental capacity for such a task. Douglass went ahead with the newspaper, and his friendship with Garrison was permanently damaged. Though deeply committed to the cause, Garrison became the Exceptional Devil by failing to consider that the struggle for black liberation

might actually belong to black people—that it wasn't about *him*. Even as
a freedom fighter, he still had to be a white guy about it and assume that
his own voice was the most important in the room.

In our own time, my vote for the Exceptional Devil myth's definitive telling is *8 Mile,* in which the real-life Eminem (Marshall Mathers)
plays a fictional Eminem (Jimmy "Rabbit" Smith) trying to make it in
hip-hop, which is represented as a closed society of people of color.
True to the myth, Rabbit not only finds his voice as a white MC, but
overpowers every black MC in the universe. Interestingly, one of the
MCs encountered by Rabbit in a parking lot is a Five Percenter. It's not
acknowledged in the script, but she's wearing the common Five Percenter head wrap and Allah pin; the character is played by Njeri Earth,
an actual Five Percent MC in Detroit.

In the final battle of *8 Mile,* Rabbit points out that his opponent, who
presents himself as a hardened gangster, actually came from a good
home and attended a private school. As a factory worker who lives in
a trailer with his single mother, Rabbit can make the argument that on
some level, he's less "white" than his black adversary. Marginalization
from white power becomes white territory.

Over the course of my years as a Muslim, I've had thousands of *8 Mile*
moments at which my disavowal of whiteness seemed to support a new
white conquest. During my first visits to the Islamic Center of Rochester,
a secret tingle rushed through me when brothers remarked with shock
that this sixteen-year-old had taught himself the prayers in full Arabic.
At the mosque's summer camp, we'd have quiz competitions on Islamic
history, and whichever team had me always won because I had read more
on our religion than all of the desi kids put together. I was Rabbit at the
end of *8 Mile,* destroying my opponent and tossing him the mic. Everyone else just wanted to go out and play basketball in the parking lot, while
I'd stay in the mosque and ask the imāms for stories about the Prophet. It
was my plan to study Islam overseas, memorize the Qur'ān, and become
an imām myself; the other kids wanted to get into good universities and

become doctors and engineers with big houses. In my imagination, I had not only *browned* myself, but out-browned them. The desi kids also seemed to notice. I had devoted myself to their cultural inheritance in ways that they were not prepared to match, and sometimes I sensed that their respect for me came with a tinge of guilt.

In larger American society, my adolescent self-exile from whiteness was thrilling. When I told a white evangelical Christian that I was Muslim, she looked quizzically into my blue eyes and asked, "Were you born in this country?" I couldn't hide my smile; Islam had succeeded in transforming this small-town white boy into an alien, and I loved it. The exchange is reminiscent of a *Chappelle's Show* sketch in which two hip-hop-loving white youths, when derided as "niggers" by a blind black man, congratulate each other.

During my first trip to Pakistan, I was adored like a shining white trophy. Brothers consistently assured me of how great the converts are, almost universally more pious and educated about Islam than those born and raised in the faith. On top of that, I was told in whispers that black converts were a "dime a dozen," but white converts were "special." Even though I was offended by their remarks, I still internalized them; my attempted treason against white supremacy only fed into it. Empowered by everyone fawning over me, I felt qualified to speak against what I perceived as Pakistan's failure to manifest a truly Islamic society. Seeing Pakistani women in public without *ḥijāb*, the white American teenager lamented their corruption by British imperialism and Hindu influence. Brothers endorsed my privilege to decide Pakistan's Muslim-ness since I was more Muslim than Muslim.

My fellow students in Islamabad, mostly West Africans, and I would hover around our television to watch CNN updates on the new Caucasian war. We cheered on the Chechen rebels against Russia, celebrating any report of success with high fives and *al-ḥamdulilāh*s. While we found inspiration in Malcolm X's pilgrimage to Mecca, and did not consciously examine the Chechen rebellion in terms of race, the struggle of our Muslim brothers looked like so many struggles of dark-skinned peoples against their white imperial oppressors—and yet, the Chechens were white. Weren't they? As far as I understood race at that time, they were white; the Caucasians were indeed "Caucasian." I still haven't fully unpacked what the Chechens might have meant to me. Even with my Islamically rooted antiracism, it comforted me to know that there were entire cultures of white Muslims, just for proof that I wasn't on some self-hating teen angst trip. At the same time, I loved that the Chechens wanted no part of the white world. For an American seventeen-year-old raised on Lakim Shabazz and Brand Nubian lyrics, Chechnya's Sunnī Muslims materialized my fantasy life: a nationless nation of race traitors waging war upon a white empire. If I dug deep enough, perhaps I could find secret white pride in my antiwhite Chechen dreams. My Chechen brothers were on the front line of a struggle for Islam, shaming the rest of the Muslim world with their bravery and sacrifice. In our global Islamic brotherhood, the *ummah*—which I saw as necessarily *not* white—it was still possible for me to envision white men as the "most awesome members."

I wanted to head to Chechnya and fight alongside my brothers, and the opportunity would have been there during my time in Islamabad, but one of my mentors talked me out of it. "You'll do more good for Islam as a writer," he told me. Years later, I'd learn of a brother who had realized his own quest for white *mujāhid* glory: the so-called American Taliban, John Walker Lindh, who was captured by U.S. forces in 2001 during George W. Bush's taking of Afghanistan. By that point, my own wannabe-*jihādī* days were long over, and the parallels between John's story and my own freaked me out a bit. John had found Islam as a teenager through hip-hop and Malcolm X, and changed his name to Sulaymān al-Fāris (adding to my freak-out, *fāris* means "knight" in Arabic). Heading overseas to learn his religion—first to Yemen, then Pakistan—he adopted what musician and producer Melvin Gibbs calls a "sort of 'wigger' version of an Arabic persona, speaking broken English with a fake Arabic accent."[17] Seeing his face on CNN was like a mirror through which I could watch myself in an alternate universe: John Walker Lindh was me, a version of myself that had once lived in my daydreams—but he manifested the dream, living it out in ways that I could not. John Walker Lindh was the real thing, while I only posed; if he was Eminem, I was Vanilla Ice.

Our religious journeys were similar enough, but moved in opposite directions. I had gone from a hardcore Salafi revivalist to building with the Five Percenters; before his conversion, John Walker Lindh had actually dabbled with the Five Percent online, even pretending to be black behind the Internet's anonymity. Posing as a black "cybergod," he would post his own lyrics and weigh in on issues such as the n-word. Finding his footing as a Sunnī Muslim, however, he mocked Nas and the Five Percent for claiming to be God.

John might have hoped to shed whiteness and dissolve in the universal Islamic brotherhood of Malcolm X's experience at Mecca, but he was not successful. John's whiteness only resurfaced in his new privilege of Sunnī orthodoxy. Because John had laid claim to a truth greater than the politics of his own identity, he felt entitled to pass judgment regarding the concerns of black men. From his position of unchallenged religious authenticity, he could mock what he saw as quasi-Islamic heresies without any respect for the histories that produced them or the power differentials between a middle-class suburban white youth and inner-city black youths—and even imagine himself to be Malcolm's true heir while doing it. With his combined white/Sunnī privilege, John decreed that all tribal, national, and racial loyalties were against Islam, and therefore invalid. Sunnī Islam's antiracism actually made him whiter than ever.

BEING WHITE in a subculture dominated by black men enabled Eminem to perform an incredible act of whiteness—the representation of himself as disadvantaged by racism. "Some only see that I'm white, ignoring skill," he complains in "Role Model," "'cus I stand out like a green hat with an orange bill."[18] Before becoming an accepted member of the closed society, the Exceptional Devil must prove that he has a right to enter; this was the challenge faced by both the fictional Rabbit and the real Eminem, for whom whiteness equaled a deficit in hip-hop's "most important credential," street cred.[19] Both Rabbit and Eminem proved themselves by battling other MCs in the Detroit scene; Eminem would later secure initiation into hip-hop's elite through the endorsement of one of its gatekeepers, Dr. Dre. Eminem remained diplomatic in his commercial ascent, choosing to focus his satire on the corniest artifacts of white America, such as boy bands and Britney Spears; in his debut video, "My Name Is," he parodies Bill Clinton, Johnny Carson, *Leave It to Beaver*, Marilyn Manson, and common trailer trash. Most of his beefs have been with other white rappers: Vanilla Ice, "Marky Mark" Wahlberg, Insane Clown Posse, Fred Durst, Everlast. He could attack Ja Rule while standing behind 50 Cent, but we haven't yet seen any dream matches against worthy adversaries that would test Eminem's cred with black audiences: no Eminem vs. Jay-Z, no Eminem vs. Nas or Kanye West or Lil Wayne.

Eminem most notoriously assimilated into hip-hop through his performance of the culture's gender norms; unable to fully achieve authentic blackness, he could at least demonstrate his authentic maleness by targeting women and homosexuals. While whiteness might have been both a blessing and a curse for Eminem, straight male privilege was less complicated; as law professor Devon W. Carbado observed, there has never been a rap song suggesting that heterosexual men be beaten or shot for being heterosexual.[20] Eminem's savagely misogynistic and homophobic lyrics secured his place within hip-hop by reminding his peers that whether white or black, he still had a dick and put it in the right place. In addition to moving attention from race to gender, Eminem was able to further appeal to young white males—who had been the biggest buyers of hip-hop heterosexism since Eminem's own youth—and play upon the long-standing fetishizing of young black males as excessively aggressive, dangerous, and hypersexual. Eminem granted young white men access to a mythic image of black masculinity, a version of the abstract surrogate black father that had been sought by both John Walker Lindh and myself.

When *The Five Percenter* referred to Eminem as the "Azreal of rap," Allah's death angel took deep offense. "I was really insulted," Azreal told me, but his outrage had nothing to do with race: "I'd never say those kinds of things about my mother that he does."

8 MILE MOMENTS occasionally transpire at Five Percenter parliaments, where gods who don't know me might ask for my credentials, checking to see if I can build on the day's degree or Mathematics. At one parliament, when I tried to buy an Allah pin, the elder god challenged my right to wear it.

"Why do you want that?" he asked.

"Respect," I told him.

"Respect for what?"

"Allah."

"Who's that?" he asked.

"He came out of the mosque," I answered, "and taught the youths that the black man is God."

"What year did he do that?"

"Nineteen sixty-four."

"That's peace," he said, handing over the pin. "No offense, but I had to test you. If you didn't know it, I wouldn't have given it to you."

After another parliament, I was riding the train downtown when a young black man noticed my Elijah Muhammad T-shirt and smirked.

"What do *you* know about Elijah?" he asked.

"What do you know about Allah's Five Percent?" I replied. "I'm Azreal Wisdom."

"Oh, that's peace!" he exclaimed, shaking my hand. "Keep seeking that knowledge!"

Can the devil fool a Muslim?

Not nowadays.

—25, 26:36

The devil's at least slick enough to fool himself, I'd try to remember, as those *8 Mile* moments left me feeling great.

It's a known fact that white people ruin everything. If there was really a "decline of hip-hop," it began when music executives realized that white kids were buying records. I'm not even talking about turn-of-the-1990s pop acts like MC Hammer; let's look at NWA's sale of black-on-black, black-man-on-black-woman violence to white male consumers. Dr. Dre's marketing scheme to portray marijuana as a hardcore drug enabled white frat boys to think of themselves as *gangster*. "No medallions, dredlocks, or black fists," as Dre says in "Let Me Ride." Exactly, and it's not limited to music. FUBU started in the urban market, but made a fortune selling clothes to white kids who wanted to identify with blackness; unfortunately, this led to FUBU becoming associated with white poseurs, which meant that black consumers didn't want to buy it anymore, which in turn meant that white kids stopped buying it, because their whole point was to avoid dressing like other white kids. Crossover success killed the brand. What would this mean for black religious and cultural movements?

There was once a time when getting access to the Five Percent, whether black or white, at least meant that you were somehow linked to the worlds in which Allah walked; but all of that has changed. The secret references in hip-hop lyrics have been decoded. Supreme Mathematics, Supreme Alphabets, and even the 120 are online now, the community's history can be found in my work *The Five Percenters: Islam, Hip-hop, and the Gods of New York,* and Five Percenters are publishing their own books. It's possible for someone to have all of the textual tools needed to be a Five Percenter without even meeting a Five Percenter in real life, let alone experiencing the traditional Five Percenter transmission of knowledge. This opening up of the Five Percent has already impacted the culture, and will not decrease with time.

Philosopher Linda Martin Alcoff writes, "In a consumer society, the core of white privilege is the ability to consume anything, anyone, anywhere."[21] In 1993, the New Age distortion of Native American religion prompted a group of "traditional spiritual leaders, traditional elders, and grassroots advocates of the Lakota people" to draw up a manifesto, "Declaration of War Against Exploiters of Lakota Spirituality." In the document, Lakota traditions are described as having been "desecrated, mocked, and abused" in "abominable and obscene imitations" by "non-Indian 'wannabes,' hucksters, cultists, commercial profiteers, and self-styled 'New Age shamans' and their followers." The document condemns theft of the holy: the Sacred Pipe, it laments, is "being desecrated through the sale of pipestone pipes at flea markets, powwows, and 'New Age' retail stores," while "pseudo-religious corporations have been formed to charge people money for admission into phony 'sweat lodges' and 'vision quest' programs," and "non-Indians have organized themselves into imitation 'tribes,' assigning themselves make-believe 'Indian names' to facilitate their wholesale expropriation and commercialization of our Lakota traditions."[22]

The declaration also includes a note against "non-Indian charlatans and 'wannabes'" who are "selling books that promote the systematic colonization of our Lakota spirituality."[23] So here I am, a white man consuming Islam, consuming Malcolm X and Elijah Muhammad, consuming the Five Percent, and selling books, caught in this double bind: by embracing what I love, I may poison it. The Moorish Science Temple offers precedent. In the 1960s, some white hipsters got their hands on Moorish Science teachings and started their own offshoot, the Moorish Orthodox Church (MOC). Existing today primarily in online groups, the MOC maintains

Noble Drew Ali's image, but has focused on his New Thought spirituality and quasi-Ṣūfism, with an added aesthetic of irony and psychedelia, while ignoring his political content. MOC members have typically rationalized white participation in Moorish Science with an urban legend that Noble Drew Ali had allowed whites to join, registering as "Celts" or "Persians." This story may or may not be true, but I remain unsure of the MOC's ultimate value in terms of subverting whiteness. A notable exception was the militantly antiracist MOC chapter in Arizona, which embraced Noble Drew Ali as their prophet in a very serious way.

There has been much debate as to whether whiteness is challenged or reinforced by white people who adopt nonwhite wisdom traditions. As we've seen, Lakota elders have made their opinions known. It's a question of what is truly transformed by white people practicing the Sun Dance: Are the white people made less white, or is the Sun Dance made more white? Allah's welcoming of "culture seeds" such as Azreal demonstrates that there's no immediate issue of theft in a white person claiming the Five Percent; indeed, Five Percenters often name their mission as the teaching of "*all* human families," and emphasize that anyone can go under the study. Nonetheless, aspiring death angels still pose a real threat of infecting the Five Percent with their own ingrained race/class issues. It's another problem with the Wonderbread God: there may be a few righteous white Five Percenters who deserve to come in the Name of Allah, but they wouldn't show up alone.

EVEN WEARING ELIJAH MUHAMMAD'S face on his body, the Exceptional Devil draws from white privilege. It's certainly easier to be a white friend of the Nation of Islam and Five Percenters than a black friend, let alone a black member; I can travel among white academics, white book publishers, agents, editors, and journalists, and speak about black supremacy to white audiences, and no one's afraid that my Elijah shirt marks me as a dangerous radical or a nutty cultist on some

Motherplane trip. Because I'm white, I can't *really* be committed to this stuff, right? So I become the translator, the trusty white man who went to a far-off land and brought back something exotic and fascinating for devils to consider. White privilege means that I can write a chapter titled "Kill All the White Men" and get away with it.

This could provide a clue as to the white Five Percenter's real purpose. Rather than worry about one's true place *within* Five Percent culture (i.e., "Can my name be Allah too?"), the righteous culture seed should perhaps consider what knowledge of self does for his/her world beyond the parliament, in dealings with other white people. Five Percenter tradition holds that as Allah's chosen death angel, Azreal was given the keys to heaven and hell and a responsibility to get the wrongdoers. Like the racially ambiguous Master Fard Muhammad, Azreal could travel undetected through white society, the perfect smuggler for a thought bomb to blow up devils. Azreal had a mandate to spread the Five Percenter message to white America, but needless to say, there haven't been too many white people interested in hearing a homeless man talk about how he met Allah in a mental institution.

One could speculate that Azreal's presence had made an impact on the Five Percent in its formative years. Prior to incarceration at Matteawan State Hospital for the Criminally Insane, Allah had taught a hard-line Nation of Islam view of race, in which all white people were devils, no questions asked. With Azreal, Allah found this view challenged; here was a white teenager enduring horrific abuses from white guards. Azreal, while clearly of European descent, was not fully "white" in any sense that made "devil" the right word for him. Unlike poor and marginalized whites throughout American history, who had clung to racism with hopes of joining the ruling white society, Azreal displayed no stake in white supremacy. He was, in Allah's words, a "righteous man," and Matteawan's hell did for Allah what Mecca's love did for Malcolm: it stretched the possibilities of who could qualify as a "poor righteous teacher."

In our travels together, Azreal didn't spend much energy on the complexities of breaking down lessons or numerology; he simply loved Allah as his father and did what he could to celebrate Allah's legacy. Azreal denied that Allah hated whites—"Allah loved everybody," the *New York Times* quoted him as pleading in 1969, after the assassination. Over forty years later, Azreal does have a special position, a unique name and title that distinguishes him among the Five Percenters. As a born devil who put himself under Allah's teachings, he has been used— perhaps problematically—as confirmation of the Five Percenters' truth ("I don't need a crazy white man to validate my culture," one god told me). In his own cipher, Azreal has largely steered clear of the Exceptional Devil trap. At least he never had himself depicted in comic-book style art as the white superhero of American Islam:

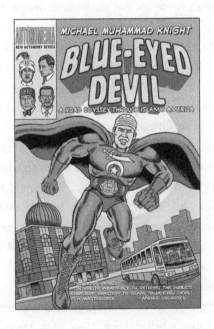

Another of my mentors on this path has been Dorothy Blake Fardan, the first white person to join Warith Deen Mohammed's deracialized Nation of Islam. In our first conversation, she directed me to words of Malcolm X that should be a required plus-lesson for any death angel:

> I have these very deep feelings that white people who want to join black organizations are really just taking the escapist way to salve their consciences. By visibly hovering near us, they are "proving" they are "with us." But the hard truth is this isn't helping to solve America's racist problem. The negroes aren't the racists. Where the really sincere white people have got to do their "proving" of themselves is not among the black victims, but out on the battle lines of where America's racism really is—and that's in their own home communities; America's racism is among their own fellow whites, that's where the sincere whites who really mean to accomplish something have got to work.[24]

Growing up on a farm in Kentucky, Dorothy had always felt connected to nature and in tune with spirituality, but would only find her sense of God properly addressed when her black husband introduced her to Elijah Muhammad's message. Since Elijah's Nation did not allow white members, Dorothy settled for conversion as a Sunnī at an immigrant mosque. Her encounter with the mosque's imām was unfulfilling:

> He was most interested in and obviously disturbed by my allegiance to the Hon. Elijah Muhammad and the Nation of Islam. I remember him saying he just couldn't understand my interest in the group nor my loyalty. He tried hard to impress upon me that these were not really Muslims and he might even had used the word *shirk* [polytheism] to describe their "wrongness."
>
> I tried hard to explain to him how the teachings of the Hon. Elijah Muhammad had helped me to understand my self and the world I lived in, and how he, through my husband, actually

saved my life and led me to God (Allah) once again. I could see
he was not convinced and I felt an immense loneliness descend
upon me.[25]

While maintaining her love for Elijah Muhammad, Dorothy understood why she was not welcome in the Nation of Islam. She could see
that the best way for her to respect and support the Nation would be
to leave it alone, to respect the importance of there being one place in
America where white people could not go. With Warith Deen Mohammed's succession to his father, however, the Nation of Islam's policy
changed, and she jumped at the chance to participate. The integrated
mosques allowed her to "experience a Muslim community that understood the heinous racial history of this country, yet reached for a way
to establish a just and righteous community for all, based on the principles of Islam."[26] In one of Warith Deen Mohammed's new mosques,
she heard an imām tell the congregation, "The Caucasians help us when
they show us that they are not what we thought they were and we help
them when we show them that we are not anymore what their fathers
made us."[27] It was the same healing that I would find in my experience
with the Five Percenters.

Unfortunately, Warith Deen moved too far from his father for Dorothy's taste, and she became dissatisfied. It was no longer the Nation—
Elijah's Nation—that she wanted:

My Islamic family, while being universal and inclusive, will always
be in its most basic and home-based way, the Nation of Islam. It
provided the door to understanding self, Creator (Allah), and the
social womb I found myself in. It nurtured my soul and supplied
an authentic "we'ness."[28]

Following the disintegration of the NOI, she maintained relationships
with Warith Deen's community, but also supported Minister Farrakhan's

NOI revival. She would regard both men as her "spiritual leaders and brothers in Islam," as "each envisioned the same day and time of peace, the Kingdom of God on earth, for the entire human family."[29]

This family can include the sons and daughters of devils. "There's a place for us under the teachings," Dorothy told me, "but we have to find that out for ourselves." Elijah Muhammad himself had said that white Muslims could attain salvation: "Good done by any person is rewarded and those white people who believe in Islam will receive the Blessing of entering into the Hereafter."[30]

> The day the Horn will be blown. And we will gather the criminals, that day, blue-eyed.
>
> —Qur'ān 20:102

It should be said that because the Nation of Islam does not believe in a bodily resurrection of the dead, Elijah's "Hereafter" will not be found in an otherworldly afterlife but rather an America after a mental and cultural resurrection. Amir Fatir, a scholar and thinker in the NOI tradition, has suggested that the "Mother of Planes" was not a spacecraft, but a plane of *consciousness,* and that the leaflets it would drop to warn of the coming inferno represented the Qur'ān. According to Fatir, this change of conciousness was what Elijah meant by the "destruction of the white man's world." Some whites will survive this destruction and take part in the future civilization when, after America burns for 690 years and cools off for 310 years, a new god will come to bring the new Islam and its new Qur'ān.[31] The bombs have already fallen, setting the devil's kingdom ablaze with suburban *mujāhidīn* and death angels, and we are still in the burning years.

FIVE

POWER AND REFINEMENT

*They didn't force me to go to church in Matteawan.
They said, "Allah, we don't have your service here." I
said, "If you did have Muslim service, that is not my
service." Because I don't have no religion. And they
didn't force me to go. They put on my paper, "Very religious man," and I said, "No, I don't have no religion."
They put on my paper that I was a leader and I said,
"No, I'm not a leader."*

—Allah[1]

*So many leaders to obey
But I was born on Savior's Day
So I choose me*

—Erykah Badu, "Me"[2]

ON THE TENTH DAY of the Islamic month of Ramadan, in the Grego-
rian year 630, Muḥammad led an army of ten thousand men on the
road to Mecca. After minimal resistance, the polytheists surrendered
their city and Muḥammad pitched his red tent near the Ka'ba. He took
a short nap, performed a ritual washing, prayed, and circled the Ka'ba
seven times before setting upon his work: the destruction of 360 idols,
the end of Mecca's old religion. He would also send troops to pagan
outposts throughout the region to ensure that every idol was smashed.

After a general named Khālid ibn Walīd crushed the statue of fertility goddess al-Uzza, she was said to actually appear to him, personified as a naked black woman screaming and pulling out her hair, grieving that she would no longer be worshiped in the Arabian Peninsula.

This idol smashing would be imitated throughout Islam's history. In 1378, an Egyptian Ṣūfī named Muḥammad Saʾim ad-Dahr, angered that Muslims were offering sacrifices to the Sphinx, destroyed its nose and was executed by the Mamluk authorities; in 1999, the Taliban dynamited two giant Buddhas that had stood for roughly fifteen centuries. A Five Percenter critique would charge that amidst the broken statues, one idol is allowed to remain: the conceptual idol of an unseen "mystery god." The Qurʾān repeatedly warns us against praying to gods that we have made with our own hands, but also against the idols we build in our heads, constructing God from our desires (25:43, 45:23). For what we call "orthodox" Muslims, it's easy to tell the false gods from the real one—Allāh the Absolute, the god of tawhīd (transcendent unity). This singular deity, however, had once been among many in the Meccan pantheon, who were worshiped in more or less the same way: as magical compensators who demanded frequent adoration and the reciting of special words. Between gods and the God, I wondered how much had really changed in the hearts and minds of worshipers. In what Muslims call the "Age of Ignorance," polytheists thanked the rain god for nourishing their crops and the sun god for not burning them. Monotheism did not seem to fundamentally alter this way of relating to divinity; rather than smash our idols, tawhīd merely consolidated them, reducing the pantheon's roster to one.

For Five Percenters, Muḥammad's remaining conceptual idol does not exist. According to the 120, humans have wasted trillions of years searching for the mystery god and were unable to find him; therefore, they decided to be their own gods (10:40). Even as a Muslim who believed in Allāh, I couldn't shake 10:40. The degree both challenged my Islam and spoke to a truth that I perceived to be at Islam's core; 10:40 was another round of idol smashing.

"When a person rationally considers God," said Ibn al-Arabī, "he creates what he believes in himself through his consideration. Hence he considers only a god that he has created through his consideration."[3] Reading this against Master Fard Muhammad's rejection of the mystery god, I would process the Five Percent's apparent atheism as an Islamic apophasis. Ibn al-'Arabī and Master Fard Muhammad would agree that my intellectual pursuits could never attain the Absolute, even after trillions of years. The Qur'ān itself seems to agree when it says, "Surely conjecture can by no means take the place of the truth" (10:36). The Arabic term for "the Truth" or "Reality," al-Ḥaqq, is one of Allāh's Names: *Surely conjecture can by no means take the place of God*. But what do any of us have beyond conjecture? In *tawhīd's* placement of God above my comprehension, I am left with only mystery gods, inadequate substitutions for the Real; whatever I pray to cannot be Allāh. Classical Islam offers a self-destruct button that, when pushed, turns me into a Five Percenter.

When I accepted the greeting of "Peace, god," it did not feel like I was committing *shirk*, associating myself with Allāh in any idolatrous manner. I was not claiming to be omnipotent, omniscient, or eternal (and this had nothing to do with "race"); the claim to godhood was really just a coming to terms with the fact that we invent God for ourselves. My personal thought of Allāh became a contradictory mix of orthodox Islamic humility and Five Percenter self-deification, as each spoke to me at different times. I could reflect upon nature, which the Qur'ān tells us to do to consider Allāh's greatness, but recognize that my conception and experience of Allāh took place entirely within me, rather than between me and a mysterious Other. As Ibn al-'Arabī said, "The thing knows nothing but itself, and nothing knows anything except from itself."[4] William C. Chittick, an authoritative scholar of Ibn al-'Arabī's teachings, explains: "In effect, everyone worships himself, because what we worship is what we conceptualize, grasp, believe, and understand. Whatever object of worship it may be . . . it cannot be outside of our own selves."[5]

Whether or not I fear the mystery god as what Sadat X called the "crazy delusions of a big white man, sittin' on the throne, magic wand in his hand,"[6] I'm still the god of my mystery god; I made him up and cannot write myself out of him. Any god that humans conceive will be a human god. To believe in a god capable of mercy, love, wrath, or justice, or even a god with knowledge and a will—whether your god has wings and a beak (ornithomorphism) or gives light to darkness like the sun (heliomorphism)—is to make the god human. "All theism is anthropomorphic," writes Esther J. Hamori, "and there is no escaping it.... Without any kind of anthropomorphism, there can be no religion as we know it."[7] On that level, while reciting the orthodox creed of *lā ilāha illa Allāh* ("there is no god but God"), I can also say yeah, God is my thought.

The Qur'ān, whatever one may believe about its origin, does not solve the problem of human limitations. A Muslim claiming to know Allāh through the Qur'ān, on the basis that s/he understands what the Qur'ān actually says, could be trapped in a more arrogant and idolatrous self-image than any Five Percenter who wears Allāh's Name. Reading words on a page with my own eyes and my own brain and my own sense of what words mean, my own abilities with Arabic, my own knowledge and/or ignorance of the book's historical context, my own cultural and personal backstory and prejudices, my own assumptions about what a scripture is or can be, and of course my own preference of scholars, translators, and mystics to guide my interpretation, should I expect to trap a god that's bigger than my cage for him? That's naked idolatry, the confusion of my individual porkshit with the Absolute.

Indeed philosophically, limiting Allah to the utterances of the Qur'ān, a specific text, would also limit Allah to seventh-century Arabia.... That is a kind of *shirk* (violation of *tawhīd*). It holds the seventh-century Arabian conceptual framework of Allah, and the epistemological constraints of that context as equal to Allah.

—Amina Wadud[8]

Wadud can actually find support for this view in the Qur'ān itself: in 18:109, the Qur'ān says, "Even if the ocean were ink for (writing) the words of my Lord, the ocean would be exhausted before the words of my Lord were exhausted, even if We were to add another (ocean) to it." The great poet Jalāl ad-Dīn Rūmī (1207–1273), considering that one could write out the entire Qur'ān with a relatively small amount of ink, read the verse as showing the Qur'ān to be a "symbol of God's knowledge; it is not the whole of his knowledge. If a druggist put a pinch of medicine in a piece of paper, would you be so foolish as to say that the whole of the drugstore is in this paper?"[9] For Wadud, the Qur'ān would serve as one window through which we can look to Allāh; but like a photograph contained within its frame, no window can show the entire scene. When people assumed that their own windows *did* show everything, it looked to me like a cheapening of Allāh, a false god produced within the frames of our human experience. Any framed conception of Allāh is a mystery god and does not exist, as no god that we can contain is great enough to be the Real.

The Qur'ān's placement of God beyond language places Allāh above the Qur'ān itself; the Qur'ān is made powerless by its own claims. The Qur'ān's declaration "There is nothing like him" is a cluster of words telling me that Allāh cannot be found in words. Just as Muslim scholars translate the Qur'ān while insisting that all attempts at translation are doomed to failure, the Qur'ān at once commands me to know God and submit to God's unknowability.

To say that there's no mystery god might just be the truest surrender (*islām*). Calling my brain God isn't *shirk*; it's the only protection against *shirk* that I have. I call my brain God to avoid calling my brain God, or—maybe worse—calling someone else's brain God.

When he asked his father and his people: "What are these statues to which you are clinging?" they replied: "We found our fathers worshiping them."

—Qur'ān 21:52, 53

And the Five Percenters, I'm teaching them that they can't go on religion because religion never did anything for them. Like my mother, she said, "Jesus, Jesus, Jesus." I know he's over there in Jerusalem dead in the earth because he hasn't showed me nothing.

—Allah[10]

The 120 lessons address the challenge of seeking transcendence in prophets, scriptures, and traditions that we inherit, asking, "What is the birth record of said nations other than Islam?" (10:10) The answer: "Buddhism is 35,000 years old. Christianity is 551 years old." At first glance, these figures are plainly absurd; but as I worked to produce my own meanings for them, they caused me to reconsider the lives of religions.

Some Five Percenters have interpreted the near-timelessness accorded to Buddhism through that tradition's concept of previous Buddhas, while Elijah Muhammad depicted the Buddha as a scientist-imām who came to India from Mecca in 33,000 BCE. I choose to read the thirty-five centuries as a lesson on genealogy. No tradition is built from scratch; founders work with what they inherit. In this sense, Buddhism is older than Siddhartha or any previous Buddha. Going back a mere thousand years before the Buddha's birth takes us to the first Indus Valley civilization, in which we find early forerunners of the religious environment that would set a stage for him: cremation, lingams, swastikas, and even depictions of figures in something that resembles the lotus position. Dating back 3,500 years, these elements were just a tenth of the age that Elijah gave to Buddhism. If Buddhism was broken down to its ingredients, and the ingredients themselves were broken down, and so on again, we could find pieces of culture 35,000 years old and beyond.

In contrast, Elijah held the religion of Christianity to date back only 551 years, perhaps since the English word "Christianity" was not much older. Doing research based on a window from 1379 to 1383, I found other possibilities. These years saw the first English translation of the Bible and also the birth of Pope Eugene IV, who is seen today as having contributed to the church's theological and political support for the transatlantic slave trade. Together, such events could be seen as creating the particular Christianity that Elijah would encounter as an African man in America. The degree reminds me that old religions cannot appear to us in exactly the condition in which they were founded; religions are constantly changed and reinvented by their travels. They are always new, and the process of "founding" a religion never really ends.

Whether or not Buddhism really dates back to the Upper Paleolithic, or Christianity can be considered less than a thousand years old—and the two traditions could just as easily trade ages—they still have "birth records." In contrast to these "nations," the Student Enrollment also asks, "What is the birth record of the said Nation of Islam?" The answer: "The said Nation of Islam has no birth record. It has no beginning nor ending. It is older than the Sun, Moon, and Stars" (9:10). This brings to mind Allāh's assurance in the Qur'ān that "the sun, the moon, and the stars are subjected to his command" (7:54) and Abraham's observations of celestial bodies that led him to realize the oneness of God. Contemplating a star, Abraham declares it to be his Lord, only to be disappointed when the star becomes obscured from view. He then takes the moon for his Lord, but the moon disappears with sunrise. Abraham finally decides to worship the sun; but when the sun sets in turn, he realizes that his only Lord can be that which created the heavens and earth and never sets. In his *Mishkāt al-Anwār*, the immensely important thinker Muhammad Abū Hamīd al-Ghazālī (1058–1111) wrote of Abraham's encounters with the star, moon, and sun as representing specific stations passed by the seeker on his/her path to realizing Allāh's singularity (*fardānıyya*) as the only existent.

A "Nation of Islam" older than the sun, moon, and stars can't be the Nation of Islam, the historical phenomenon whose birth record starts with Master Fard Muhammad's arrival in Detroit on July 4, 1930. Nor can it be the Islam of Muhammad in seventh-century Mecca, the Islam of my Qur'ān, or the earlier prophets who taught their respective nations—even Abraham, who recognized Allāh through comparison to those celestial bodies. There's nothing timeless in Mecca, no piece of religion without a birth record attached. As Five Percenters read the sun, moon, and star as representing man, woman, and child, an Islam with no birth record would therefore exist beyond human beings, any particularities of language or the capabilities of a cerebral cortex, deeper than scripture and theology and theories of religion and anyone's thought of God.

I imagined an auto-critique in these degrees, as though the 120, like the Qur'ān, was admitting its own inadequacy: the failure of language to be more than language. If the 120 makes this confession about words, the Universal Flag says it about symbols. Displaying that same sun, moon, and star, the Universal Flag becomes a symbol that kills symbols:

At the center of the Universal Flag stands the 7, a placeholder for that which is beyond place—that which is "everywhere," says the RZA, "but you still can't locate"[11]—the Absolute Reality that manifested the universe in order to evolve a brain and know itself. Call it al-Ḥaqq or the Black Mind.

DEGREES 9:10 AND 10:10 force me to consider that my religion is not outside the world, that it travels through history to reach me, and therefore travels through power. I get my Qur'ān from Sunnism's third caliph and first mass burner of Qur'āns, 'Uthmān, who sent his own codex to the major cities of the empire and demanded that all other versions be destroyed. I desire an Islam without history's interference, but this is impossible. Nearly everything that we take for granted as inherent or essential to Islam is the result of human power struggle, even the idea that prophethood ends with Muḥammad. Nowhere in the Qur'ān does it clearly state that Muḥammad is the final prophet; the reading of "seal of prophets" (33:40) to signify finality took hold after Muḥammad's death, when the challenges of competing prophets and apostate tribes called for a new doctrine that could stabilize the Muslim community and protect the fledgling state against insurgency.[12]

Likewise, the Nation of Islam's lessons and earliest publications do not explicitly identify Master Fard Muhammad as God in person but rather as a prophet. A 1938 sociological study of the Nation of Islam, describing Elijah Muhammad's faction as an "even more extreme branch" of Fard's followers, marked the belief in Fard as God as a major point of difference between supporters of Elijah and the rest of the movement.[13] Fard's divinity was Elijah's innovation in the early post-Fard years, and came with political advantages. In *Black Crescent,* Michael A. Gomez observes that Elijah's reports of Fard revealing his divinity always have Elijah asking the question and Fard answering him; the narratives represent Elijah as more insightful than Fard's other students, for which Fard rewards him by surrendering this privileged information. In the competition for power after Fard's disappearance, the idea that Fard had shared his greatest secret with Elijah would elevate Elijah's own claim to authority.[14]

Even the vision of Islam that I found in Malcolm X, which I had sought as a resistance against power, arrived as the product of power: the first time that I saw Malcolm's face was on MTV, and the image of Malcolm that drove my conversion was actually Denzel Washington in a $34 million Warner Bros. film. The U.S. Postal Service hasn't yet put out an Elijah Muhammad stamp, and there's no big-studio biopic telling Elijah's side of the story—but, of course, the *image* of Malcolm that triumphed over his teacher might not have been the Malcolm that Malcolm himself would have chosen.

I eventually moved from my MTV/Warner Bros. mythology of Malcolm to an Islam defined by literature coming from Saudi Arabia. Politically advantaged through the control of Mecca, and financially advantaged through the twentieth-century oil boom, the Saudis have been empowered to push their own version of Islam across the globe. Lacking the means to critically examine what was presented to me as "real" Islam, I spent some time going crazy with it.

The question is no longer what kind of Muslim I am, but what kind of Muslim history has allowed me to be. As an American in these years, my choices are not the same as they might have been in Almohad Spain or Mughal India or Safavid Iran, or twelfth-century Abbāsid Baghdad as opposed to twelfth-century Fāṭimid Cairo, or the first generation after the Prophet's death, or during the Prophet's life, or even the Prophet's first Mecca period as opposed to his Medina period. Whatever constitutes "real" Islam in a given setting has no more objectivity than indexicals like "here," "now," and "me."

So here's what I've got: God is an idea in my head. The ingredients that went into my idea of God were transmitted to me by culture, and culture is human, and human beings are always competing with one another for dominance, so these things—theology, culture, dominance—are inseparable. In a nutshell, that's my Five Percenter understanding of religion.

Historically, what exists is the church. Faith, what is that? Religion is a political force.

—Michel Foucault[15]

Christianity is our slave master's . . . He gave you something to
enslave your brains. That is where you are tied up at: it's in your
brains, from the slave master . . . He says to you and me that, "I've
taken Jesus and I killed him. I've hung him up on a cross. Now
nigger, come on and worship it, because I'm going to do you the
same way."

—Elijah Muhammad[16]

Master Fard Muhammad's response to religion was a political act.
People who believe in a "mystery god" are described in the lessons as
"deaf, dumb, and blind, slaves to mental death and power" (14:40). The
degree warns against surrendering agency in our lives to other humans
based on their supposed knowledge of what invisible beings desire
from us—that is, for a family in abject poverty and an overcrowded
house to ask the Pope if God allows birth control, or for slaves to ask
the slaveowner if God has endorsed their captivity.

Nineteenth-century Russian radical Mikhail Bakunin connected religious authority with the elite's control of the masses in a breakdown that
would be closely mirrored in the thought of Master Fard Muhammad—
who, as a child, had reportedly envisioned himself throwing the Carne-
gies and Rockefellers of the world into a pit of fire. Bakunin dismissed
the majority of society as "kept in ignorance by the systematic efforts
of all the governments, who consider this ignorance, not without good
reason, as one of the essential conditions of their own power."[17] The
holders of power in society encourage people to "accept religious traditions without criticism and in a lump," as provided by "official poisoners
of all sorts, priests and laymen" until the delusions of the church have
become "more powerful even than their natural good sense."[18] These
masses are the 120's Eighty-Five Percent, "slaves from mental death and
power," ignorant of God and "their origin in this world" (14:40). One
god advised that I specifically remember the words "and power," suggesting that one's personal belief was less of an issue than the social

consequences of that belief. The real point is that we don't ask a phantom buddy to do our work for us, or surrender our wills to others who claim to represent the phantom buddy's wishes.

Bakunin recognized another class of people, "who, if they do not believe, must at least make a semblance of believing:"[19]

> This class comprising all the tormentors, all the oppressors, and all the exploiters of humanity; priests, monarchs, statesmen, soldiers, public and private financiers, officials of all sorts, policemen, gendarmes, jailers and executioners, monopolists, capitalists, tax-leeches, contractors and landlords, lawyers, economists, politicians of all shades, down to the smallest vendor of sweetmeats, all will repeat in unison those words of Voltaire: "If God did not exist, it would be necessary to invent him." For, you understand, "the people must have a religion." That is the safety-valve.[20]

In the 120, these are the Ten Percenters, described as "bloodsuckers" and "rich slavemakers of the poor," who depict God as a "spook who cannot be seen by the physical eye" (15:40). It is explained that such a god is advocated by the devil to "make slaves out of all that he can, so that he can rob them and live in luxury" (12:40). An attack on the Ten Percenters' god can be found in Frederick Douglass's "The Meaning of July Fourth for the Negro" address, delivered in Rochester, New York, on July 5, 1852. Douglass condemned an American Christianity which "favors the rich against the poor; which exalts the proud above the humble; which divides mankind into two classes, tyrants and slaves; which says to the man in chains, *stay there*; and to the oppressor, *oppress on*; it is a religion which may be professed and enjoyed by all the robbers and enslavers of mankind."[21] Even when a religion is manipulated to endorse social inequality, it can find its most loyal support among groups with the least security and comfort. The consequence is that a political party whose tax and health care policies favor the rich can still win votes from the poor by emphasizing social issues of religious import, such as gay marriage, abortion, or the "Ground Zero Mosque."

To use Allah's phrase, to be Ten Percent is to bring the minds of others *under the capture,* usually based on the notion that God withholds knowledge of himself from the masses but grants it to a privileged few, entitling these chosen ones to power. An early example would be depictions of Hammurabi receiving his code of laws as a revelation from the sun god Shamash. The 120's definition requires that Ten Percenters attain their power through lies and use it for unethical purposes, that is, the exploitation of others to make life more comfortable for themselves. This means that not every spiritual leader is necessarily a bloodsucker. I suspect that someone who uses a tradition's power for the good of humanity could escape categorization as a Ten Percenter. Supported by his mystical visions and biblical knowledge, Nat Turner inspired slaves to rise against their masters; it might be difficult to call him Ten Percent. In his rebellion against the Shah, Ayatollah Khomeini read Shi'ī millenarianism as a call to action: rather than simply wait for the Mahdī to come, Muslims must actively struggle to set the stage for him, striving to create a better, more just world for themselves. Perhaps a leader such as Khomeini, whose religious authority enabled him to stand up to an unjust power but ultimately become the unjust power himself, can move from Five to Ten Percent over the course of a career. Whether prophetic figures such as the seventh-century Muḥammad or Joseph Smith, or religious leaders such as the Pope, the Dalai Lama, the Aga Khan, or Louis Farrakhan should be denounced as Ten Percenters is up to our personal assessments of their motives.

To be a Ten Percenter is not a theological position as much as a political one; anyone can be a Ten Percenter, whatever s/he believes. The great philosopher Ibn Rushd (1126–1198) could potentially be called an agent of the Ten Percent. While holding the highest reality of Allāh to be abstract and beyond comprehension, Ibn Rushd advocated a simpler, more explicitly anthropomorphized god that the uneducated masses could grasp. For Ibn Rushd, preserving Islam (and social order) required lower classes to avoid the dangers of intellectualism and stick to worshiping what he saw as an inferior conception of the divine.

There's even room for secularists to be Ten Percenters; they can also take control of the people through an idea of what religion is or should be, transforming religion in the process. The notion of religion as a private, personal choice, (theoretically) unrelated to politics and national identity, comes to us through the culture fostered by a secular document: the Constitution of the United States of America. "Separation of church and state" is a power play, a cutting of religious institutions from the state's business. In France, where Catholicism's ties to the monarchy framed religion as a rival to the Republic, the appearance of Islamic head scarves is seen as threatening to the modern democratic nation-state and its construction of shared French identity. Divorcing religion from rituals of the state can allow the state itself to *become* religion, to bring minds *under the capture* by taking religion's place. In the rituals of civil religion, America offers repeated chances at transcendence: immortality in our cult of dead soldiers, communal worship in our festival of fireworks, pilgrimage to our national capital of statues and monuments, and hymnals in the form of patriotic country songs.

American religious freedom meets capitalism to make religion a competitive market. Ten Percenters can sell the sacred as a product; Walmart has reportedly made annual sales exceeding $1 billion in Christian books, music, and jewelry. It has been charged that calling Barnes & Noble a "secular" bookstore could be a bit off the mark, as its stores in America's more religious areas devote huge amounts of floor space to Christian material.[22] This intersection of church and commerce leaves an impact on the message; just as good business sense calls for Pepsi and Sony to avoid political controversy, the intense marketing of religion has little space for preachers challenging the social order. As media scholar Mara Einstein points out, "Instead of marching in the streets demanding a more equitable distribution of wealth, we get a personalized, market-driven Jesus, with the ultimate goal that God will make you rich."[23]

When celebrities like Madonna and Britney Spears took to wearing Kabbalah's red string (blessed as protection against the evil eye) on their left wrists, the Kabbalah Centre began selling red strings at Target (there was also an attempt to trademark the religious artifact). At the height of its pop culture presence, the Kabbalah Centre even peddled a Kabbalah Energy Drink, a "delicious citrus fusion" infused with Kabbalah Water and produced by the same company that makes 7Up. The Centre depicts Kabbalah Water—bottled spring water from Canada—as endowed with healing powers because it had been blessed by Rav Philip S. Berg, the sect's founder. "If the damn FDA would just let me put that the water cures cancer on the label," the Rav was quoted as saying in 2005, "I wouldn't need marketing."[24] A complete set of the Kabbalah Centre's essential texts, the *Zohar*, sells for $415; because of "positive energy" in the books, the Centre suggests that you buy more than one set, blessing both your home and workplace with the power. This energy within the Hebrew letters also means that one does not even have to understand Hebrew to benefit from them. "I have no idea what it says," remarked a Kabbalah practitioner to ABC News, "but that doesn't matter, this is powerful stuff."[25]

As the sacred merges with a secular marketplace, not only does the sacred become a product, but products become sacred, endowed with religious principles. Superstar athletes become shields for dirty corporate religion, their hard work and human power remade into symbols of the magical properties imbued in a pair of sneakers. Advertisers, like Ten Percenters, will never say that what you need is already within you; salvation must always be obtained from outside. Through myths of personal transformation that can be achieved by the ritual of purchase, the devil strives to "make slaves out of all he can so that he can rob them and live in luxury" (12:40). Remembering Master Fard Muhammad's statement that the devil had taught his uncle to "eat the wrong foods," which made him "other than his own self" (10-13:14), we can find a Ten Percenter in Den Fujita, the founder of McDonald's in Japan. Fujita had reportedly promised Japanese consumers, "If we eat McDonald's hamburgers and potatoes for a thousand years, we will become taller, our skin will become white and our hair blond."[26]

Between Kabbalah Water and Coca-Cola stands Oprah Winfrey. In marketing spiritual health and personal growth without emphasizing overtly religious material, Oprah has become a "post-modern priestess—an icon of church-free spirituality" and from one perspective, the world's most powerful televangelist.[27] The image of Oprah as personal guru to masses of people is a mystery god: an empty promise of what cannot be real, the selling of a personal savior between commercials as another life-changing product that instantly makes everything perfect forever. "Oprah's religion is one that doesn't take too much effort," says Einstein; "it is created by the consumer, and just like the American Dream, if you keep on working it, it will cure whatever ails you."[28]

The bloodsuckers and "deaf, dumb, and blind" in all their varieties leave a mere five percent of the population to be neither a mental slave nor slavemaker. Naturally, both Bakunin and Fard saw themselves in this class. For Bakunin, the materialists and revolutionary socialists were those inspired by the "love of truth" and passions for logic and justice.[29] The 120 describes the Five Percent as consisting of "poor righteous teachers" who reject the lies of the Ten Percent, recognize the true and living God as the Asiatic Black Man, and "teach freedom, justice, and equality to all the human families of the planet earth." (16:40). At a time when American socialists such as Howard Kester reimagined Jesus not as a "worker of miracles," but rather a "workman struggling with the problems of his people," Fard asserted that "freedom, justice, and equality" were Christ's true teachings (5:14). It was also during Fard's active years that Langston Hughes wrote his poem "Goodbye Christ," published in the *Negro Worker* in 1932. "The popes and preachers've made too much money from it," he laments. "They've sold you to too many kings, generals, robbers, and killers." Hughes tells Christ that his usefulness has run out: "Make way for a new guy with no religion at all. . . You're getting in the way of things Lord."[30]

Fard's particular use of Islam essentially presented a Marxist/anarchist critique of religion while also making use of religion's power to remake culture. Though normative Islam may be no less "spooky" than normative Christianity, the imagery of Islam placed African Americans in a new world in ways that white-defined Marxism or anarchism could not.

While Fard dressed up his message in religion, his solutions to social inequality were more practical than supernatural. In Fard's *Problem Book*, Muslims are shown the way to salvation through basic math word problems. Fard promises that mastering the "Mathematic Language" leads to "luxury, money, good homes, friendship in all walks of life" and then tests our multiplication skills, offering prizes of cash and Qur'āns for students who answer them correctly: "the reward is awaiting for the best and neatest worker." If Saturn orbits the sun at 1,037⅓ miles per hour, how many miles are covered in a Saturnian year—29½ Earth years? If one-hundredth of a cubic inch contains 200 million atoms, how many atoms are in fifty square miles? Some of the questions manage to include ideological content. One describes a lion pacing in a cage for "nearly four centuries" before finding the door—easy enough to interpret, recalling the 40:40 degree: original people have been waiting 379 years for the devil's destruction. The lion has 17 million keys, which he turns at the rate of sixteen and seventeen one-hundredths per minute; in 20:36, Fard tells us that there are 17 million "original Muslims" in North America. How long will it take the lion to turn all 17 million keys? Another problem states that in Detroit, people only have money to eat twice a day, and the average person consumes 10⅕ ounces of "poison animal," which destroys his/her brain at a rate of

$\frac{1}{60}$ of an ounce of brain for every 10 ounces of poison animal. If a person of one-third destroyed brain can be robbed by the devil, how long would it take for the devil to rob these poison animal eaters?[31]

Master Fard Muhammad came to the poorest of the poor and spoke of luxury, but he wasn't selling a name-it-and-claim-it prosperity gospel or the power of positive thinking, and he wasn't trying to make people into mystical masters. Fard wanted his Muslims to learn how to manage their finances, spend less and save more, work hard, keep a household, and stay away from the wrong foods, while recognizing these practical skills as divine virtues. "It took this real teaching to make us real," wrote Warith Deen Mohammed in 1976.

> When he saw that our problem was that we were already too spiritual (too wrapped up in the Bible), he devised a plan. He knew he could not get us if he came at us with the Holy Scripture. . . . Our churches were filled with more spirit than anybody else's churches. No one could come to us telling us that we needed spirit. . . .
>
> People had come to us with God and religion and they have approached us with the spirit, talking to us about holiness, righteousness, divinity, God and the saints. Master Fard discovered that that is not the way Almighty God develops the community of His people. . . . When you find a people completely dead, you do not come to them with the spirit. . . . He did not say that the streets were filled with spirits playing on invisible harps, walking around with golden slippers that did not really exist. He said to tell us that there was real gold over there. . . . [32]

Hip-hop legend Afrika Bambaataa isn't a Five Percenter, but he sounds like one when he describes two distinct categories of American religion: the "go to sleep slavery type of religion," and its antithesis, the "do for self and others type of religion." The latter, he says, relates to "knowledge, wisdom, [and] understanding of self and others."[33] As with the Ten Percent, my comprehension of the Five Percent deals more with the social impact of a theology than the theology itself. The issue seems to be less about the mystery god's existence than his usefulness; religions that advocate a mystery god tend to claim that we can interact with him, negotiating through pleas and gestures to persuade him to improve our conditions. Of course, not all believers in mystery gods simply "wait at home," as the lessons say. During our 2008 interview for *Vibe*, the RZA told me that such deeply religious personages as Mahatma Gandhi and Martin Luther King, Jr., qualified as Five Percenters in his view of the term. I can't imagine anyone arguing that Sunnī Islam's mystery god had pacified Malcolm, who stated in the last month of his life, "I believe in religion, but a religion that includes political, economic, and social action." Malcolm even mocked his former mentor, who denounced both the ballot and the bullet, for his willingness to "sit and wait on God to come."[34] For Nation of Islam insiders, it would appear that Malcolm had referred to the Nation's own lessons—"Will you sit at home and wait for that mystery god to bring you food?" (11:40)—to call Elijah Muhammad a "deaf, dumb, and blind" Eighty-Five Percenter.

Before a distinct group called the Five Percenters existed, the Nation of Islam claimed to be this Five Percent—but the Nation's discourse would nonetheless resemble a Ten Percenter's claim to power. Elijah Muhammad's unquestionable authority came from his endorsement by a long-lost Fard, whom he portrayed as having been elected by an unseen council of scientists that secretly ruled the universe. Sometimes, the demarcations between Five, Ten, and Eighty-Five aren't so clear. This was Allah's complaint of his time in the mosque, as he mentioned in a 1968 interview comparing the Nation of Islam with the Catholic Church:

I can show a religious man that he never led anyone to God. Not the Pope or anyone. They all died and all the people in the Bible died. Now where are they? Where are they? The only way you will find God [is] if you keep on reproducing until he make himself known. And the Pope, he's supposed to be a successor to God. Where they show the people? Have they? Elijah says W. D. Fard is God. Where is he? They make me sick. . . . My wife wanted to teach me Elijah Muhammad. She tried to put my mind under the capture of that man. I said, "Woman, you crazy!" She said, "What, what, what." I said, "What, what."[35]

Despite my Five Percent–inspired notion of Islam as I Self Lord And Master, I still hoped for new ways of having Muslim community. Around the time of my first encounters with the Five Percent, I began building with a nascent movement called "Progressive Islam." The scene appealed to me most for its call to Islamic gender equality.

Progressive Islam's first wave found its climax in early 2005, with an act of radical ritual: an Islamic prayer service in which women and men prayed together behind our female imām, Amina Wadud. As an open feminist challenge to ritual norms, the prayer brought worldwide attention to the cause. The prayer also served as the public launch of a new organization, the Progressive Muslim Union (PMU). I accepted an invitation to serve on PMU's board of directors, but the organization collapsed within a year.

It was during PMU's one and only board meeting that I realized my true problem with the movement. We were discussing plans to hold woman-led prayer events across North America, and board members made suggestions of distinguished Muslim women who should lead in various cities. Each prayer, it was assumed, had to be led by a recognized scholar at the level of Amina Wadud. While heavy names were thrown about and their star power debated, I thought of the Five Percenter parliament, where poor righteous teachers gather in a cipher to take turns offering their own interpretations of the day's Mathematics, degree in the 120, or whatever's on their mind. At parliament, there are no imāms, no priests, and no requirement that you learn six dialects of Arabic and study all of the classical *tafsīr* and *ḥadīth* before claiming your right to speak. Imagine a church or mosque service in which every member of the congregation gave a piece of the sermon. You could be an elder who walked with Allah, or a teenager who's only on the Student Enrollment, but you still step into the cipher and give what you have. Comparing Progressive Islam's bourgeois academic scene with the Five Percent, I couldn't help but feel that we had missed something: the chance to make a real movement of the people.

"Why can it only be scholars?" I asked the board. "Why not have some fifteen-year-old girl lead a prayer? You know, find some kid who has never imagined that she could have any respect in the community, and put her up in front and have her lead the prayer and let her remember for the rest of her life that this radical fringe movement told her that she can be an imām."

A board member named Hussein Ibish shot me down quick. These prayers were political performances, he explained; for the movement to find legitimacy, we needed women with "proper gravitas" to lend their authority. No sooner were the words out of his mouth than I understood that PMU could never ease my spiritual static. For me, heartbreak over Islam wasn't just about interpretations of scripture and jurisprudence; my problem was organized religion itself.

Debate over woman-led prayer and its Islamic legitimacy leads to a challenge for proof from authentic sources. While thankful for the intellectually rigorous Muslim feminists who can answer the call, I wasn't climbing into that ring. When pious reformers used words like "permissible" or "legal" in their discussion of intergender congregations, it made my skin crawl. *Legal as opposed to what?* To even humor the question would mean that we regarded some forms of worship as "illegal," which didn't strike me as "progressive" at all. It seemed that for some reformists, the solution was not to rethink religious authority or the assumptions upon which our current Islam had been built, but to merely replace the conservative imāms with liberal imāms and keep the whole machine running as normal.

"A spirit is subjected to us and not we to the spirit," said Elijah Muhammad.[36] Rather than prove myself with authentic sources, I ask the authentic sources to prove themselves to me. In the enterprise of defining Islam, I do not have a source better than my conscience; that's the meaning of I Self Lord And Master. There's no waiting at home for imāms and jurists to bring me a religion, and no sneaking around the old structures. When making this point at readings and lectures, I am sometimes asked if this means that Islam is simply "whatever we say it is." I have no choice but to shrug. Yes, Islam is what we say it is. I'm embarassed to say this, because it looks like a cop-out—which actually worries me, as Progressive Islam has given public voice to some flaky people. Still, it's less a cop-out than the easier answer of blind imitation, because I've struggled for years on my religion. I confess to having an inner Sherman Jackson voice that wants to distinguish some Islams as more legitimate than others. I've desperately wanted to say that the tradition's not just a buffet of texts, that it's more than a matter of filling my plate with what I like, and that I can name an Islamic truth that's nonnegotiable.

Reading Omid Safi's *Progressive Muslims* anthology, I found a jewel in Ebrahim Moosa's chapter, "The Debts and Burdens of Critical Islam." Moosa calls for us to admit that "all we really know about what we call 'Islam' is what humans have ever told us": we get our Islam first from the Prophet, then from "the Companions, the imams, the scholars, jurists, and authorities" all defining Islam within their own experiences. [37] Muslims must submit to these limits of representation, argues Moosa, "unless they claim to being God themselves—which surely takes the debate out of the realm of sanity."[38] I read Moosa's words in a context for which he could not have been prepared—riding the train uptown on my way to a place called the Allah School, where sane men did in fact call themselves God. In my interpretation of Five Percenter thought, the claim to godhood was not a denial but an acknowledgment that human representation is all that we have.

If I'm not Allah, who is?

—Allah[39]

I'd still go to the mosque and pray, but who or what was I praying to? My actions gave every appearance of a conventionally pious Muslim; I performed ritual washings, pressed my face to the carpet, and recited the same Arabic formulas that I had learned early in my conversion. This was my script for approaching Allāh, as good a script as any, but no longer a conversation between me and a mystery god. If Allāh was really al-Ḥaqq, my prayers could not tell Absolute Reality anything about my spiritual condition, intentions, or needs that it did not already know. During a long flight, my recitations of Allāh's Name at moments of turbulence did not imply that I expected Absolute Reality to steady the plane. The value and purpose of prayer was what I said to myself, the mental state that I created with my prayer, the peace that I found in Islam. In a sense, I was my prayer's addressee.

Prayer still came with blessings and rewards, but it wasn't anything spooky like checking boxes on Allāh's cosmic scorecard, asking the King for charity or pleading my case to the Judge. Prayer opened up a quiet moment for me to step out of my self-absorption and petty stresses and recognize my smallness in Allāh, submitting to my smallness. The feelings of peace that I found in such moments would integrate with Qur'ānic verses and stories from the Prophet's life that taught me how to treat people, and I'd step out of the mosque refreshed and ready to deal with the world again. The Qur'ān, Sunna (Muḥammad's example) and centuries of accumulated Islamic tradition gave me a beautiful technology for becoming more human. It all remained sufficiently "real" to me, not for a superhuman source but for what I could do with these tools. When I missed prayer with my Muslim brothers and sisters, I forfeited real-life, nonspooky blessings.

Though Five Percenters often express a desire to "kill all religion," they inadvertently rescued mine. The Five Percenters helped to resolve my defining crisis: the matter of drawing benefit from a religious life when no religion can be everything that it claims to be. For Islam to be of the earth and not the clouds became a comfort, not a problem. With the insanely heretical idea that perhaps I know what's best for me, I can love my religion more honestly than ever.

SIX

BATTLEFIELD EARTH:
FIVE PERCENTER FEMINISM

*I think that 'twixt the Negroes of the South and the
women at the North, all talking about rights, the white
men will be in a fix pretty soon.*

—Sojourner Truth (1797–1883)[1]

IN A SOCIETY THAT is both white supremacist and patriarchal, the racist
and sexist white male is never forced to choose between conflicting loyalties. He doesn't have to worry that masculinist ideology will undermine the
white family structure, or that rallying for white unity will betray the need
to empower men. It's all the same, really. Racism and sexism cooperate to
serve him, and they both have the prestige of being "traditional values."

This setup could be the greatest genius of the devil's kingdom, because
if the right hand doesn't get you, the left hand will; people who resist one
form of oppression may be trapped into reinforcing the other. If a feminist happens to be racist, s/he could favor the liberation of some women
over others; if a black nationalist is sexist, s/he might defend the black
community against outside oppressions while perpetuating oppressions
within. The argument could be made that you can't really be a feminist
without also challenging white privilege, and you can't really be antiracist
if you think that women should be controlled by men. The intersection
of oppressions, however, is also an intersection of privileges—meaning

that white women are still white, black men are still men, and black women may be forced to choose which fight matters more.

Such tensions have been present throughout American freedom movements. In the time of slavery, abolitionists were divided on the question of whether women should speak publicly to audiences of men; such scandalous behavior might have associated the antislavery cause with loose morals. Patriarchy stood in the way of black and white women who wished to contribute to black freedom, but women asserting their right to speak against slavery challenged both racism and sexism. Sarah Grimké (1792–1873) insisted that women's liberation was crucial to black liberation: "We cannot push Abolitionism forward with all our might until we take up the stumbling block out of the road. . . . What then can woman do for the slave, when she herself is under the feet of man and shamed into silence?"[2]

Abolitionism's rhetoric of human dignity inspired those who would extend its promise to include women. Angelina Grimké (1805–1879), Sarah's sister, described abolitionism as "the high school of morals in our land—the school in which *human rights* are more fully investigated" and revealed, "The investigation of the rights of slaves has led me to a better understanding of my own."[3] In 1848, a gathering of sixty-eight women and thirty-two men in Seneca Falls, New York, resulted in a feminist "Declaration of Sentiments." Modeled after the Declaration of Independence, the text demonstrates parallels between racial and gender subjugation: even in the white ruling caste, a woman had no representation in the making of laws that ruled her, no choices of vocation or education, "all colleges being closed against her," and no rights of property or control of her own wages. Man had denied woman "all the avenues to wealth and distinction which he considers most honorable to himself" and made her "civilly dead" through the domestic enslavement of marriage, which put her completely under the legal power of her husband.[4] The Declaration also noted the psychological impact of this social order upon woman, charging that patriarchy worked "to destroy her confidence in her own powers, to lessen her self-respect, and to make her willing to lead a dependent and abject life."[5] Among the men who signed the Declaration was Frederick Douglass.

While some male abolitionists advocated the merging of women's rights with abolitionism, others held that attaching these two struggles made poor political sense. It was feared within the movement that a white man would be less open to the freeing of black slaves if this also meant freeing his white wife. A male abolitionist warned Angelina Grimké that her advocacy for women's rights brought harm to the slaves' cause. She answered, "The time to assert a right is when that right is denied."[6] When the Declaration's primary author, Elizabeth Cady Stanton (1815–1902), was similarly challenged by a man saying, "One war at a time . . . This hour belongs to the Negro," she replied, "Do you believe the African race is composed entirely of males?"[7]

By instigating dialogue about the participation of women in public affairs, and causing women to think about commonalities between racial and sexual injustice, the campaign to abolish slavery gave rise to American feminism. The struggles against racism and sexism remained connected, at least until black men and white women were compelled to choose between them. After the Civil War, abolitionism grew into a movement to grant voting rights to African Americans and women, but suffragists disagreed over which group should be given top priority. If voting rights became possible for black men, should suffragists settle for what Douglass called "the culmination of one-half of our demands" or risk losing it by fighting to include women? While staunchly advocating suffrage for all, Douglass regarded black suffrage as the more pressing concern. Stanton and Susan B. Anthony (1820–1906) also believed that both African Americans and women should be granted their rights, but held that if universal suffrage was not possible, women's rights should come first.

"If colored men get their rights," Sojourner Truth foretold, "and not colored women get theirs, there will be a bad time about it."[8] The suffrage debate pitted supporters of black (male) enfranchisement against champions for (white) women, with neither side promising the vote to black women. Douglass argued that even if only men could vote, black women would still benefit from voting rights given to black men. Stanton decried the Republican party's choice to push male suffrage at the expense of universal suffrage as creating "antagonism between black men and all women."[9] As the division widened, white feminists betrayed their abolitionist heritage and even played into white racism. With a claim that black women weren't likely to vote if given the chance, women's suffrage was promoted as a means of increasing white electoral power. Stanton expressed resentment that (white) women would have to "stand aside and see 'Sambo' walk into the kingdom first"[10] and went so far as to suggest that for a black woman, "It is better to be the slave of an educated white man, than of a degraded, ignorant black one."[11] For their racist rhetoric, Douglass unsuccessfully attempted to have Stanton and Anthony expelled from the Equal Rights Association.

Forced by the white male devil to fight against itself, the American struggle for social equality would never fully recover. The wounds could still be detected a century later, when second-wave white feminists ignored the particular experiences and concerns of black women, and even in the 2008 Democratic presidential primaries, when deciding between Barack Obama and Hillary Clinton reenacted, for many voters, the choice of which painful history must be corrected first. It has been argued that Obama won in part because while Clinton represented an older generation of white women who treated feminism as a white project, Obama spoke to younger voters who recognized feminism and antiracism as interrelated. When the Clinton campaign exploited race, it actually made Obama the feminist choice.[12]

> The sexual question and the racial question have always been entwined, you know. If Americans can mature on the level of racism, then they have to mature on the level of sexuality.
>
> —James Baldwin[13]

This tension can also be felt in the Five Percent, a tradition that speaks on both race and gender. For the black man to be God, as I understood it, was a reclaiming of his power to create himself and his world in his own image, by his own vision. The black man calling himself Allah meant that he was no longer enslaved by the crippling narratives of the white man. The question of whether this power also belongs to the black woman, and to what degree, sparks heated debates among Five Percenters.

Controversy centers around the question of women possessing an equal claim to the Name of God. My teacher, Azreal, was sympathetic to the idea, and my own logic would suggest that control of the Name should be shared among all; but having been the object of neither racism nor sexism, we're not part of that conversation. The wisest approach would be for me to take a neutral position, but as James Baldwin said, there's no such thing as a neutral position; the refusal to speak is still a political act with consequences. To say that whiteness prevents me from speaking on maleness means that I owe something to my whiteness that I do not owe to my maleness. But I am also pulled in the other direction, with the knowledge that challenging maleness does not entitle me to ignore my whiteness. I must formulate a position without much confidence that I have the right to one.

Because Five Percenters are as diverse as any community, the matter is never as simple as saying that I side with the men or the women. Within the culture, there are male sexists but also male progressives, along with feminist women and antifeminist women, and people in gray areas between these categories. I can't be the devil who steps in to impose my own values; all I'm really qualified to say is what fits my situation, being both white and male, with my own readings of American history and the Five Percent.

I have been asked countless times how, as a white person, I can call myself a friend of the Five Percenters; it is assumed that the gods must be virulent racists who insult and threaten me whenever I come to the

Allah School, and that I accept heapings of abusive rhetoric for the sake of my self-hating white liberal guilt. This has been far from the case; in my dealings with the Five Percent, I am consistently treated with respect and even friendship. Meanwhile, I find this tradition commanding me to perform inner investigation, to look at myself as a white person and recognize just how much of my world and identity have been created by injustice and the suffering of others. Race, however, is not the only means in America by which identity is created. For the fuller humanity promised with the Five Percent's knowledge of self, I would need an equally serious treatment of what it means to be male.

Everything that the Five Percenters had taught me about examining myself as a white person could also be applied to my self-examination as a man. Like white supremacy, patriarchy creates a sense that conditions of inequality are "natural." Such a mentality produces devils: a ruling class whose members remain so enmeshed in their privilege that they cannot help but act it out. Like white people, men—even well-intentioned and enlightened men who remain ideologically cool on paper—can appear to be devils by nature, since they don't even know what they're doing when they're doing it. For exhibit A, I give you Sherman Jackson, who writes in *Islam and the Problem of Black Suffering* that he has no idea what it's like to be in a dominant group:

> I sometimes wonder . . . how I might respond from a posture of unearned privilege, where I become the object, rather than the subject, of social protest from voices whose history of subjugation at the hands of my group confers on their cause an automatic semblance of legitimacy. What kind of social morality might I embrace?[14]

The professor answers his own question by forgetting that he travels through the Muslim community (and America at large) while owning a penis. For exhibit B, I'd look at the portrayal of female characters in

my own novels, in which women have existed primarily as sexual challenges through which messed-up males can work out their issues. I
could reevaluate material that I had written consciously *against* sexism
and still find it exposing the pins and needles in my own head.

> Women have had the power of naming stolen from us. . . . To
> exist humanly is to name the self, the world and God.
>
> —Mary Daly[15]

God has long been a factor in women's freedom struggles. Like abolitionism, early American feminism required a conversation with the
religion of power. In her famous "Arn't I a Woman?" speech from 1851,
Sojourner Truth made theological defenses for women's liberation.
"Then that little man in black there," she remarked, "he says women
can't have as much rights as men, 'cause Christ wasn't a woman." To this
argument she countered, "Where did your Christ come from? From
God and a woman! Man had nothing to do with him." Secondly, she
answered to the blame of women for the sin of Eve: "If the first woman
God ever made was strong enough to turn the world upside down all
alone, these women together ought to be able to turn it back, and get
it right side up again! And now they is asking to do it, the men better
let them."[16]

When religious leaders objected to women speaking in public, Angelina Grimké attacked the "deep laid scheme of the clergy against us" for
its claim that "every time we open our mouths for the dumb we are
breaking a divine command."[17] Sarah Grimké, attributing the "corrupt
public opinion" regarding women to "perverted interpretation" and
"false translation" of the Bible, asserted her own authority upon scripture: "I believe it to be the solemn duty of every individual to search
the Scriptures for themselves, with the aid of the Holy Spirit, and not
be governed by the views of many men, or set of men."[18] "The Grimkés
simply sought to delegitimate a tradition of biblical interpretation that

had grown out of what they saw as warped male commentary," writes Robert H. Abzug in *Chaos Crumbling.* "The sisters thus followed a precedent set in the abolitionists' biblical argument against slavery, one that sought to overthrow dominant proslavery Biblical interpretation based upon parallels with slavery among the Hebrews."[19]

Similar to his attack on American Christian racism, Douglass spoke on the church's hand in sexism. Comparing the Methodist Episcopal Conference's failure to include women with its earlier opposition to abolition, Douglass referenced his negative impressions of Islam, lamenting a Christianity that could "enforce this Mahometan idea of woman upon American women," in which woman "has no recognized moral, social, or religious existence. In the mosques of the East, her presence among the faithful is held a defilement. She is deemed incapable of self-direction—a body without a soul."[20]

What power is it that makes the Hindoo woman burn herself upon the funeral pyre of her husband? Her religion. What holds the Turkish woman in the harem? Her religion. By what power do the Mormons perpetuate their system of polygamy? By their religion. Man, of himself, could not do this; but when he declares, 'Thus saith the Lord,' of course he can do it.

—Elizabeth Cady Stanton[21]

In addition to statements on sexism in American economics, politics, and law, the Convention's Declaration of Sentiments charged that "religious degradation" had contributed to women feeling "aggrieved, oppressed, and fraudulently deprived of their most sacred rights." In the church, man gave woman "but a subordinate position, claiming apostolic authority for her exclusion from the ministry, and, with some exceptions, from any public participation in the affairs of the church. . . . He has usurped the prerogative of Jehovah himself, claiming it as his right to assign for her a sphere of action, when that belongs to her conscience and to her God."[22] Stanton made an attempt at the solution with her *Woman's Bible*, created with the help of twenty-six other women and published in two parts in 1895 and 1898. In the text's introduction, Stanton explicitly rejects all stories of human beings walking and talking with the mystery god or getting their sacred laws from him, since these encounters have produced nothing good for woman: "all the religions on the face of the earth degrade her, and so long as woman accepts the position that they assign her, her emancipation is impossible."[23]

The conversation continued into the twentieth century with second-wave feminism, as radical women embarked on deconstructing male-centered representations of God. "If one purpose of deity," writes Margot Adler, "is to give us an image we can *become*, it is obvious that women have been left out of the quest, or at least have been forced to strive for an oppressive and unobtainable masculine image."[24]

Just as a white god speaks for the interests of white people, glorifying whiteness as divine, feminist theologian Mary Daly wrote in 1973 that "If God is male, then male is God." Echoing more than a century of black criticisms of the blue-eyed, blond-haired Jesus, Daly argued that images of He-God sanctified the power of men over women:

> The Judaic-Christian tradition has served to legitimate sexually imbalanced patriarchal society. Thus, for example, the image of the Father God, spawned in the human imagination and sustained as plausible by patriarchy, has in turn rendered service to this type of society by making its mechanisms for the oppression of women appear right and fitting. If God in "his" heaven is a father ruling "his" people, then it is in the "nature" of things and according to divine plan and the order of the universe that society be male dominated. . . . Within this context, a mystification of roles takes place: the husband dominating his wife represents God himself.[25]

Similarity to the Five Percent's mission should be obvious, as Daly calls for an "awakening of women to their human potentiality by creative action," which reveals the "Second Coming of God incarnate," the "manifestation of God in themselves."[26]

Considering what exactly one means by reference to the "Goddess" in women's spirituality movements, Carol P. Christ articulates what she has found to be the three most common definitions:

1. A divine female, a personification who can be invoked in prayer and ritual.
2. Symbol of the life, death, and rebirth energy in nature and culture, in personal and communal life.
3. Symbol of the affirmation of the legitimacy and beauty of female power.[27]

Daly was critical of the idea that problems with God the Father could be solved simply by calling him Goddess the Mother; but for some participants in goddess religion, it would seem that the Goddess was essentially a feminization of the Abrahamic He-God, a creator/protector described by Christ as "out there." Other women would see the Goddess not only as "out there" but also "within themselves and in all natural processes."[28] "I have spoken of the Goddess as psychological symbol and also as manifest reality," writes neo-pagan feminist Starhawk. "She is both. She exists, *and* we create Her."[29]

Christ opens her essay, "Why Women Need the Goddess," by quoting Ntozake Shange's play, "For Colored Girls Who Have Considered Suicide When the Rainbow Is Enuf": "I found God in myself and I loved her fiercely." Christ holds that a woman who lives by these words affirms "that the divine principle, the saving and sustaining power, is in herself, that she will no longer look to men or male spirit-figures as saviors."[30]

As I read these texts, it seemed that a woman who realized her divine inner self, rather than appeal to a mystery goddess "out there," would be a feminist Five Percenter. Within or without, the redefining of God as feminine performed the same function as the Five Percent's "I Self Lord And Master" or even a black Jesus on the wall: "to name God in oneself, or to speak the word 'Goddess' again after many centuries of silence, is to reverse age-old patterns of thinking in which male power and female subordination are viewed as the norm."[31] For women to redraw the divine was also to redraw themselves, allowing for a "new naming of women's power."[32]

Goddess spirituality even corresponded to the Five Percent in its use of mythic prehistory. Both movements attributed the world's present condition to a past shift of consciousness, in which people were blinded to the true knowledge of themselves. For Five Percenters, this fall occurred with the rise of false religions and worship of nonexistent mystery gods, causing the black man to look for God outside himself. The goddess movement calls to a forgotten time when religions were built upon representations of the divine as feminine—sun goddesses, warrior goddesses, and female creators of the universe. It is claimed that humanity began its decline when men rose to power, smashed all of the goddess statues and replaced them with God as Man. In both goddess thought and the Five Percenters, these golden ages illustrate that our current state of affairs is out of harmony with the natural order of things, but also capable of being restored to its idyllic original state.

With so much common ground between Five Percenters and the goddess movement, it seemed natural to me that they should form an alliance and tear down their shared enemy, the World-Raping Church of the White Man. Unfortunately, old hostilities have forced a choice between God as a black man and God as a white woman. God as a black woman is not on the ballot.

Feminist spirituality movements have been dominated by white women who faced one type of oppression, largely failing to speak to the experiences and concerns of black women, who faced multiple oppressions. Black lesbian poet and essayist Audre Lorde wrote a well-known

"Open Letter to Mary Daly," in which she charges Daly with failing to think through her own white privilege. In Lorde's critique, even Daly's promotion of the Goddess is found to be steeped in racism:

> So I wondered, why doesn't Mary deal with Afrekete as an example? Why are her goddess images only white, western european, judeo-christian? Where was Afrekete, Yemanje, Oyo, and Mawulisa? Where were the warrior goddesses of the Vodun, the Dahomeian Amazons, and the warrior-women of Dan?[33]

"Assimilation within a solely western european herstory," she tells Daly, "is not acceptable."[34]

If Lorde could not find herself in Daly's reimagining of God, I don't believe that she would have had an easier time at parliament. Though the Five Percent interpretation that most resonated with me named both men and women as gods, it became clear early in my research of the culture that this was not a popular idea. Rather than challenge my maleness, I often found Five Percenter materials expressing sexist attitudes, such as the common description of black women as "secondary but most necessary."[35] I wanted to ask, *Secondary to what?*

The black man is Knowledge (1) to the black woman as Wisdom (2); mathematically, Knowledge precedes Wisdom in the natural order of things, and Wisdom cannot exist without Knowledge. The notion of a female god has been often dismissed as reversing the natural order, placing Wisdom in front of Knowledge. In Five Percent discourse, putting Wisdom before Knowledge implies that you've made a judgment without having obtained all the necessary information, speaking on what you do not know.

The black man is the Sun; the black woman is Earth, and as gods have told me, "It's called the solar system, not the earth system." For a black woman to call herself God is seen as analogous to the Earth straying out of orbit and attempting to play the role of the Sun. As Earth/

Moon, the woman receives/reflects her man's light, but does not produce light of her own.

Let now my penis be praised, and serve as a reminder to you!

—Enki, Mesopotamian deity[36]

Ancient Sumerians worshiped Enki, possessor of the Tablet of Destinies, as the deity of fresh water and also the god of semen. He dug irrigation ditches with his penis, and his ejaculation produced the waters of the Tigris and Euphrates. The myths of Enki struck me as resonant with Five Percenter imaginations of gender; Five Percenter male sexuality is reproductive, as an Assyriologist wrote of Enki, "on both the metaphoric and concrete levels."[37] In popular Five Percent thought, the penis and vagina are treated as symbolic indicators of man and woman's cosmological significance. With gods sometimes comparing their doctrines to traditional sky father/earth mother mythologies, woman is seen not so much as the cocreator of life, but rather the fertile soil in which man plants life. Receptivity is then equated with passivity. "The feminine is the receptive principle and the male is the active principle," argues Knowledge Scientific Cipher.[38] "Stating that the Black man is God is not meant to degrade or debase the Black woman, but to affirm HIS role, and not take anything away from hers," explains Supreme Understanding Allah. "God represents the creative force in the universe."[39] To be the creative force in the universe is seen as essentially *not* feminine.

When Five Percenters, avoiding the word "religion," choose instead to call their community a "God-centered culture," they unapologetically designate the Five Percent as a *man*-centered culture. "When one titles the Black woman as a 'goddess,' " argues the Five Percenter anthology *Knowledge of Self*, "then one is implying that the only difference is gender, yet that the duties are the same. . . . 'God' and 'Earth' clarifies the fact that the duty of the Blackman and the duty of the Black woman are different, yet complementary in nature."[40] These complementary opposites are based on essentialist ideas of what it means to be a "real" woman and "real" man.

Five Percenter media typically idealizes man as the "intellectual, economic and cultural head of his family."[41] One Five Percenter author praises the black woman as vital to his own success by comparing her to the queen on a chessboard. In this analogy, man is not only the king on the board but also the supreme hand that controls all pieces: "God directs her movements both at home and abroad. It is a grave mistake in chess to be careless with the movement of your Queen."[42] This attitude may help to explain the severely uneven male-female ratio that I have observed among Five Percenters, both online and in physical space.

As with racial essentialism, ideas of gender essentialism are socially constructed. Amina Wadud slices up the notion of "natural complementarity" in more orthodox Muslim communities: "While positively stressing relationships, it keeps their inequality central, by evaluating each player on a separate and unequal standard, leaving the relative power and privilege to men and male roles."[43] According to Wadud, "complementarity" ends up meaning that "[a] woman can complement a man like a tie complements a suit."[44]

For me, the Five Percent's black and male supremacies worked to undo one another, particularly as I heard anecdotes of a white male Five Percenter in 1980s Brooklyn who had a son with a black woman. In the standard Five Percent view, their child qualified as an Asiatic Black Man, and was thus entitled to the name of Allah, though he received his blackness from a woman and his Y chromosome from a devil. The child's father proudly displayed the baby to his Five Percenter friends, none of whom had sons, and asked, "If *I'm* not God, and *she's* not God, how did we *make* God?" The gods had no answer; their racial and sexual exclusivisms had trapped them.

Five Percenter discourse, whether at a rally in Harlem or in community media or posts on a god's Facebook page, often reacted to the suggestion of a divine feminine with such disdain and venom, I had to wonder whether it was black women, not white men, who were really seen as devils. At the very least, white devils and black women were sometimes portrayed as conspiring together to keep the black man from achieving his full potential as God. Five Percent hip-hop artist King Sun, who also calls the black woman "secondary but most necessary," clearly says as much: "If not drawn to the fullest of equality/She is equivalent to devil in society."[45] "Equality" in this context ironically signifies the woman's inequality; representing the number 6 in Supreme Mathematics, Equality is often seen as the ceiling for both white people and black women, who are unable to pass 6 to reach 7 (God). A woman cannot transcend *her* Equality to take part in God's Equality.

There are Five Percenters who, while undoing the harmful myth of Ham (in which black people are portrayed as descendents of a cursed, wicked son of Noah), would hold on to the equally damaging paradigm that blames Eve for Adam's downfall.[46] Examining Five Percenter statements on gender, and comparing these with statements on race and the evidence of my own reception at parliaments, I was shown a troublesome reality: even within Five Percenter culture, a white man could receive unearned privilege over black women. Additionally, a heterosexual white man is without question privileged in the Five Percent over gay black men. The black man is God and the white man is the devil, but because I'm straight, I would be more welcome as a Five Percenter than James Baldwin or Langston Hughes.

Some Five Percenters denounce homosexuality because the black community needs "soldiers," but I can't name a Five Percenter who has been a soldier on the level of Angela Davis. Despite her years of work against the American prison-industrial complex—which has caged and abused many, many Five Percenters—Davis, as a feminist and open homosexual, is less acceptable for many gods than a grafted pale devil who hadn't even been born yet when she was building with the Black

Panthers, losing her teaching position at the decree of Ronald Reagan, gracing the FBI's Ten Most Wanted list, or living in exile in Cuba. Somehow, this doesn't seem right.

FIVE PERCENTER IDEAS of manhood are the products of a certain history that challenges my right to speak, because white men interfering in the black family is what has caused these problems in the first place. Religion scholar and social ethicist Jonathan Walton has described narratives of "the 'Strong Black Man' as savior of the race" originating as a "counteroffensive against white masculinist terror during slavery."[47] Africans in America faced a racist and patriarchal society in which white men were exalted as providers and protectors of their families, lords within their homes, while black men lived with essentially no chance of securing health, safety, stability, or comfort for their loved ones. When white men could sell slave children away from their parents, split up married couples, and even rape black women and girls—or black men and boys, for that matter—the natural result was a "symbolic castration" that would not end with the abolition of chattel slavery.[48] In the twentieth century, black families continued to struggle with poverty and powerlessness, while film and television presented a mythic *Leave It to Beaver* image of "Wait until your father gets home" white masculinity, which set a standard of racist patriarchy that even most white men failed to meet.

The urge for a united black front against white supremacy absorbed these frustrations and anxieties. Cornel West describes a "vulgar form of racial reasoning: black authenticity → black closing-ranks mentality → black male subordination of black women in the interests of the black community in a hostile white racist country."[49] Racism and sexism have combined, as feminist author bell hooks has observed, to make the deification of black womanhood impossible in America for "white folks, and even some black folks."[50] According to hooks, the "insistence on patriarchal values, on equating black liberation with black men gaining access to male privilege that would enable them to assert power over black women, was one of the most significant forces undermining radical struggle."[51] The need to control black women was in agreement with the bionationalist emphasis on reproduction: as genocidal white power threatened black survival, nonreproductive sexuality was linked with race treason: birth control pills, abortion, and homosexuality were parts of the devil's plan. Homosexuality is seen not only as diminishing the black population but also weakening black men: "Because of my sexuality I cannot be Black," said the late filmmaker Marlon Riggs. "A strong, proud, 'Afrocentric' black man is resolutely heterosexual, not even bisexual. . . . Hence I remain a sissy, punk, faggot. I cannot be a gay black man because, by the tenets of black macho, a black gay man is a triple negation."[52] Such a paradigm should crumble under the weight of evidence that the Strongest and Blackest of Strong Black Men, Malcolm X, had engaged in same-sex encounters during his hustler days.[53] If Malcolm X is no longer qualified to be a "soldier" for black liberation, what hope can anyone have?

Association of racial empowerment with straight male power provides much of the foundation for Five Percenter godhood. Historically, the Five Percent has been a movement for young black men, with its central message being that the black man had created the universe and therefore held limitless potential to overcome adversity and achieve success and happiness within it. Female participation was nearly nonexistent at the beginning, and developed slowly as gods brought their girlfriends to parliaments. Significant founder figures of the movement—Allah, the Elders, and First Born—were all male, and much of the culture's later spread occurred in the all-male society of prison. It does not appear that any serious thought was given to the role of women in the Five Percent until years after Allah's assassination, and the issue is still not settled. The foremost concern remains that the black man is God; for this to mean anything requires that someone else is *not* God, whether the distinction is drawn by race or gender (or both).

The Five Percenters are not the only ones to build a theology centered on the Strong Black Man. Five Percenter rhetoric on gender closely matches that of leading black Christian televangelists such as T. D. Jakes, Creflo Dollar, and Bishop Eddie Long. Jakes speaks and writes on the "restoration of man to his God-given masculinity, strength and purpose." In a gender essentialism that echoes what I've heard among the Five Percent, Jakes describes women as natural "receptacles" and "receivers" while men are naturally "givers."[54] Woman's role is chiefly that of divine helper, supporting her man's fulfillment of his own destiny.[55]

Walton criticizes Dollar for demonstrating "antiquated views of gender" in the public performance of masculinity with his wife:

> Creflo Dollar cannot be a "real" man unless Taffi is a "real" woman. Power becomes a gendered zero-sum game. If Taffi is independent, forceful, and self-assured—"womanish" in black southern parlance—then Creflo must be dependent, weak, listless, and emasculated, the spirit of Ahab to her spirit of Jezebel. For Creflo to take his rightful place, he must first put Taffi in her rightful place.[56]

Bishop Long, flexing his muscles under stretch fitted shirts, preaches on the need for men to be "warriors" and avoid getting "wimpified" so that they can best carry out the divine order, man's "rulership" over his own kingdom. For both Long and Dollar, this means a chain of divine command from God to man, and man to woman. For the woman to obey her man is thus to obey God and submit to the divine order; closeness to God requires a "man to instill authority and maintain it."[57]

To be a man is thus to control a woman; this leads to an image of lesbians as invaders of male territory, and gays as not only failed men, but in fact anti-men, active destroyers of their maleness. During our conversation at a drag show, a Five Percenter once told me that while he had received important knowledge from the gods, and had learned to see himself as the Original Man, overwhelming homophobia allowed no place for him in the community. A gay Five Percenter confided to me that if he came out, he would be immediately "exiled." In 2005, when two gods were discovered kissing at a New York parliament, some Five Percenters accused them of being FBI agents who had been sent to "poison" the cipher with homosexuality.[58]

Bishop Long led a march in favor of a constitutional ban on gay marriage, and would later compare the gay community's protests against him with segregationists who had jeered Reverend Martin Luther King, Jr.'s march in Selma in 1965.[59] Long's campaign against homosexuality ended as these things often do; in 2010, he faced accusations of having coerced four young men in his church into sexual relationships. Long initially vowed to fight the conspiracy against him, and then settled out of court.

THE HISTORY THAT PRODUCED the Strong Black Man narrative also produced *me*, defining manhood as I once understood it. The Strong Black Man, compensating for the historic emasculation of black men by white patriarchy, encouraged an identification of blackness with excessive masculinity—powerful, aggressive, dominant, uncompromising—that would play a significant role in my conversion to Sunnī Islam. Delivering the eulogy at Malcolm X's funeral, Ossie Davis remarked, "Malcolm was our manhood, our living black manhood;" he was mine too. While other boys in my hometown were learning how to drive a car or skin a deer or having their first beers with their dads, I took lessons in manhood from Malcolm's autobiography: "The true nature of a man is to be strong," Malcolm taught me, "and a woman's true nature is to be weak, and while a man must at all times respect his woman, at the same time he needs to understand that he must control her if he expects to get her respect."[60] Malcolm's Strong Black Man mythos left me well prepared for the Strong Muslim Man mythos that I would receive from Sunnī literature printed in Saudi Arabia and Pakistan.

I converted to Islam with an awareness of race issues that, while itself flawed, was not accompanied by equal sophistication in gender issues. This is not to say that I never thought of myself as committed to justice and equality for women. I did take sexism seriously, but within the limits of my patriarchal religious views. Islam honored and respected women more than American culture, I believed, chiefly because Islam shielded women from being made into prostitutes and sex objects. This would lead to my critique of American sexism focusing on women's obligations: America's hypersexualization of women and commodification of the female body was blamed less on men (because all "real" men were "naturally" helpless slaves to their lust) than women who failed to understand the wisdom of dressing Islamically. I even imagined that in Muslim countries, there was no such thing as rape.

Rather than awakening me to the interconnectedness of racism and sexism, my Islamic antiracism gave shelter to my sexism. Subscribing to ideologies in which the primary conflicts were racial (black vs. white), national (colonized vs. colonizers), or civilizational ("Islam" vs. the "West") seemed to require the defense of one male-dominated identity against another. If someone criticized Islamic attitudes about women, I could dismiss him or her as having been brainwashed by Western imperialist propaganda. This response would not be completely invalid—look at how the Orientalist mythology of "rescuing" brown women from brown men has been used to support U.S. conquest in Afghanistan—but in my eagerness to combat racial injustice wherever it showed up, I defended the right of brown men to dominate brown women. This has been an observable trend in my interactions with both white and black male converts to Islam, who have often displayed a heightened sensitivity on racial matters while unapologetically advocating patriarchy.

The Strong Black Man and Strong Muslim Man scripts spoke to what

I wanted at the time. As a fatherless son of an abused woman, what I valued most were the things that had been denied to my mother and myself. For the majority of my childhood, there was no man in the house to provide for us and protect us, or guide me on the road to manhood. Islam, through both indigenous and immigrant sources, presented itself as the remedy to this absence, with an idealized vision of what men should be. Concentrating on our shared lack of a husband/father figure, however, I completely missed the fact that my mother had always fulfilled the "masculine" duties in our house: she kept her child safe, warm, fed, and ontologically secure. In doing so, she also modeled important values and provided an example for me to follow; what, then, makes "manhood" "masculine?" Describing the roles of men and women as "different, yet complementary in nature" cannot mean anything in my life or have any bearing on my thoughts of God and who can wear the Name.

Years after my conversion, I was shaken by a statement of bell hooks: "There is no justification for Malcolm's sexism."[61] By the time these words found me, I was intellectually open to them, but I still ran over that sentence again and again, forgetting that I had to finish the rest of her essay. I underlined the sentence and then reproduced it in my handwriting, making her words my own, in the margin of her page in all caps: THERE IS NO JUSTIFICATION FOR MALCOLM'S SEXISM. A hard thing to digest. Malcolm was *my* manhood; I'll say it again, my living black manhood.

Hooks at least attempts to rehabilitate Malcolm, attributing his distrust and hatred of women to his background as a hustler and the ideological support later bestowed upon his misogyny by the Nation of Islam. She notes that after Malcolm's break from the "patriarchal father embodied in Elijah Muhammad," his views on gender began to evolve.[62] "He no longer endorsed the sexist notion that black male leadership was essential to black liberation," she writes.[63] Her view is shared by James Cone, who suggests that Malcolm realized a changing approach to women as necessary for "mobilizing the forces needed to revolutionize society."[64] Malcolm founded two organizations after his split from the Nation, one strongly rooted in Islam (Muslim Mosque, Inc.) and one more secular and black nationalist (Organization of Afro-American Unity); Malcolm appointed a woman, Lynn Shifflet, to head the latter. It is said that she was "directly at odds" with James 67X, who led Muslim Mosque, Inc.[65]

"Had he lived," hooks considers, "Malcolm might have explicitly challenged sexist thinking in as adamant a manner as he had advocated it."[66] Judging by his life up to 1965, we can consider that had Malcolm survived, his long series of rebirths and self-transformations would have continued. This makes what would have been Malcolm's future a blank screen on which any of us can project our messianic fantasies: Sherman Jackson imagines Malcolm evolving to become a formative figure for a "properly constituted orthodox Islam in America, in effect from Malcolm X to Ibn Taym-X."[67] Humanists have made their own claim on Malcolm, which is no less justified.[68] One can argue that as the 1960s progressed, Malcolm—who was spending time with socialists in his last year, and experiencing tensions between his secular and religious constituencies—would have felt more at home with organizations that were not defined by faith. Just three days before his death, Malcolm told a reporter, "I'm man enough to tell you that I can't put my finger on exactly what my philosophy is now."[69] Just about any of us can claim him; for those who wish to imagine a feminist Malcolm X bringing together a variety of radicals, the dream is not out of line.

"AS A UNIQUELY MASCULINE divinity loses credibility," Mary Daly predicts, "so also the idea of a unique divine incarnation in a human being of the male sex may give way in the religious consciousness to an increased awareness of the divine presence in all human beings."[70] To me, Daly reads here like Malcolm X's enlightenment at Mecca, where the absence of God's incarnation in a human being of light or dark skin allowed people of all colors to come together as one—an experience that Malcolm describes repeatedly in his autobiography as "brotherhood."

I would later find more inclusive representations of gender in Islam than what I had read in Malcolm X and mosque literature. With her "*tawhīdic* paradigm," Amina Wadud imagines a oneness of humanity within the pure unicity of Allāh: if *tawhīd* could be experienced on Earth, it would mean a "single global community without distinction for reasons of race, class, gender, religious tradition, national origin, sexual orientation or other arbitrary, voluntary, and involuntary aspects of human distinction."[71] The *tawhīdic* paradigm reflects a sense of shared humanity that manifests in both feminist and antiracist refuge from white male gods.

"Woman," writes Rūmī, is "not the being whom sensual desire takes as its object," but rather a "beam of the divine light . . . she is creator, it should be said."[72] I found Ibn al-'Arabī treating women and men as united in essence and equally capable of reaching the highest point of development, *al-Insān al-Kāmil* or "Complete Human." Though Ibn al-'Arabī did believe that woman was created from man, he also taught that woman was equally a host of Allāh's manifestation; a husband and wife could realize Allāh by contemplating the divine attributes in each other. Regarding women, Ibn al-'Arabī wrote, "I am the most tender of people toward them, and the most observant of their due, because of the insight that I possess in this matter . . . only one given knowledge and understanding from God knows the value of women."[73]

One of Ibn al-'Arabī's Ṣūfī guides was a woman, Fāṭima bint al-Muthannā, who told him, "I am your divine mother, and the light of your earthly mother." She taught him the esoteric science of letters, and it was even reported that the beginning passage of the Qur'ān, *al-Fātiḥa*, would materialize before her in a three-dimensional form and carry out her orders.[74] For women to hold religious agency was not an issue for Ibn al-ʿArabī. In a gender progressivism that puts him at odds with Islamic orthopraxy even today, Ibn al-ʿArabī supported the right of women to lead prayers for both women and men. If the Shaykh could have been here in 2005, when Amina Wadud led an intergender congregation in prayer, he might have been in the front row.

That man over there says that women need to be helped into carriages, and lifted over ditches, and to have the best place everywhere. Nobody ever helps me into carriages, or over mud-puddles, or gives me any best place! And ain't I a woman? Look at me! Look at my arm! I have ploughed and planted, and gathered into barns, and no man could head me! And ain't I a woman? I could work as much and eat as much as a man—when I could get it—and bear the lash as well! And ain't I a woman? I have borne thirteen children, and seen most all sold off to slavery, and when I cried out with my mother's grief, none but Jesus heard me! And ain't I a woman?

—Sojourner Truth[75]

There has also been room for negotiation within the Five Percent itself. One Five Percenter told me that to divide human beings with any kind of dualism, whether black/white or male/female, means that we don't know God.

In Allah's own lifetime, a Brooklyn god's girlfriend called herself Goddess. When another young woman claimed to be God, some Five Percenters brought her to Allah, certain that she would surrender her claim in his presence. When she persisted, Allah remarked that she was a goddess.[76] Regardless of what titles are used, there are Five Percenters who view women and men as sharing divine power. In my time with the community, I occasionally observed Five Percenters advocating full theological equality—sometimes delicately stated with care to respect all sensibilities, sometimes adamantly and without compromise. Some Five Percenter women have claimed righteous names such as Goddess and Allat (based on the pre-Islamic goddess al-Lāt, whose name is a feminine equivalent of Allāh), with or without also calling themselves Earth. According to controversial thinker Prince Allah Cuba, any Five Percenter who sees "Goddess" and "Earth" as irreconcilable terms needs to hit the books. In a synthesis of Five Percenter mythic history with the claims of feminist spirituality writers, Cuba envisions a past golden age of matrilineal and matriarchal societies whose religions centered around an Earth Mother, which were destroyed by Aryan invaders who then instituted a "patriarchal 'white man is god' astral religion" and capitalism.[77] For Cuba, there's no either/or; when a woman represents herself as the Earth, she's also calling herself Goddess, and vice versa. In *The Universal Truth*, a Five Percenter publication for which he worked as editor in the 1990s, Cuba gave voice to writers such as Goddess Earth Equality, whose "A Letter with Love to Allah" asserts female godhood while attributing discord within the black family to the devil's kingdom.[78]

> I know this uncivilization has caused you to forget my greatness, my ability to lead Nations and love my BlackMan willingly and compliantly. We have battled and degraded each other for so many hundreds of years that our division has blurred us. . . . Now, we are of the 5% and our third eye is open.[79]

In efforts to make the culture more empowering for women, Cuba published an alternate version of the Student Enrollment's first degree:

Who is the Original Woman?
The Original Woman is the Asiatic Blackwoman, co-maker, co-owner, womb of the planet Earth, mother of civilization and Goddess of the universe.[80]

Cuba's work is less inclusive on race, condemning what he calls the "Baby Yakub Devil Worship Cult" of Five Percenters who attempt to make the movement more friendly to whites, and arguing that changes in Allah's positions on race were only for political expediency and did not reflect his true teachings. Regardless of how Cuba would feel about it, his writings have contributed to this devil's understanding of gender in the Five Percent. I can't call Cuba a feminist with full confidence—at one point he puts the word in quotation marks, as though smirking at the idea—but he has nonetheless brought Five Percenter and feminist ideas closer to dialogue with each other, creating an opening in which I Self Lord And Master could represent total liberation.

It seemed that a Five Percenter feminism would rescue this white male from having to choose between white-dominated feminism and male-dominated black power. The stories of both Ham and Eve can be erased. Taking the devil off the planet would mean recognizing the ways in which sexism and racism feed each other, causing black men to be hurt by sexism, white women to be hurt by racism, and everyone's lives to be shaped by both.

As the beneficiary of both racism and sexism, I have seen my reality written by them. Apart from the countless ways in which whiteness and maleness define me every day, I can trace histories through which racism and sexism lured me into each other. Taking my views on gender as a teenager from Malcolm X, my treatment of women was therefore influenced by the psychological impact of slavery, poverty, and disenfranchisement upon black men: the legacy of racism made me a sexist. Similarly, if commitment to antisexism causes me to forget my whiteness and all that comes with it when in dialogue with Muslim communities or the Five Percent, then the legacy of sexism has made me a white supremacist. I have to respect what Malcolm X and Mary Daly could say to me, but also what they would say to each other.

Considering the interplay of these American tragedies, I cannot imagine that it would benefit anyone for me to see women as less representative of God than men: for a white man to do so in the face of black women repeats more than one old crime. If self-possession after everything that America throws at her means that an Original Woman names herself God, I'm the very last person who can say no, but this does not mean that I can decide the place for women in the Five Percent. There are also Five Percenter women who don't want to be God, and who find fulfilling meanings exclusively in their title of Earth, just as there are Muslim women who find empowerment in the Nation of Islam or Sunnī tradition, and Christian women who feel empowered by T. D. Jakes. It's not my question to answer. On this map, my only rightful territory is what happens inside my brain, and the manifestation that behavior gives to my thought. Unable to say what will work for everyone, I have no option but to support every individual's right to name himself or herself, whatever name is chosen. "Knowing the ledge" and surrendering to my limitation is the single appropriate response for a white male in the Five Percent.

SEVEN

GODS OF THE WORD

Every existent thing finds in the Qur'ān what it desires.

—Ibn al-'Arabī[1]

We are all mediators, translators.

—Jacques Derrida[2]

IN HIS COMPARATIVE STUDY of Ibn al-'Arabī and Jacques Derrida, Ian Almond arrives at the conclusion that the medieval Ṣūfī master and twentieth-century French philosopher are making essentially the same point, but for very different reasons.

As Allāh's Absolute Reality (al-Ḥaqq) is beyond comprehension, Ibn al-'Arabī regards Allāh's literary self-expression, the Qur'ān, as a similarly "shoreless ocean" in its capacity for meaning. Attempts to define and contain the message of the Qur'ān are as problematic as defining and containing al-Ḥaqq itself. Readings of the Qur'ān in a strictly literal and "straightforward fashion," writes Almond, are "not enough: the infinite richness of the Word of Allāh yields different meanings when read in different manners—and every single one of them is intended."[3] Almond compares the Qur'ān in this view to the plays of Shakespeare— if, before having written a word, Shakespeare was aware of every way in which his work would be read in the centuries after him: every critical study, every film or stage adaptation, every high school term paper, every influence and reference found in the work of other artists, even every instance in which a man is called "Romeo," whether in earnest or sarcasm. That the Qur'ān contains this wealth of possibilities could be seen as leading to disunity and confusion; for Ibn al-ʿArabī, it is rather an essential sign of Allāh's perfect unity and boundless knowledge. "To the degree that we understand the Qur'ān, we come to understand God's self-disclosure within ourselves," writes William C. Chittick. "Given that no self-disclosure is ever repeated, no two understandings, even by the same individual, can be exactly the same."[4]

This comes with a serious mandate, pointing to what Muslim scholar and activist Laury Silvers calls the "extraordinary extent of our responsibility in being human."[5] For Allāh to intend every possible meaning of the Qur'ān does not imply that all interpretations should have equal value. To perfect our character through the Qur'ān requires that we guard our reading with critical self-examination, a constant checking of our own intentions with every verse. Some readers will do better than others.

For Silvers, Ibn al-ʿArabī's treatment of the Qur'ān provides a key for Muslim feminists struggling with verses such as 4:34, which appears to express the right of men to beat their wives. Silvers argues that because Islam's model for humanity, Muḥammad—whose nature was described by his wife Āʾisha as a personification of the Qur'ān itself—did not take advantage of 4:34 by beating his wives, the verse cannot be taken as simply a green light for spousal abuse. The Prophet's own example demonstrates the Qur'ān's multiplicity of meanings, and also that our interpretive choices render the Qur'ān a mirror of our own personal development. How we read each verse reflects our success or failure in fulfilling our humanity, which the Qur'ān calls "the Trust."[6]

Ibn al-ʿArabī remains a highly divisive figure in Islamic tradition, and many charge that his engagement of the Qur'ān has exploded the book and destabilized the structures of religion. In his liberties with the scripture, Ibn al-ʿArabī not only changes the meanings of stories but specific words; Abraham's title of *Khalil Allāh*, ordinarily understood to mean "intimate friend of God," is given an alternative etymology. Ibn al-ʿArabī chooses to derive *khalil* from *takhallul,* meaning "penetration" or "permeation," to signify a closer relation to the divine: Allāh appears *in the person* of Abraham, manifesting in Abraham's every thought and deed.[7] Going further in his manipulation of language, Ibn al-ʿArabī assigns meanings even to individual letters. Interpreting the Arabic word *kun,* "be," Ibn al-ʿArabī reflects on its short vowel as a missing letter, a hidden long vowel; *kun* as secretly *kūn.* With two "manifest letters," *kāf* and *nūn,* and one "non-manifest letter," the missing *wāw,* the word *kun/kūn* is read to signify God's union of the manifest (*ẓāhir*) and non-manifest (*bāṭin*), and also the perfected human master who brings these opposites together.[8]

Religious bodies tend to prefer that their scriptures remain consistent. Ibn al-ʿArabī's approach to the Qurʾān, however, potentially kicks out the legs of Ten Percenters who rule the masses through control of fixed meanings. Scholars invested in Ibn al-ʿArabī's Islamic legitimacy may defend him against the charge, emphasizing his loyalty to the Qurʾān's "literal meaning;" but what can "literal meaning" even mean when letters are no longer mere letters?

Jacques Derrida is also seen as a destabilizer of language. The limitless potential that Ibn al-ʿArabī sees in the Qurʾān, Derrida extends to all texts—not because they are loaded with infinite meanings but the opposite: in themselves, they are empty.

A word's meaning is only produced by relation to the context in which it appears. The word "run," for example, means nothing by itself. "Run" acquires its meaning when we add words: a man can run down the street, the president can run the country, my nose can run, my refrigerator can run. Even if "run" appears alone as an imperative, its meaning is created by the situation, that is, "run" as a computer command or "Run!" as someone alerting others to danger. This happens not only with individual words but entire scriptures. A text's meaning is constantly recreated as it drifts between readers, always an orphan and homeless, always vulnerable to the strange environments into which it is inserted, which are "only contexts without any center of absolute anchoring."[9] An example would be Ibn al-'Arabī's account of his mystical encounter with Adam: "And on his right I saw the 'black ones of the ancient origin' (aswīdat al-qidam), and on his left I saw the 'black ones of non-existence' (aswīdat al-adam)."[10] The significance of aswīdat could change in accordance with its reader, depending on whether the passage is examined at a symposium of the Muhyiddin Ibn Arabi Society or a 120 class at the Allah School.

Due to the unstable relations of countless forces both inside and outside the book, ten thousand Muslims can interpret the Qur'ān and show it to be saying ten thousand different things, with each one promising to have the only "faithful" or "literal" reading and accusing others of "diluting" or "corrupting" the message. This is also why the Qur'ān's "literal" meaning has changed for me numerous times. Khan Abdul Ghaffar Khan, an Indian Muslim pacifist and close friend of Mahatma Gandhi, interpreted Islam as commanding nonviolence, and named "patience" as the Prophet Muhammad's greatest weapon; he read the same Qur'ān as Osama bin Laden. Anyone trying to make a claim on what the Qur'ān really says, whether pious Muslim or bigoted Islamophobe, is getting it wrong: the Qur'ān doesn't "really" say anything apart from the meanings that we inject into it.

Derrida would agree with Ibn al-'Arabī's assertion that the Qur'ān transforms as it moves from reader to reader, but without Ibn al-'Arabī's faith that this signified the Author's own inexhaustible capacity. Instead, texts produce new meanings when they break free of their authors. Every text faces the "possibility of extraction and citational grafting . . . a possibility of functioning cut off, at a certain point, from its 'original' meaning and from its belonging to a saturable and constraining context."[11] There are no "deeper meanings" to uncover, only new misreadings.

As in the case of Ibn al-'Arabī, Derrida's conclusion is not that we should say, "Nothing means anything," and throw our books away.

Rather, with knowledge that the pieces are always in motion, reading becomes a path of high vigilance. After a phenomenal career of writing and teaching philosophy, Derrida considered himself to be only at the "threshold" of reading Plato and Aristotle: "I feel I have to start again and again and again. It is a task which is in front of me, before me."[12]

Almond writes that both Ibn al-'Arabī and Jacques Derrida "raise in us the unsettling possibility that all the things we have felt so comfortable about ('God,' 'truth,' 'literature,' etc.) may actually be radically unthinkable, formed more from our own beliefs and experiences rather than embodying the things themselves."[13] For the mystic and the atheist, there is no center.

IN ITS VARIOUS PHASES, the Nation of Islam has always sought to maintain a center; interpretation has never been a democracy. In the formative period, meaning was the domain of Master Fard Muhammad, who pulled it from a variety of sources. He is said to have taught not only from the Qur'ān, but also made use of radio sermons by apocalypse-heavy Christian evangelists; whatever the source material, it was Fard's role to properly interpret and explain the message. With his student Elijah Muhammad (who Fard described as having answered his exam questions "near correct"), Fard also produced his own text, the Supreme Wisdom Lessons, which would speak for him in his absence.

After Fard's disappearance and Elijah's victory in the factional disputes, Elijah assumed control over the lessons' power, which would amount to control over the community's memory of Fard himself. With Elijah's death, mastery of the text would in turn be claimed by competing heirs. The NOI's reorientation toward Sunnism led by Elijah's son, Warith Deen Mohammed, depended upon popular acceptance of Warith Deen's authority to interpret the lessons; it was only as the divinely appointed successor to his father and Master Fard that he could alter their doctrines. Preparing the community for drastic changes, Warith Deen would claim that in reforming the Nation, he was fulfilling a promise made to his father, and that he occasionally spoke to the long-lost Fard on the telephone.

Muhammad Speaks, March 21, 1975

Warith Deen's Sunnification of the NOI, while moving the tradition away from the lessons, still took place within their degrees. Shortly after taking over the Nation in 1975, he described the lessons as a "kind of catechism for the students of Islam in North America," designed to teach a "new language or knowledge of words" and bring its students "back in touch with reality."[14] In articles for *Muhammad Speaks* and its successor paper, *Bilalian News,* Warith Deen pulled a different reality from the language: the terms "Black" and "Original Man" referred not to mere racial identity but the "man who was born in darkness . . . and whose mind developed so strongly that it was able to bring light out of darkness."[15] Meanwhile, "Colored Man" did not condemn a racial group wholesale, but specifically referred to the "Caucasian white supremacist . . . because his mind is colored," that is, consumed by obsession with "skin color classification . . . the most ignorant classification for people that anybody could come up with."[16]

The imām's article that defined devils as wicked mind states, rather than people signified by certain phenotypic traits, was titled "The Destruction of the Devil"—a clear reference to the fortieth degree of Lost-Found Muslim Lesson No. 2, "What will be your reward in regards to the destruction of the devil?" The issue's front page displayed a cartoon of four heads—one white, one black, one yellow, one brown—each containing a brain filled with "lies," "weak ideas," and "wrong thinking"— surrounded by the blazing fire of "Divine Truth and Knowledge." While a departure from traditional readings of the lessons for allowing that different races could be capable of the "devil mind," the image of four heads also made a subtle reference to Lost-Found Muslim Lesson No. 1. The lesson's tenth degree states that by presenting four devils— portrayed often in the NOI/Five Percent imagination as decapitated heads—a Muslim would be rewarded with a special lapel pin and free transportation to Mecca to "see Brother Muhammad." In those uneasy years of change, any counterargument against the lessons had to be justified by the tradition itself. Raymond Sharrieff, who had been Supreme Captain in Elijah Muhammad's FOI (Fruit of Islam), would write that "Muslims have grown to be seriously attached to the Lessons and old language," while assuring Muslims that Elijah had desired to "rewrite the Lessons and bring them up to date."[17] Soon enough, everything changed. By 1980, Warith Deen had sufficiently transplanted Fard's authority upon himself to boast, "I have been able to peep his card. . . . Dr. Fard is beneath me in the understanding of the religion."[18] Scholar and Malcolm X biographer Manning Marable writes that over the course of Warith Deen becoming the new center of meaning, the Nation of Islam's archive was purged of countless internal records, publications, photographs, and audiotapes, erasing the communal memory and effectively producing an empty new archive on which "a new memory, branded by orthodoxy, was imposed."[19]

In his own resurrected Nation of Islam, Louis Farrakhan would also position himself as Elijah's rightful successor, the chosen student of God's chosen student. As such, it became Farrakhan's perogative to interpret the lessons for his community; like Warith Deen Mohammed, he occupied the top of his pyramid and disseminated meaning to the base. At first glance, this would additionally appear to have been the case with the Five Percenter movement, founded when Clarence 13X left the mosque and claimed ultimate authority by renaming himself Allah, the "best knower." The teenagers who called him Allah were willing to give that power to him, if he wanted it; but Allah chose to share the power. In the spring of 1967, following his release from Matteawan, he informed his Five Percenters that each of them was the Allah of his own universe, living out the lessons by his own understanding.

Some readers of the lessons, believing literally that Master Fard Muhammad had received advanced knowledge from a hidden council of wise scientists, study the degrees as Ibn al-'Arabī studied the Qur'ān: as a bottomless reservoir of supreme guidance. These readers dive deep into the 120, hoping to reveal the meanings that Fard had buried in every word and punctuation mark. For such gods, even the 120's statements on geographic and astronomic data must tell us something *more*; behind the measurements of an ocean's square mileage or a planet's distance from the sun, one finds a greater encounter with reality, "higher knowledge," as a god told me; *bāṭin* behind the *ẓāhir*. To study the 120 in this way is to engage in a lifelong process of unlocking Fard's treasure chest and retrieving the precious items that are already inside. For the lessons to produce a diversity of interpretations, therefore, points to Fard's immeasurable genius.

Five Percenters dislike words such as "religion" and even "belief," but attempting to dig into the 120 and recover its hidden meaning remains an act of deep faith. One must believe that there is really such a meaning to be found, that Fard had left behind a pregnant text containing either traces of his transcendent wisdom, clues to riddles, or hints of knowledge for which the world was not yet ready. Like any worthwhile scripture, the 120 rewards the reader's faith; whatever you're looking for in those degrees, you find it.

The ethos of I Self Lord And Master can lead to another way of reading the lessons. As opposed to Ibn al-'Arabī, for whom "it is infinite presence which causes the text to multiply and proliferate," Almond explains, "Derrida is challenging us to read texts without worrying about what their authors are trying to say to us."[20] This latter approach struck me as more "Five Percent" for its deemphasizing the lessons' transcendence and placing power in the hands of the interpreter.

Fard is not waiting for us at the end of this road. In his disappearance, Fard acted out a phenomenon that literary theorist Roland Barthes would later call the "death of the author:" a de-authoring of the text, or the supplanting of the author by the reader as the real producer of meaning. Or, to say it with a rephrasing of 10:40:

There is no Mystery Author. The Reader has searched for that Mystery Author for trillions of years and was unable to find a Mystery Author. So they have agreed that the only Author is the Reader. So they lose no time searching for that which does not exist.

Literary theorist Terry Eagleton would describe this phenomenon as a turning away from the treatment of any text as a "closed entity, equipped with definite meaning which it is the critic's task to decipher" and instead seeing the text as "irreducibly plural, an endless play of signifiers which can never be finally nailed down to a single centre, essence or meaning."[21]

While Fard gave students a block of stone with which to work, each god must bring his or her own chisels and hammers. In the manner that I engage the 120, these degrees are less about finding Master Fard's secret than exercising the imaginative power of our own minds; the search for a degree's meaning does not bring anyone closer to the 120's "essence," because no text has an essence. To be God, and to be human, is to *create* meaning. One Five Percenter told me that during his training with the 120, his teacher instructed him to internalize every degree: "When it talks about retaking Jerusalem from the Devil, make that about *you*. What's *your* Jerusalem, and what's *your* Devil?" The Five Percenters' emphasis on this value could be the real point of difference between them and the Nation of Islam. For the Five Percent, Fard is long gone, and there is no Holy Apostle or Honorable Minister to feed meaning to you; as God, you have to read for yourself.

WHETHER WORKING to retrieve or produce meaning, Five Percenters have a special set of tools for approaching the degrees: Allah's Supreme Mathematics and Supreme Alphabets. In these systems, numbers and letters are assigned attributes that are then used to interpret corresponding degrees in the lessons, allowing each degree to stretch its meaning beyond what seems immediately self-evident.

The codes were reportedly inspired by Fard's *Problem Book*, which commands the student, "Sit yourself in Heaven at once! That is the greatest desire of your Brother and Teachers."[22] According to the *Problem Book*, Heaven is achieved through mastery of all "twenty-six letters in the Language" and "ten numbers in the Mathematic Language." In my face-value assessment of the text, this would mean improvement in reading, writing, and arithmetic—through which one could attain the "luxury, money, good homes, friendship in all walks of life" that Fard promised. A more esoteric reading of the question surfaced sometime in the Five Percent's prehistory, between Clarence 13X's attrition from the Nation of Islam and his sparking of a new movement as Allah. John 37X (later Abu Shahid), who had befriended Allah while they were both in the Nation of Islam and followed him out of the community, believed that mastering the ten numbers meant "sciencing out" their inner characteristics. John 37X's process led to assigning attributes not only for numbers 1 to 10 but also 11 and 12, in a code he called "Living Mathematics." The system was refined by Allah and his friend Justice into a 1–9 code (followed by an attribute for 0), Supreme Mathematics:

1 Knowledge
2 Wisdom
3 Understanding
4 Culture
5 Power
6 Equality
7 God
8 Build or Destroy
9 Born
0 Cipher

Allah and Justice developed a similar code for the twenty-six letters, the Supreme Alphabets. Together, these systems would amount to Allah's hermeneutical intervention in the reception of Fard's lessons (I write "hermeneutical" while mindful that folk etymology derives the term from the mythical character of Hermes, messenger between gods). On the first day of the month, for example, the first degrees in Supreme Mathematics (1 = Knowledge) and Alphabets (A = Allah) would be used as lenses for reading the first degree in a lesson from the 120, such as "Who is the Original Man?" (1:10) and/or "Why isn't the Devil settled on the best part of the planet Earth?" (1:14).

Supreme Mathematics and Supreme Alphabets act as agents of inter-textuality, the process by which texts obtain their meaning through relations to other texts—such as reading Ibn al-'Arabī's mention of aswīdat alongside the 120. It is intertextuality that unsettles every text, because these relations are always in flux. To comment upon a degree with its appropriate attribute in Supreme Mathematics comes with a certain potential for multiple meanings; to use Supreme Alphabets adds a different set of possibilities, and to use both adds even more. The potential for meaning is further expanded when Five Percenters use the day's degree from more than one lesson, relating corresponding degrees to one another as well as to the Math and Alphabets. Double-digit dates add more options, as the twelfth day of the month could be read as 12 (Knowledge Wisdom) or digit-summed to read as Understanding (1 + 2 = 3). Someone could even use both of these numbers and their appropriate degrees in the various lessons, Supreme Math, and Supreme Alphabets in relation to one another. The combinations are virtually unlimited, and I've witnessed some amazing exegetical gymnastics from older gods who had been living in the degrees since the 1960s.

Add to this whatever a god brings to the texts—previous books read, languages studied, life experiences, backgrounds in other wisdom traditions, and the context of that particular day—and the lessons overflow with messages. The Five Percent's speed-of-thought scripture lives and moves, always transforming, always reinventing itself and reinventing its reader/creator, showing God's knowledge—whether we're talking about God in the Five Percenter sense or something more recognizably Abrahamic—to be a shoreless ocean, because we are shoreless.

This practice is a ritual enactment of the first degree from Lost-Found Muslim Lesson No. 2, in which the Original Man is described as renewing history at the start of every 25,000-year cycle by authoring the next cycle's Qur'ān. A Five Percenter renews history at the start of each day, determining in advance how s/he will live out the day's reality with a blend of text and imagination. With Supreme Mathematics and Supreme Alphabets celebrating the unpredictability in this "endless play of signifiers" rather than attempting to suppress it, every day means a new Qur'ān.

As a Muslim approaching the Supreme Mathematics and Supreme Alphabets, I held an interest in appearances of similar practices throughout Islamic history. It turned out that Islam abounded with this kind of thing, which would ease my own transitions between one realm and the other.

> I am the Qur'ān and the seven doubled.
>
> —Ibn al-'Arabī[23]

Islam inherited number and letter esotericism from the ancient world. In Mesopotamia, certain numbers were used to refer to gods: the number 20 corresponded to Shamash, the sun god; the number 30 corresponded to Nanna-Suen, the moon god.[24] Gematria, the interpretation of words through the numerical value of their letters, was used by the Assyrian king Sargon II (reigned 722–705 BCE), who built the wall of Khorsabad 16,283 cubits long because it matched the numerical value of his name.[25] The Greeks used gematria for dream interpretation, and Pythagoras equated mathematics with the ultimate reality of the cosmos. Pythagorean ideas of numbers influenced Neoplatonism, which in turn influenced the Jewish number mysticism of the Kabbalah. Neoplatonism would also find its way into Islamic thought, while rabbinical gematria would inform the treatment of letters for Hebrew's cousin Arabic.

In the Near East, the number 7 held special significance. Mesopotamians believed in a group of gods called the Seven, often represented with seven dots and identified with the Pleiades star cluster.[26] Seven "planets" were known to Babylonians: the sun, the moon, Mercury, Mars, Venus, Jupiter, and Saturn. These "planets" were seen as corresponding to seven celestial spheres, and Babylonian ziggurats were built to have seven levels.[27] The number's importance passed into Jewish tradition and would later surface in the Islamic tradition: seven levels of heaven, earth, and hell; seven circuits around the Ka'ba; and seven verses in the opening *sura* of the Qur'ān, *al-Fātiha*.[28]

Early Ismāʿīlī cosmology named the first created beings as Kūnī (a feminization of Allāh's command *Kun*, "Be") and her vizier, Qadar, with their names totaling seven consonantal letters—the "higher letters" (*al-hurūf al-ʿulwiyya*). Each of these seven letters became an archetype for a "speaking prophet" (*nātiq*) who would appear in his respective cycle. The seven speaking prophets would each be succeeded by his own legatee (*waṣī*), each of whom would start a line of seven Imāms; the prophets matched the seven heavens, while the Imāms matched the seven earths. The seventh Imām of a cycle would become the *nātiq* of the next one—with the exception of the Seventh Imām of Muḥammad's cycle, recognized by Ismāʿīlīs as the Imām-Mahdī, whose mission was the lifting of all textual veils, symbols, and allegories, destroying the line between exoteric (*ẓāhir*) and esoteric (*bāṭin*) meanings.[29] Anti-Ismāʿīlī writers, meanwhile, would distort Ismāʿīlī hierarchies to make the sensational claim that Ismāʿīlī converts were taught atheism at the seventh and final stage of initiation.[30]

Letter mysticism might have been a natural outgrowth of the cosmic significance that Islam assigned to a written text, the Qur'ān. Early in the development of Islam, argument over the Qur'ān's true nature was won by those who believed the revelation to be uncreated and eternal, which therefore meant that the letters of Arabic script themselves had existed before the universe. Within the Qur'ān, Muslims would read that creation began with an act of language, Allāh's *Kun*. Language was eternal with Allāh and the means by which Allāh's Attributes manifested, whether in the creation of physical existence, the revelation of the Qur'ān, or the conception of Jesus through a command spoken to Mary's womb.

Describing the *ilm al-hurūf* (science of letters) as *ālam al-anfās* ("world of breaths"), Ibn al-ʿArabī viewed everything in the universe as a word from Allāh, spoken with the Divine Breath, which gave a cosmological role to each letter. In his *Futūhāt al-Makkiyya* (Meccan Illuminations), Ibn al-ʿArabī writes extensively on each letter of the Arabic alphabet as corresponding to Names of Allāh, cosmic principles, celestial bodies, days of the week, and prophets. The letter *nūn*, for example, corresponds to the fourth heaven, God's Attribute as *an-Nūr* (the Light), the sun, Sunday, and the prophet Idris/Enoch.[31] "Existence is entirely letters, words, *suras*, and verses," he wrote, "and it is the macrosmic Qur'ān."[32]

Words were seen as bottomless wells of divine knowledge. Ismāʿīlī thinker Abū Yaʿqūb al-Sijistānī (d. after 971) broke down the words of Islam's first testimony, *Lā ilāha illā Allāh* ("There is no god but God"). That *lā* contained half the letters of *Allāh* and *ilāh* was missing one letter (*lām*) that was present in *Allāh*, while *Allāh* consisted of four letters and four was the "most complete of numbers," were all given symbolic importance.[33] Muhammad's name received similar treatment. The Şūfī martyr al-Hallāj (d. 922) authored a mystical work (whose title, *Ţā-Sīn of the Lamp*, employs letter symbolism) in which he broke down the four letters of Muhammad's name into units of meaning: the first *mīm* represented the Prophet's rank (*mahall*); *ha* represented his spiritual state (*hāl*); the second *mīm* expressed his speech (*maqāl*); the *dāl* signified his permanence (*dawām*). "Never has anyone departed from the *mīm* of Muhammad," the saint tells us, "and no one has entered the *ha*."[34]

South Asian mystic Ahmad Sirhindī (1564–1624), who formulated a more conservative Şūfī response to Ibn al-ʿArabī's teachings, also expressed his point with the hidden meanings of letters. In his own breakdown of Muhammad's name, Sirhindī found the two *mīms* to symbolize Muhammad's two natures, the "bodily-human" and "spiritual-angelic." Over time, the bodily-human *mīm* disappeared and was replaced by an *alif,* causing Muḥammad to become Aḥmad—thus pointing to Sirhindī's own name as proof of his supreme spiritual rank.[35]

In addition to its esteemed status as the Word of Allāh, the Qur'ān could be said to have encouraged letter esotericism through its use of "mystery letters." Twenty-nine *suras* began with unexplained combinations of letters, such as *Alif Lām Mīm* or *Ya Sīn.* The meaning of these *al-ḥurūf al-muqaṭṭaʿah* ("disconnected letters"), also called *fawātih* ("opening letters"), has not been clear; conflicting narrations attributed to the Prophet's companion Ibn Abbās describe *Alif Lām Mīm* as either Allāh's Greatest Name, an oath by which Allāh swore, or an abbreviation for the phrase *Anā llāhu al-Alīm* ("I am God, the Knower").[36] Islam's first generation is said to have generally regarded these letters as belonging to *al-mutashābihāt,* the Qur'ān's obscure verses whose proper interpretation is known to Allāh alone.[37] Regardless, the tradition has been littered with elaborate explanations of the letters' secret meanings. Both mystics and philosophers got in on the project; for the philosopher al-Rāzī (d. 925), the mystery letters actually exposed the Qur'ān as a created thing. "God knew that a group of this community would assert the eternity of the Qur'ān," al-Rāzī wrote; "thus he mentioned the letters to indicate that his words are made up of letters and that therefore the Qur'ān could not be eternal."[38]

Ibn al-ʿArabī broke down the *alif* in *Alif Lām Mīm* as Allāh's Essence, the foundation of all existence; *lām* signified the angel Gabriel, the "middle point of existence," while *mīm* signified Muḥammad, the "end of existence," the completion of the circle. In this scheme, Ibn al-ʿArabī saw Gabriel as manifesting Knowledge and God's Attribute of *al-Alīm* (the Knower), while Muḥammad manifested Wisdom and God's Attribute of *al-Ḥākim* (the Wise).[39]

Not all interpretations focused on hidden messages. Mahmoud Ayoub reports that according to some commentators, the Qur'ān had opened *suras* with disconnected letters "to shock the Meccan Arabs into listening to the rest of the recitation. They refused to listen to the Qur'ān, but when they heard apparently meaningless letters being recited, they listened to what followed out of curiosity."[40] It has also been argued that to begin a poem with ostensibly random letters was simply the literary convention in pre-Islamic Arabia. Contemporary secular scholarship has made an intriguing suggestion: the mystery letters were added to the Qur'ān during its compilation after Muḥammad's death, as a method of citing sources. These letters could have been the initials of trustworthy Muslims who provided sections of the Qur'ān, helping to establish the authenticity of 'Uthmān's version.[41] It's possible that the sources of inspiration for centuries of mystical writings, poetic allegories, and magical talismans were simply 'Uthmān's footnotes.

APPROXIMATELY A CENTURY after Ibn al-'Arabī, Fazlallāh Astarābādī (d. 1394), leader of the Hurūfīs ("letterists"), interpreted the "names" that Allāh had taught to Adam as letters in a higher alphabet: thirty-two sound-letter pairs that formed a "divine metalanguage."[42] To fully comprehend the universe as an expression of Allāh, and the human being as the heart of the universe, required comprehension of this alphabet.[43] Shahzad Bashir writes that in the science of letters as understood by Astarābādī, the letters of God's metalanguage could be discovered if one endeavored to "break words down to letters and sounds and analyze them to see their metalinguistic referents."[44]

I have often seen Five Percenters mocked by normative Muslims for their interpretations of "Allah" as "Arm Leg Leg Arm Head" and "Islam" as "I Self Lord And Master," since these acronyms do not work in Arabic. This would not have discredited them for Astarābādī, who, as Bashir observes, believed that "all human languages could be related to the Qur'ān in some shape or form."[45] Regarding letters and sounds as "greater bearers of truth than the words formed from combining them," Astarābādī himself would recite the Qur'ān in Arabic sounds, but interpret the sounds as Persian words.[46] In his own version of Arm Leg Leg Arm Head, Astarābādī saw the shapes of letters as establishing a connection between Allāh and the human being. Astarābādī pointed out that Allāh was spelled with one straight letter (*alif*), one bent letter (*lām*), and one rounded letter (*ha*). These shapes corresponded to three postures of Islamic prayer (standing up straight, bending with hands on knees, and prostrating oneself on the ground).[47] For Astarābādī's belief that the Qur'ān's Arabic words could be understood through other languages or the shapes of their letters, Bashir describes the Ḥurūfī movement as "threatening for scholars invested in conventional interpretations of religion."[48] In 1394, Astarābādī was arrested and executed.

Ottoman Ṣūfī commentator Meḥmed el-Niyāzī el-Miṣrī (1618–94) believed himself to be a prophet and the messiah, as well as successor to Ibn al-'Arabī's role as "Seal of the Saints."[49] El-Miṣrī claimed that while chained up in prison for his teachings, he became endowed with the secrets of *cifr*, his own mystical gematria.[50] Growing obsessed with *cifr* during his exile, he would apply the science to verses of the Qur'ān based on instructions from the angel Gabriel (who spoke to him in Turkish). He also used *cifr* as a key to interpreting Ibn al-'Arabī's mystical works.[51]

The "existential letters" of Shaykh Aḥmad al-Aḥsā'ī (1753–1826) bore a close resemblance to Supreme Alphabets, assigning a Name of God and metaphysical level to each letter. Drawing a distinction between dotted letters and those without dots, Shaykh Aḥmad believed that dotted letters would return on the Day of Resurrection as complete words, whereas undotted letters would appear in random order.[52]

It's easy for outsiders to see Five Percenter treatments of numbers and letters as nonsensical; but the more I looked at Islamic history, the clearer it became that Supreme Mathematics and Supreme Alphabets had a place in the tradition—which could actually present a challenge to our understanding of the Five Percent. Due to Five Percenter use of words like "Allah" and "Islam," scholars writing on the possible origins of Supreme Mathematics and Supreme Alphabets have automatically pounced upon these traditional Ṣūfī alphanumerics. It's problematic for a few reasons.

First, similarity does not prove a direct connection. We cannot demonstrate that Allah himself did any reading in Ṣūfism. Abu Shahid/ John 37X has stated that the systems were inspired by Master Fard Muhammad's *Problem Book*, which contains no clear references to Ṣūfism, and comes with the similar problem of identifying Fard's sources (i.e., having a cyclical concept of time does not prove Fard to have been Ismāʾīlī).

Second, the assumption that Allah had studied Ṣūfism ignores the non-Islamic materials that Allah, Abu Shahid, and Justice were more likely to have encountered. Number/letter esotericism had enjoyed a presence in Western culture long before the rise of the Five Percent. In the nineteenth century, European groups such as the Hermetic Order of the Golden Dawn attempted to link their own numerology to ancient Egypt, often with spurious lineages.[53] Mitch Horowitz writes that by the 1920s, America was home to a "widespread industry in modern number mysticism," and by midcentury, the practice had become "as widespread as bridge games and crossword puzzles."[54] Noble Drew Ali has not been shown to have read traditional Islamic sources, but would pose with his hand on his heart to form a 7 with his body. Elijah Muhammad made frequent reference to the properties of 6 and 7; prior to Muhammad Ali's bout with Sonny Liston, Malcolm X predicted an Ali win through digit-summing his own seat number in the arena, 34, to get 7; and Jonathan Walton even describes 7 as "the number of completion according to televangelist lingo."[55] Before jumping into medieval Islamic cultures for the source of Supreme Mathematics, it would be salient to look at materials that more directly impacted twentieth-century America, such as Rosicrucianism, Theosophy, or Hebrew gematria; in Kabbalah's Sefirotic Tree, the numbers 2 and 3 correspond to Wisdom and Understanding, their respective attributes in Allah's code.

My third concern with "Ṣūficizing" the origins of Allah's number and letter sciences would be that it unjustifiably places the Five Percent in further debt to classical Islam. While investigating the Five Percent is certainly relevant for the study of Islam in America, there are too many other things going on within the community for someone to frame the Five Percenters as an "Islamic" movement. Approaching the Five Percent exclusively as heretical quasi/pseudo/proto-Islam keeps us from comprehending what the Five Percent tradition actually means for so many of its adherents.

For my personal purposes, however, the shared language of letter and number science built a bridge by which I could pass from one tradition to the other, and remain conscious of one while absorbed in the other. When spotting letter/number mysticism in medieval Ṣūfī works or seeing the number 786 (the numerical equivalent of *bismillāhi r-raḥmāni r-raḥīm*, "In the Name of God, Most Compassionate, Most Merciful") painted on a bus in Pakistan, I thought of the Allah School back in Harlem and Fard's statement, "Islam is mathematics." When building on Supreme Mathematics with gods at parliament, I felt like a dervish.

Though I had access to the lessons, and teachers who would build with me from time to time, my encounters with these materials did not occur within the Five Percent's traditional process of initiation. A new entrant into the knowledge would ideally have a committed personal guide ("enlightener") who exposed him/her to the texts piece by piece; after memorizing an item and working through its interpretation, the student could move on to the next. I initially studied these materials as a detached researcher, but by the time that I desired a more personal relationship to the lessons, it had already happened; I was thinking in the language of the text. When Five Percenters asked, "Do you have 120?" I knew what they meant—had I gone through the process of memorizing the lessons and drawing them up through the Math?—but I did not know how to answer. Did I *have* 120? "Yes" or "No" would not have been enough.

I went to Allah B and told him that I would like to go under the formal study. We could not pretend that I did not already have access to the lessons, or that I had not already put in work, but he agreed to build with me. Before dipping into the 120, Allah B started me off on Supreme Mathematics and Supreme Alphabets, asking that I draw them up in my own way and get back to him.

To draw up the Math and Alphabets meant taking each number's attribute and finding its meaning through the attribute of the corresponding letter. After I shared my breakdowns with Allah B, he gave some helpful comments and assigned me the first portion of the 120, the Student Enrollment. My exercise with the Mathematics and Alphabets had been preparation for approaching these ten questions. I could additionally interpret the degrees with any materials that I chose, Allah B told me: "How you see it, that's how it is." So I went through the questions and answers, scribbling thoughts or relevant quotes in my notebook. After filling up enough pages that I had become a reference for myself, I could see the project that Allah B had put on me: the creation of my personal scripture, a customized Book of Life. The 120, Supreme Mathematics, and Supreme Alphabets were not themselves the scripture, but rather the plywood skeleton for a private Allah School that I would build in my mind.

I began with the number 1, which signified Knowledge, and the letter A, which stood for Allāh. Knowledge is information, data, actual facts. Allāh is al-Alim, the Knower, and Muḥammad said, "The men of Knowledge are the inheritors of the prophets."

The Student Enrollment's first degree tells me, "The Original Man is the Asiatic Blackman, the Maker, the Owner, the Cream of the planet Earth, father of civilization, God of the universe." Arabic is an Afro-Asiatic language, so my name for God (like all names for God, and all language, and everyone's biological origin) can be traced to Africa. The parallel degree in Lost-Found Muslim Lesson No. 2 asks, "Who made the Holy Koran or Bible?" We all write our own Qur'āns because we create our personal experiences of the book with what we bring to it, and that could be what it means to have an Original mind.

The first letter of the Arabic alphabet, *alif,* is the first letter in both "Allāh" and "Adam." Allāh is the foundation for the universe; Adam is the foundation for humankind. Ibn al-'Arabī regarded *alif* as the foundation for all letters. In Ṣūfī commentaries and poetry, *alif* would represent Allāh's Essence from which the Attributes flow. The Punjabi Ṣūfī poet-saint Bulleh Shah (1680–1752) tells us to look only to *alif* instead of wasting our time with religion: despite all of their books and prayers and pulpits and sermons, the vain hypocrites accomplish nothing. "You have no self-knowledge at all," says Bulleh Shah. "One *alif* is all you need."[56]

Alif is the first letter in *'ism,* the Arabic word for "name." To know is to name; to claim the power of naming is to know the named. Adam, teacher of angels, knew the names of all things, and so the world belonged to him. Master Fard Muhammad was an Adam of the time (*Ādam az-Zamān*), the Adam of his own time. When Master Fard Muhammad brought the knowledge of self—"He who knows himself, knows his lord," said the other Muḥammad—he gave his Muslims new names. *You are not Lindsey Garrett, you are Hazziez Allah; you are not William Blunt, you are Sharrieff Allah.* In the Student Enrollment, the Original Man is named "God of the universe" (1:10); in the first degree of English Lesson C-1, Master Fard Muhammad says, "My name is W. F. Muhammad" (1:36).

A single straight penstroke, *alif* happens to look like the number 1, expressing Allāh's singularity. When it starts a word, *alif* stands alone, disconnected from the letters that follow it. Singularity is Fard's name—literally. Fard's name is the root for Arabic words meaning loneliness, isolation, separation, uniqueness, solitude, incomparability, seclusion, individuality, and individualism; the state of being matchless, peerless, unrivaled, or odd-numbered; and performing singlehandedly or possessing alone, standing alone, doing alone, being alone. *Fard* (pl.

afrād) was the name for a category in Ibn al-ʿArabī's classifications of knowers. The *afrād*, "singular ones" are those outside the hierarchy of saints, beyond the control of the Pole of Saints, the Quṭb; among these singular ones are the Quṭb himself, Alī, and even Muḥammad, who was a *fard* prior to his prophethood.[57]

Ibn al-ʿArabī described Muḥammad's wisdom as *fardiyya* "because he was the most complete existent in this humankind, and thus the Order begins with him and ends with him."[58] Master Fard Muhammad came to North America by himself, a *fard min afrād* ("singular one from among singular ones"), a solitary *alif* from which later names would multiply: Elijah Muhammad, Malcolm X, Louis Farrakhan, Clarence Smith's names as 13X and Allah, and the thousands of names that would spring from these men, names of NOI Muslims, Sunnī and Shīʿī Muslims, and Five Percenters, an endless proliferation of letters from one. The names that I adopted both as a Sunnī (Mikail Muhammad) and a Five Percenter (Azreal Wisdom) are multiplications of Fard's *alif*.

The number 2 corresponds with Wisdom; the letter B represents "Be" or "Born." Wisdom is the interpretation or application of Knowledge. Wisdom is the womb from which Knowledge becomes Born. In "The Birth," the RZA calls Wisdom the "wise word spoken"; in the Qurʾān, Allāh creates the world through speech. There's also correspondence to the second letter of the Arabic alphabet, *bā*, which is the first letter of *bismillāh*, "In the Name of God," the first words of the Qurʾān. While *alif* represents the Essence, *bā* signifies the Attributes. If you were to write out the sound made by *bā* in Arabic letters, you'd have to use an *alif*; *bā* contains the manifestation of *alif* and all letters that follow are manifestations of *bā*. Fard's *bā* is the Honorable Elijah Muhammad. Bringing this back to real life: the wisdom that you speak in the world, your own *bā*, manifests *you*, and that wisdom in turn will be manifested by its future effects.

Even the dot under *bā* has been the subject of esoteric commentaries. Ṣūfī tradition would come to understand the dot as representing the

Perfect Man, the "site of emanating grace," developed from the saying attributed to Alī, "I am the point under the *bā* of *bismillāh*."[59] The dot under *bā* is a mark between the Absolute and existence.

In my continuing play with these signs, Allah's Math and Alphabets provided the shovel and I only dug to find *myself* buried in Fard's text. I didn't see the systems to be "real" beyond the borders of their own logic, but that didn't change what these things could do for me—or what I *made* them do, the ways that I could manipulate these attributes and their relationships.

The number 4, for example, signified "Culture." I wrote in my notebook: "Culture = the shared beliefs, attitudes, and behaviors of a group." The fourth letter of the alphabet, D, represented the attribute of "Divine." As I saw it, all of our experiences and articulations of the Divine were produced by Culture; even Muḥammad alone on the mountain still had a Cultural background and experienced the Divine through what his Culture had given him, its symbols and stories and language.

In the theory offered by nineteenth-century sociologist Émile Durkheim, religion is a sacralization of the clan and its social order. We project our own tribal/national values and moral norms on to supernatural beings who are then said to have authored our values for us as holy commandments. Durkheim said, "God is society," and the Five Percenter anthem "The Enlightener" says, "The Culture is I-God." In the actualization of this degree, people who have been disenfranchised by the dominant totems of their society realize their own power to create Culture and define the sacred for themselves. This helped me to find my way around the Qur'ān's "wife-beating verse," 4:34. Using Supreme Mathematics, I read the verse as 4:3+4 to get 4:7, which manifests as Culture:God. Witnessing those two terms juxtaposed, Culture and God, I could see the verse for what it was.

Over the course of my encounter with Five Percenter hermeneutics, something else happened. Building with the lessons, Mathematics, and Alphabets, and integrating these materials into my Islamic life, raised questions that I had about the very nature of religion and what I wanted from it. What did I actually *believe*? And what place did belief even have in my religion, the new religion that I've made up for myself?

For many of us, when we're talking about religion, we mean belief. I entered the Muslim community through a testimony of belief in the oneness of Allāh and the prophethood of Muḥammad. I am also an American, and have inherited a Christian history through which religion is defined by belief in a particular creed. The Five Percenters, as respondents to this same Western Christian society, likewise tend to equate religion with matters of faith, which is a primary reason why they reject that term for their culture. Religion is understood as an institution's claim to be rooted in supernatural knowledge and authority; to be "religious" means that you accept the institution's claims as true. But that wasn't the entirety of my experience with religion; belief has not always come first.

I recently tried but could not remember the exact moment at which I achieved full *belief* in the claims of Islam. I do remember how it felt to read Malcolm X and the arguments of Muslim scholars for Islam's concepts of monotheism, the Day of Judgment, and so on. I can remember *feeling* something when I first picked up a Qur'ān, though I couldn't yet say that I had "converted." It was not long after these initial encounters that I was spending most of my time at a mosque—in Pakistan.

When did my comprehension of Islam go from "This makes sense" to "This is *true*"?

On the other side of that history, I would later experience a collapse of Islam's truth claims in my heart. Disillusioned, I could no longer say what I believed; but there were times when, even if I did not meet every condition of faith, I retained my sense of *being* Muslim. Today, I can say that most of my personal growth as a Muslim came after the point at which I no longer had—to use Derrida's phrase—a "stable position" on articles of doctrine. I went to Mecca while in my unstable condition, and had genuinely transformative experiences while performing ritual imitation of Abraham and Hajar, despite the fact that I viewed these people as fictional characters. Sometimes I catch a glance of a nearby Qur'ān and feel a rush of affection for the physical object; I pick up the Qur'ān and don't even know what to do with my love, gritting my teeth and unsure of whether to squeeze the book or try to eat it. To see and hear the Qur'ān can bring me to trembling and tears—but my feelings are in no way connected to whether the Qur'ān actually came from a supernatural source outside Muḥammad's mind. My experience of the Qur'ān does not depend on the Qur'ān's promises about itself actually being true. Maybe that's just the pro wrestling fan in me.

I had a similar experience with the Five Percent. As a researcher, I found the community's doctrines and history to be endlessly fascinating, and the unique phrases and concepts in the lessons and Math to make for natural poetry. Even before I had embarked on the project, my encounters with personalities such as Azreal felt magical, and I had been preoccupied with the figure of Master Fard. But there had to be some moment at which things turned—I became a changed person, a "convert"—and I could say with some confidence, "I am part of this, and/or it is part of me."

I did not believe in claims that Master Fard Muhammad had come from Mecca, that he was trained by a secret council of scientist-imāms, or that he possessed transcendent knowledge. I did not treat Fard's lessons as a source of empirically grounded history, or consider that Yakub's grafting of the devil could explain variations in skin color better than the modern science of population genetics or studies of ultraviolet radiation across the planet. Nor did I believe that Supreme Mathematics expressed mystical properties of numbers rather than the imagination of human beings. But apart from *believe*, I did other things with these items.

Somehow I reached a point at which I could be sitting in a Sunnī mosque, listening to the imām talk about Moses/Mūsā, and find myself interpreting the sermon through alternative texts that the imām couldn't know: the 2:14 and 4:14 degrees from the 120. And I don't even assume Moses to have been historical, but I'm still retrieving/producing truth from these fictions.

In 2:14, Moses is described as having a "hard time civilizing the devil" because he had lost the knowledge of himself and took on a "beast life." Moses, you could say, had undergone a conversion experience. By going among the devils, he became like them.

Moses had come to the devils to teach them, two thousand years after they were exiled from the Root of Civilization (Mecca) into Europe. In 4:14, the devils are said to have been exiled for causing discord and strife among the righteous people. The devils were marched across the hot desert, forced to walk every step of 2,200 miles. Later material from Elijah Muhammad would describe a character named General Monk Monk who led the devils with a high-powered rifle.

"We took from them everything," says the degree, "except the language."

This became my answer to questions of conversion. The gods did not take the devils' language because it would have made them devils too; Moses lost his knowledge of self and became "half-Original" because he adopted the devils' language as his own. In the corresponding degree from English Lesson C-1, Master Fard Muhammad says, "My uncle cannot talk his own language" (4:36). Fard's uncle (the black man in America) had been converted from his own self, like Moses, through the devils' language, the "wrong food" (10:36). Taking "Colored" off black people and putting it on whites, rewriting meaning for "God" and "Devil," and getting rid of everyone's slave names, Fard seems to have understood that a complete overhauling of both society and the self would begin with words. Equality could not have been achieved in the old vocabulary.

Without making value judgments on how this relates to my "own self," I recognize that like Moses, I was changed by words. My true conversion to Islam was the moment of its language becoming naturally my own, my coming to think in Islam's terms, speaking both belief and disbelief (and all points between them) through Islam—the time from which a mention of "God" would always refer me to the concepts, texts, practices, and cultures of Islam. By the time I reached Mecca, the stories of Abraham and Hajar were a symbolic language in which I could express my own thoughts and emotions. This conversion could have taken place before or after my statement of *shahādah*. Or it might have been the moment at which a word such as "convert" no longer applied, since I had outgrown that in-between place and Islam was embedded too deep to ever be pulled out of me.

There also came a time when I would think in Supreme Mathematics, when the 7 on a football jersey would strike my heart the same as Allāh's Name in elaborate Arabic calligraphy. What I believed about Supreme Mathematics did not matter; for a language to be "real" only means that it is understood. I had become so comfortable in Supreme Mathematics that I understood it without trying, never having to stop and think about its rules.

For me to object to the logic of Supreme Mathematics would be like asking why a *D* has to be shaped like that, or why a dog is represented by the sound *dog* and why those three letters represent the sound, or why a green traffic light has to mean "Go" and a red light always means "Stop." That's the language; green means "Go," 8 means "Build or Destroy." I have also integrated the doctrines of the Five Percent into my life, but I'm not sure if this came before or after the language. I'm guessing that it all kind of happened at the same time, and that the two processes encouraged each other. I entered the system as it entered me. Perhaps I was a Five Percenter at the moment when, upon seeing a book titled *Is God a Mathematician?* at Borders, my first thought was "All the gods that *I* know are mathematicians."

It has been said that poetry cannot really be translated, only rewritten; considering religion as language, I wonder if religion can be translated. In *Chinese Gleams of Sufi Light,* Sachiko Murata discusses the challenge faced by early Chinese Muslims who needed to express their Islamic concepts in terms that could be locally understood. Their biggest problem was that the language had no equivalent for *Allāh*. They tried a few things: "Heaven," "Buddha," and eventually "Lord," "Real Lord," "Real One," and "Real Ruler." Meanwhile, Muhammad was described as "the Utmost Sage," and angels were "heavenly immortals." Paradise was "ultimate happiness" and Hell was "earth prohibited" or "earth prison." Mosques were called "temples of the pure and real."[60]

These terms could have transformed Islam, especially when the names had previous histories with their users: "Utmost Sage" had been a title used for Confucius, and "heavenly immortals" had a Taoist backstory.[61] To trade in a word like "Prophet" and all of its baggage for "Utmost Sage" gives Muhammad an entirely new character. Even if the doctrinal matter remains untouched, I don't know if it's exactly the same Islam, or if it should be. A Muslim with a Buddhist past who refers to Allāh as Buddha is effectively writing her own Qur'ān.

For religion to be language has to mean something for pantheons with gods of writing and knowledge. To worship Thoth or Ganesh is to glorify the human mind, but it's the same with pursuits of Allāh through Arabic words on ornamented pages, and the contemplation of meanings hidden in letters that were made by people. *Mīm,* one of the Qur'ān's "mystery letters," has been read to signify God as the All-Comprehensive and Muhammad as the all-comprehensive prophet, and also humanity as Allāh's all-comprehensive creation; even its shape has been interpreted. As part of the Qur'ān, *mīm* is taken to be much more than a *mīm,* but the letter also has a birth record. *Mīm* is the first letter of the Arabic word for water; it goes back to a character that was doubled to spell the Phoenician word for water, *mem,* and the Phoenician character was derived from the Egyptian hieroglyph for water. Not sure if this changes the price of bread for Hurūfīs. Even *alif* derives from an ancient picture-letter for "ox," but I don't know how you'd work that into Ṣūfism.

Through systems of writing, humans built and disseminated sophisticated theologies. In this sense, the esoteric letterists are completely right, because Allāh *is* within the words; there's no mystery god because we have no Allāh independent of our words, just words on words on words for trillions of years. When Ibn al-'Arabī witnessed a vision of the Divine Essence, it appeared to him as text: the two letters that spell *Hu* ("He"), *ha* and *wāw*, resting within another *ha* signifying Allāh's *Huwiyya* ("He-ness"), seated on a red carpet, emanating light in all directions. "He, who had revealed His words in the letters of the Koran," writes Annemarie Schimmel on the vision, "could be 'seen' only in a symbol taken from the letters, from the Book."[62]

In another of his mystical experiences, Ibn al-'Arabī was visited by an angelic/theophanic being, "the Scribe who writes upon all the pages of the intellect," in the physical form of a youth. Ibn al-'Arabī pleaded with the Scribe to reveal the Qur'ān's inner meanings, only to receive this answer: "You are a cloud over your own sun. First of all, know the reality of yourself."[63] Alī was right when he called himself the dot of the first *bā* in the Qur'ān, because it's his *bā* and his Qur'ān; as the dot, he drives the *bā* and everything that follows, wherever he wants it to go. In your Qur'ān, no one can be the dot but you.

EIGHT

SUNNĪ GODS: THE PRAYERS OF FIRST BORN PRINCE ALLAH

Don't ask me if I'm Muslim, don't say nothin' to me.
—Gang Starr, "2 Deep"[1]

THE WATERSHED EVENT in Nation of Islam history, the death of Elijah Muhammad in 1975, forced a momentary shift in the Five Percenters' position. In the brief span of time between Warith Deen Mohammed's dismantling of his father's teachings and Louis Farrakhan's NOI revival, Five Percenters could not have been considered an "offshoot" or "heresy" of the NOI, because the NOI did not exist. In this vacuum, they became the Nation's primary traditionalists. Upholding interest in Elijah Muhammad's message and rejecting the innovations of his son, Five Percenters would have been the closest thing to an NOI Salafism. Insiders and outsiders alike may have seen them as such; it is believed that many NOI Muslims who disagreed with Warith Deen's changes, seeking Elijah's doctrine in something closer to its original form, joined the Five Percenters.

A mass influx of adherents from the destroyed Nation of Islam left a permanent—and for many gods, troublesome—mark on Five Percenter culture. The earliest record of Five Percenters calling themselves the "Nation" dates to November 1976, just one month after Warith Deen renamed his NOI the World Community of Islam in the West (WCIW).[2]

Numerous Five Percenters even referred to their movement as the Five Percent Nation *of Islam*. Also in 1976, a Five Percenter known as Malik Al Hadi reportedly called for the movement to become more structured and organized, with a chosen leader.[3] No other information is available on Malik Al Hadi, but his name may provide clues to his inclinations, as all-Arabic names (without one of them being Allah) are virtually unheard of among Five Percenters.

It is probable that as Farrakhan developed his group, Five Percenters initially supported him as a reviver of their own heritage; Five Percenter history mentions figures such as Father Bushawn drifting back and forth between the two movements during this period. Farrakhan's rising profile, however, would lead to confusion between his Nation of Islam and the Five Percent Nation of Islam. By the mid-1980s, a clear break had to be made, repeating Allah's original divorce from the NOI in the 1960s.

This was achieved in part by a growing creedal impulse among the Five Percent. A religion's creed is its border, separating those who have light from those lost in ignorance. By stating what it believes, a religious institution additionally states what it does *not* believe, and who does not qualify for inclusion within the community. It is for this reason that scholar John B. Henderson writes that creeds from early Christianity provide "hidden heresiographies."[4] Creeds appear after confusion; as an attempt to freeze doctrine, a formal creed is written because circumstances call for this explicit redrawing of boundaries. To study a proclamation of Five Percenter doctrine could therefore reveal controversies and debates that divided the community at the time of its writing, such as the culture's relationship to Islam.

A text commonly accepted as the Five Percenters' creed, "What We Teach," first appeared in 1986, nearly two decades after Allah's assassination.[5] The statement was drafted by Beloved Allah, Allah Mind, and Allah Supreme, and appeared on the back page of their newspaper, *The WORD*. Both *The WORD* and "What We Teach" were landmark events in the Five Percenters' formulation as a textually stabilized tradition, and have permanently affected the community's vision of its own history, identity, and purpose. The establishment of *The WORD* and its close relationship to the Five Percenters' physical property, the Allah School in Mecca, allowed an increasing sense of structure to spread throughout the movement. It was only through a centralizing medium like *The WORD* that a god such as Dumar Wa'de Allah could claim to be the movement's "official spokesman" and issue formal dictums to all members.[6] With new institutional power, the Five Percenters could more clearly define "correct" and "incorrect" teachings, having brought the formulation of doctrine to a halt. Not everyone accepted this development; for some, such as Prince Allah Cuba, it appeared that the Five Percent was on the fast track to becoming an organized religion.

"What We Teach" is presented in nine points, each of which can be read to match its corresponding attribute in Supreme Mathematics; the third item mentions "understanding," which is the attribute for the number 3, and the seventh item discusses God, which is the attribute for the number 7. As a clear and concise mission statement—a pledge of allegiance for Allah's nation—the document plainly names the conditions of belief by which someone can be accepted as a Five Percenter:

1. That black people are the original people of the planet Earth.
2. That black people are the fathers and mothers of civilization.
3. That the science of Supreme Mathematics is the key to understanding man's relationship to the universe.
4. Islam is a natural way of life, not a religion.
5. That education should be fashioned to enable us to be self-sufficient as a people.
6. That each one should teach one according to their knowledge.

7. That the blackman is god and his proper name is ALLAH. Arm, Leg, Leg, Arm, Head.

8. That our children are our link to the future and they must be nurtured, respected, loved, protected, and educated.

9. That the unified black family is the vital building block of the nation.[7]

The third, fourth, and seventh items make a clear break from the identification of Five Percenters as Muslims, whether NOI or otherwise. By designating Supreme Mathematics as the most essential source of guidance, "What We Teach" privileges this unique Five Percenter system over texts that would bind the movement to other traditions, such as the Qur'ān or even the Supreme Wisdom Lessons. In contrast, the creed's description of Islam as a "natural way of life, not a religion," may not seem too drastic; it actually repeats similar statements made by Elijah Muhammad and even Sunnī apologetic materials. However, Five Percenters have used this vision of Islam as a means of disavowing categorization as Muslims: a Muslim is one who *submits* to God, but a Five Percenter *is* God and submits to no one.

Obviously, the statement that the blackman's proper name is Allah distinguishes Five Percenters from orthodox Muslims. With no mention of Master Fard Muhammad, it also marks a subtle but crucial distinction from Nation of Islam doctrine; the black man is Allah with no Allah above him.

Five Percenters also distanced themselves from the Nation of Islam through increasing emphasis on their own history. In 1987, *The WORD* published "The Bomb: the Greatest Story Never Told," the first hagiography of Allah. The narrative serves an ideological purpose, showing Five Percenters as possessors of a rich heritage independent of the Nation of Islam, and repeatedly illustrating a complete separation between the two groups. In "The Bomb," the Five Percent's patriarch is identified as Allah (not Clarence 13X, his name in the mosque).[8] It is claimed that when Allah was Muslim, Elijah Muhammad gave him the honorific title Abdullah, meaning "servant of God;" however, as "The Bomb" tells us, "Allah had been a man who always thought for himself, he was no follower."[9] After unlocking the true meaning of the Nation's lessons, the would-be Abdullah revealed himself to instead be Allah, and was banished from the mosque as a heretic.[10] While the historical circumstances behind Allah's attrition remain mysterious— reasons have been given ranging from gambling to drug use to domestic violence—"The Bomb" insists that Allah left due to "irreconcilable" differences of scriptural interpretation, his advanced understanding of Fard's message placing him hopelessly at odds with Elijah Muhammad's institution.[11]

"The Bomb" describes Allah after his exit from the mosque as "teaching Islam to the people in the community," but "Islam" should be understood here as defined in "What We Teach": a way of life, not a religion.[12] There is no mention of Allah teaching theology or rituals, only that black people "had to clean themselves up in order to regain their long lost stature of prominence in this world. That they should abstain from smoking cigarettes, drinking alcohol, and eating pork."[13] Frustrated at his inability to affect change on Harlem's streets, "The Bomb" asserts, Allah then developed Supreme Mathematics as a better means of teaching the youth.[14]

"The Bomb" goes on to describe Allah's incarceration and later prominence as a City Hall–endorsed community leader, as well as detailing events that illustrate the birth of a new culture: "Allah was very particular at distinguishing his nation from the Muslims."[15] Distinction was created through the Five Percenters' adoption of their own emblem, the Universal Flag; Allah's order that Five Percenters drop their "Muslim names" (i.e., Hakiem) in favor of names drawn from their own code of Supreme Mathematics and Supreme Alphabets (i.e., Born Allah); and a declaration allegedly made by Allah when confronted by NOI Muslims:

You or any Muslims can't judge me or my sons and your lessons
say that anything made weak and wicked from the Original Man
is devil, and you are running around worshiping a Half-Original
man [Fard] and not the blackman.[16]

"The Bomb" also presents an apocryphal account of Allah making
an announcement that would forever separate his legacy from the par-
ent tradition: "After this year there won't be any Five Percenters anymore. You will be the Nation of Gods and Earths, not the Nation of
Islam."[17] The statement, purported to have been made in 1968, implies
Allah foreseeing his own assassination one year later, and that his death
would bring forth a new phase in the movement. There is no historical
evidence that Allah had ever uttered the words "Nation of Gods and
Earths"; the term does not appear in Five Percenter or outside media
prior to the emergence of The WORD in 1986.[18] In opposition to "Five
Percent Nation of Islam" and similar names in circulation (including
Allah's Nation of the Five Percent and Allah's Nation of Islam[19]), The
WORD declared itself the "national newspaper of the Nation of Gods
and Earths (NGE)"; with authority for the new name projected back-
wards upon Allah, the paper helped to settle the community's naming
dispute.[20] Today, despite occasional dissent, Nation of Gods and Earths
is generally regarded as synonymous with Five Percenters.[21]

This production of a new Five Percenter knowledge falls into the
pattern that comparative religion scholar Wilfred Cantwell Smith calls
"reification," the process "of crystallization, of communalization, of
systematization" by which a master teacher's message takes shape as a
distinct religion—even if this appears to betray the spirit of the teacher's
original mission.[22]

The master teacher, having transcended symbol systems and realized
a "personal and cosmic reality," speaks of a truth beyond sectarianism;
but after the master teacher's death, his/her followers protect the teacher's message and community from disintegration by consolidating into

yet another sect. Smith uses the example of Guru Nānak (1469–1539), who is regarded as the founder of Sikhism. Guru Nānak, Smith tells us, "attacked religious formalism of all kinds," denied that truth could be owned by one community or book, and advocated only faith and righteousness. After Guru Nānak's passing, however, those who sought to uphold his teachings reformulated them as a system of knowledge and practices that could be kept separate from other systems. Through the crystallizing work of later Gurus such as Arjan Dev (1563–1606) and Guru Gobind Singh (1666–1708), Guru Nānak's blend of Hindu and Islamic elements evolved into Sikhism, a unique religion complete with its own systematized piety, and distinguished from both Hinduism and Islam. Smith thus asserts that it would be wrong to regard Guru Nānak as Sikhism's founder: "Nānak had never heard of Sikhism, and would have rejected the idea if he had; just as Jesus Christ did not and could not conceive of 'Christianity,' nor Lao Tse of 'Taoism.'"[23] Fred M. Donner has presented a similar case regarding Muḥammad, arguing that the "single shahādah" ("There is no god but God") was supplanted by the "double shahādah" ("There is no god but God, and Muḥammad is the Messenger of God") decades after Muḥammad's death, as part of an Umayyad effort to exclude Jews and Christians from the community of believers and mark "Islam" as a separate religion.[24]

In Five Percenter reification, Allah's significance was celebrated through his posthumous distinction as "the Father," a title he had never claimed for himself, while aspects of his inclusivism—such as holding a Christmas party for Five Percenters and giving Universal Flags to non–Five Percenters—largely fell out of favor. Tradition relied on innovation to survive, while innovation relied on tradition for purpose and meaning. As the Nation of Gods and Earths became an institution of sorts, it carried the paradox that Derrida observes in each "instituting moment:" when the birth of an institution "starts something new, it also continues something, is true to the memory of the past, to a heritage, to something we receive from the past, from our predecessors, from the culture."[25] It seems a bit problematic to say that the NGE was "founded" by Allah; rather, the NGE emerged as a 1980s reification of Allah's 1960s career, shielding the Five Percent from absorption into other communities. As a natural consequence of this process, Allah's antireligious intervention became its own religion.

In opposition to the NGE, a faction called the Allah Team has performed a rival form of reification, attempting to re-Muslim the ideas that the former Clarence 13X had worked to de-Muslim, pull him back into the mosque that he rejected, and crystallize his movement as the Five Percent Nation of Islam, a subset *within* the NOI. Allah Team member Wakeel Allah authored two books, *In the Name of Allah: A History of Clarence 13X and the Five Percenters, Vols. 1 and 2,* arguing that Allah consistently viewed himself as a follower of Elijah Muhammad and even decreed that in the event of his death, Five Percenters should join the NOI. The NGE, in Wakeel Allah's view, constitutes a break from authentic Five Percenter tradition, having unjustly "idolized" the former Clarence 13X above Master Fard Muhammad and strayed from the lessons.[26] Categorizing Five Percenters as representing either "division" (NGE) or "extension" (pro-NOI), Wakeel Allah even speculates that the NGE may be acting as part of a government conspiracy to sabotage the Five Percent.[27] Wakeel Allah's work has been widely rejected by NGE Five Percenters as little more than NOI propaganda. Online discussions in NGE newsgroups and message boards frequently host attacks on the Allah Team:

Religion is the enemy of Free Thought and Free Expression. ALL religion. Even though I think it's hilarious y'all are trying to link that 7th century camel riding religion to what Fard taught, I don't care if "Islam" started with a Black face or a White face. If it's a RELIGION, then it's not my service. You're obviously joking by saying Elijah didn't have a "slave religion." He said HIMSELF that HE was a slave to Fard and that WE MUST BE SLAVES TO

FARD TOO. That is, if we didn't want Fard to kill us and murder our families!! That, my disingenuous trouble-making friend, is the very foundation of a slave-making religion. . . . Individuals Submitting Lowly Acting Muhammad IS NOT the same as I Self Lord Allah Master. Who you fooling? Not me.[28]

IN 2009, pro-NGE Five Percenters produced *Knowledge of Self: A Collection of Wisdom on the Science of Everything in Life,* an anthology of essays. Like *The WORD* before it, the book speaks with a voice of communal power; its "FAQ" section functions as a creed, giving the impression of a united NGE response to controversies relating to race, gender, and religion. In answer to the question, "Are you Muslims?" the text states plainly, "No, we do not consider ourselves Muslims," while adding the claim that "Muslim" could technically mean "one of peace." The answer to "Are you a part of the NOI?", while rejecting ties to the formal organization, expands the meaning of "Nation of Islam" to signify the "fundamental structure of the universe"—supporting Five Percent independence while also negotiating with the 120's description of the Nation of Islam as older than the sun, moon, and stars. The field of acceptable Five Percenter discourse is narrowed with the question, "Are all of those rappers really 'Five Percenters'?" The provided answer—that most hip-hop artists who claim affiliation with the Five Percent are not "true and living" in their relationship to the culture—pushes out artists who fail to adequately represent NGE norms. *Knowledge of Self,* perhaps most explicitly in its final pages, takes part in the construction of an orthodoxy, a community's setting of its limits.

Knowledge of Self positions the Five Percenters as possessors of their own tradition, not as an "offshoot" of a larger tradition, and affirms that any exchange between the NGE and other knowledge systems will occur on the NGE's terms. The question of whether Five Percenters follow the Qur'ān or Bible is answered in a way that empowers the Five

Percent to use these materials without owing commitment to any outside institution:

> We don't "follow" any text. We do realize that such written texts
> are a collection of history, moral directives, and mythology of the
> Original Man. By critical analyses we can assess which portion of
> the texts are relevant to our current conditions in the Wilderness
> of North America and which portions are being used to oppress,
> confuse, and stagnate us.[29]

KNOWLEDGE OF SELF'S contact directory, providing information on
Five Percenters in various cities, does not include Allah Team members.[30] No essays in *Knowledge of Self* identify Five Percenters as Muslims, and more than one stresses the difference. Popa Wu, an elder Five
Percenter known as a mentor to members of the Wu-Tang Clan, writes,
"I'm no Muslim, so I don't pray to Allah. I don't submit. I bear witness
to the teachings of Allah. That's what makes me show and prove Allah
is the God, always was, and always will be, through the knowledge that
He blessed."[31] I Majestic Allah's essay, "Is the NGE a Muslim Community?" acknowledges that confusion over the Five Percent's connection
to Islamic religion exists even *within* the NGE, but argues that relief
from the "limited parameters of 'Proto-Islam'" is necessary for the Five
Percent to be properly understood.[32]

Despite its disagreement with the Allah Team's Muslim affiliation,
Knowledge of Self does contain numerous references to canonical Islam;
editor/publisher Supreme Understanding Allah asserts that Ṣūfism teaches
that "the Black man is God" and quotes the Qur'ān to produce an
image of God as man,[33] while contributor Shaikhi Teach Mathematics
Allah references Qur'ānic verses to argue that white people are devils.[34]
Perhaps demonstrating influence of the Ansaru Allah Community,
Knowledge Infinite Supreme Allah examines God's creation of Adam

as described in the Qur'ān: "Here, we have Allah breathing His Spirit into the Original man. This goes back to the Higher Self, the Original man's true essence, which is Allah."[35] A writer named I Medina Peaceful Earth states that she chose her name after reading about the Prophet's *hijra* in *The Life and Times of Muhammad*, and later learning of Five Percenter history in Brooklyn, which the community has renamed Medina.[36]

The Five Percenters' relationship to the NOI and classical Islamic tradition has remained the community's central source of tension for decades, much more so than the questions of goddesses or white gods. On one side of the tension, it is rightly stated that Allah did not self-identify as a Muslim, nor did he consider his Five Percenters to be under Elijah Muhammad's command. However, one could also raise doubts as to whether Allah, who defined "Five Percenter" as merely a person who was "civilized," advocated a narrow sectarianism. In my personal relationship to the Five Percent, I was not asking whether Five Percenters should properly see themselves as Muslims, but whether anyone could cross the line—real or imagined—that divides these traditions. I found my answer in one of Allah's esteemed companions.

FIVE PERCENTER HISTORY recognizes nine youths from Harlem as the First Born, the original disciples of Allah in 1964. They have been granted a status in Five Percenter history comparable to that of Christ's Twelve Apostles, or Islam's Companions of the Prophet, and have been immortalized in Five Percenter publications and hip-hop lyrics.[37] Some within the community have questioned the concept of the First Born; Prince Allah Cuba treats the First Born as part of the Five Percent's reification into an organized religion, providing the basis for a "priesthood" and thus antithetical to Five Percenter egalitarianism. He also challenges the historicity of the First Born, claiming that the concept did not emerge as a list of named individuals until the mid-1970s, and that this list underwent politically motivated revision. According to Cuba, the original list included Sha Sha, a Latino Five Percenter from Brooklyn, and his absence from later versions could have been an attempt to render the First Born more Afrocentric and/or Harlem-centric.[38]

Conflicting versions of the First Born appeared in print in the early and mid-1980s, with different names appearing in four to five of the nine positions.[39] One version appeared in "The Bomb"; another was presented by Universal Shaamgaudd Allah, creator of the Universal Flag, in his newsletter, *Sun of Man.* In "The Bomb," the First Born includes Sha Sha, who is not on Shaamgaudd's list. While his own First Born roster recognizes only Harlem youths, Universal Shaamgaudd additionally provides lists of the First Born in other boroughs, marking Sha Sha (and himself) among the First Born of Brooklyn.[40] The "Bomb" version contains Ubeka (Ebeka), who had left the Nation of Islam with Allah; the removal of his name from Universal Shaamgaudd's version would serve to distinguish "Elders," adult Five Percenters who had formerly belonged to the Nation of Islam, from the earliest teenagers to join Allah's new movement. Despite the more widespread circulation of "The Bomb," Universal Shaamgaudd's prestige contributed to his First Born becoming the canonical version. Today, online versions of "The Bomb" are edited to conform to Universal Shaamgaudd's roster.

First Born Prince Allah (not to be confused with Prince Allah Cuba) may appear on both lists; the question arises from a possible misreading of names. Prior to the Father's order that Five Percenters no longer use Islamic names, Prince had been known as Al-Jabbar; "The Bomb" list includes an "Al-Java," which could be a misspelling or confusion of Prince with another god. Prince addressed the issue in a 1991 letter, stating that Al-Java was another individual who did not qualify as First Born.[41] Regardless of his standing in "The Bomb," First Born Prince Allah does appear in Universal Shaamgaudd's triumphant text, and has been uniformly recognized as one of the true First Born.[42]

First Born Prince Allah was born Leslie Stanley on June 20, 1946, in New York. Five Percenter narratives report that in the early 1960s, his cousin William Craig introduced him to an underground scene of youths who studied Nation of Islam lessons and trained in martial arts.[43] Though these youths were not registered with the local Nation of Islam mosque, and had obtained their lessons through attritioned members, they regarded themselves as Muslims and adopted Islamic names. William had taken the name Amin; after deciding to convert, Leslie renamed himself Al-Jabbar, "the Compeller."

Al-Jabbar, 1960s

For Al-Jabbar and other members of New York's Islamic under-ground, according to a Five Percenter elder, "basic Islam" at this stage consisted primarily of three items: "white man is the devil, don't eat no pig, and be strong."[44] Converts were additionally taught judo and techniques to "smack police off horses."[45] In the summer of 1964, Amin and five other Muslim youths would gain notoriety as the "Harlem Six," falsely accused of the murder of a Hungarian woman in her store.[46] New York media ran wild stories of the "Blood Brothers," an alliance of "Harlem hate gangs" trained to kill white people by former members of the Nation of Islam.[47] We cannot say for sure whether Harlem's pockets of rogue NOI Muslims were so organized, or even called themselves by a common name before reporters dubbed them the Blood Brothers. It would not have been the first time that white hysteria drummed up myths of black freedom fighters. After a Georgia lynching in 1904, whites throughout the state became paralyzed with fear of the "Before-Day Clubs," a rumored network of black vigilantes determined to avenge any lynching before the next day. The Before-Day Clubs did not exist, however, and have been described as most likely a "combination of black fantasy and white paranoia."[48] The Blood Brothers may have been a similar specter, a nightmare for one side and messianic for the other. Today, oral tradition regards the Blood Brothers as a concrete fact of Five Percenter prehistory, and one can find Five Percenter elders in Harlem who claim to have been aligned with the group. *Knowledge of Self* recognizes Prince as a former Blood Brother.

According to one narration, Al-Jabbar was studying Nation of Islam lessons with two youths who had taken the names Karriem and Niheem, when Karriem's brother arrived with shocking news: a man at one of the local gambling spots claimed to be "Almighty God Allah." Karriem armed himself with a meat cleaver and told the rest of the group to stay behind. When he returned, he revealed that he had been taught a new system called Supreme Mathematics, a numerological key to unlock the Nation of Islam's lessons. That day, October 7, happened to be the birthday of Elijah Muhammad. Three days later, the man who claimed to be Allah would bring Al-Jabbar and other youths together under his tutelage.[49] October 10, 1964, is thus marked as the beginning of the Five Percenter movement.

In Prince's account, the First Born were not simply the original nine teenagers to encounter the Father's teachings, but a group of elites chosen from among numerous youths who followed the Father at the time. In his letter on the issue, Prince names several individuals who were present in the early period, including one who "was around before we met ALLAH," but should not be counted among the First Born. For Prince, who consistently referred to himself as "First Born Prince," the title represented more than seniority; it was a special endorsement, and perhaps designated its wearers as successors to the Father's authority—hence the "priesthood" of Cuba's critique. When clarifying the proper names of the First Born, Prince writes, "There is always one among us who is the best knower."[50] The statement echoes Elijah Muhammad's belief that all black men are gods, but only the "best knower" can call himself Allah. When it came to revising the canonical list, Prince saw himself in that position:

Now, if a God knows that I am one of the First Born, what the fuck makes him think that I didn't know how to spell or pronounce my own fuckin name or who isn't one of the First Born?[51]

Among the First Born, Prince became a particularly prominent figure, for a number of reasons. First, his longevity within the culture: of the nine youths designated as First Born, Prince was one of three who could still be found at parliaments in the year 2000. The rest had either left the community or passed away. Karriem/Black Messiah, regarded as the very first teen disciple of the Father, was active in the movement until his death in 1989; Al-Salaam was reportedly exiled during the Father's lifetime. Other First Borns, such as Niheem and Akbar, are virtually anonymous, with little or no information available on their fates. In contrast, Prince remained a prolific teacher, with possibly thousands of Five Percenters now tracing their lineages back to him. He attained legendary status not only for his close relationship to the Father and the origins of Five Percenter culture, but also from oral traditions suggesting that he was an important figure among the Attica prison inmates during their 1971 rebellion.[52] Additionally, Prince's distinct personality, quick wit, and confrontational teaching style have been memorialized through numerous anecdotes that circulate within the culture.

First Born Prince Allah was also a controversial figure, criticized and even reviled by some for his continued identification with traditional Islam.[53] He was known for attending Friday prayers at Sunnī mosques such as Masjid Malcolm Shabazz, wearing a *kiffeyeh,* and even performing Sunnī prayers in the Five Percenters' Allah School.[54] Prince's recorded recitation of the 120 also includes short *suras* of the Qur'ān, which he recites in Arabic.[55]

When asked by Five Percenters whether a member of the movement could also be a Muslim, Prince is said to have answered that Allah allowed participation in any tradition, as long as the Five Percenter knew that he was the locus of whatever transcendent power the tradition presented: the black man, when in a mosque, must know that he is Allāh; in a church, he is Christ; at a stupa, he is Buddha. Every tradition offered a portal through which one could realize the divine self. Prince propagated his views by writing "plus-lessons," interpretive texts, which he sold at the Allah School. Wakeel Allah describes his encounter with one such lesson:

> While I spoke with Yahse briefly 1st Born Prince walked outside by us and sat back in his chair. This time he put a stack of papers on the little table outside. It was a lesson called "Lost Found Muslim Lesson #3, The third Prophecy" I was like what??? I asked him about it and he said he wrote this lesson . . . I was still taken aback by the Title . . . to me it was real bold of him . . . but I didn't question him on it because after all he was 1st Born Prince and nuff respect due . . . He told me it was for sale . . . I think it was $2.00 . . . I thumbed through the lessons and it was

full of the teachings of the Holy Quran, meaning of certain Arabic words and knowledge of Islam as taught in the East and in the West.[56]

The lesson addresses points of division between Five Percenters and the Nation of Islam, and also between these groups and the larger Islamic tradition. Prince defines Islam as "mathematics," and also a "complete way of life. It is the guidance provided by Allah through His Messenger for the human families of the planet Earth."[57] Recognizing the concerns of orthodox Muslims, Prince states that the last prophet of Allah was "Muhammad Ibn Abdullah of over 1,400 years ago," but adds that the seal of prophethood had been broken by Master Fard, and Elijah Muhammad was the last "Messenger of Allah." It would appear that he is attempting to satisfy both sides, or justify his own space between them.

The Third Prophecy, like other lessons in the 120, is written in a question-and-answer format. Two of the questions and answers present Prince's rebuttal to anti-Muslim Five Percenters:

4. What is the meaning of I-S-L-A-M?
   Answer: Islam. Islam is an Arabic word which means "submission and obedience to Allah," the proper name of God. It also means "I Self Lord and Master."

8. Who is a Muslim?
   Answer: A person who accepts the Islamic way of life and acts upon it is a Muslim. Muslim means "one who submits to the will of Allah."[58]

PRINCE GIVES two definitions of Islam, one orthodox and one Five Percenter. Defining "Muslim" as a "person who accepts the Islamic way of life and acts upon it," Prince may be appealing to what orthodox

Muslims would call *adab* (etiquette), and Five Percenters would call being "civilized," as well as shared gender constructions and dietary norms such as the prohibition of pork.

As Wakeel Allah mentions, the lesson's title was bold. With the 120 containing sections titled "Lost-Found Muslim Lesson, Nos. 1 and 2," the title of Prince's text—"Lost-Found Muslim Lesson No. 3, the Third Prophecy"—suggests that Prince assigned an enormous weight to his work. Considering Prince's understanding of prophethood both in orthodox Islam and the Nation of Islam, one could also speculate on his use of the word "prophecy." Considering his previously noted allusion to there always being a "best knower," Prince seems to have viewed himself as a seal or fulfillment of the tradition. At the very least, he desired for his works to be accepted within the permanent Five Percenter canon.

In another plus-lesson, Prince offered "9 Pertinent Points of Islam," intended to be given to neophyte Five Percenters before they begin study of the 120. Prince's definition of Islam, as constructed in these nine points, reads vaguely enough for possible acceptance by Five Percenters, NOI Muslims, and Sunnīs:

1. Islam teaches of the one supreme being, Allah (God).
2. Islam teaches one a true knowledge of oneself.
3. Islam teaches a way of life that is in accord with one's own nature.
4. Islam teaches one to love and be tolerate [sic] of one's brother.
5. Islam teaches one to work and achieve the higher planes of thought and action.
6. Islam takes the mystery out of religion, making it tangible, and feasible.
7. Islam offers living proof in God of its mathematics expounded.

8. Islam teaches a true knowledge of all things and can be applied to any given situation.
9. Islam teaches freedom, justice, and equality.[59]

Possibly referring to his Third Prophecy, the essay promises "other short lessons which also outline the basic ideas and purpose of Islam." The "9 Pertinent Points of Islam" essay then takes a defensive tone, as Prince anticipates criticism:

> To the narrow mind, they may appear too Muslimish for the God's taste who has not scienced up the origin of this world, and can [not] view truth or light with an open mind.
> Al yawma akmaltu lakum dinukum wa atmamtu alaikum ni'mati um raditu lakumul islama dinan. (Quran: 5:3)
> The mere fact that I did not break-down what is written above, is causing you to wonder of its meaning; makes you want to reject what's being said. You know why? Because it's translated [sic] Arabic. If it was Spanish or French, you'd jump on it. But because it's Arabic, the mind says, "Oh shit that's Muslim," and rejects it. They do not try to learn what causes all this to happen by letting the 5% teach them. They believe in the 10% on face value.[60]

In English, the quoted passage from the Qur'ān reads: "This day have I perfected for you, your religion, and have completed My favor upon you, and chosen for you Islam the religion." Verse 5:3 is widely held to be the last verse revealed to Muḥammad, representing the completion of Islam and Muḥammad's mission. It may be that with this document, Prince Allah is completing his own favor upon his community, presenting Islam in a form that he hopes will be accepted.

In his closing words, Prince paraphrases the question from the twenty-third degree in Lost-Found Muslim Lesson No. 2: "What did he promise his people he would do?" Due to the importance of

memorizing lessons, Prince knows that his reference will be instantly
recognized; but to be sure, he prefixes the question with the number 23.
The question refers to Yakub's determination to create a devil; however,
Prince has given the text a new meaning. It should be noted that Prince
replaces "people" with "Nation," that is, the Five Percent Nation, or
Nation of Gods and Earths, and capitalizes the male pronoun. Rather
than give the lesson's memorized answer, reflecting on the past—"That
he would make a devil, graft him from his own people and that he
would teach them tricknowledge and how to rule his own people for
6,000 years"—Prince speaks with hope for a perfect and endless future:

> 23—What did He promise this Nation He would do?
>
> Ans: that He would manifest Himself through His own people
> and that He would teach them mathematics and how to rule for-
> ever.[61]

The essay is then signed, "Wa Salaam! Prince."[62]

In addition to his own texts, Prince's understanding of the Nation of
Islam/Five Percenter lessons demonstrates a middle position between
the two movements. He does accept that Allah had made changes in the
lessons, such as the variation in Lost-Found Muslim Lesson No. 2's
thirty-ninth degree:

> I fast and pray to Allah, in the name of His Prophet, W. D. Fard,
> that I live to see the hereafter when Allah, in His own good time,
> takes the devil off our planet.[63]

In the version used by Prince for his recorded recitation of the
120, the phrase "in the name of His Prophet, W. D. Fard" is absent.[64]
According to Prince, Allah had instituted the change because prayers
offered in the name of "somebody outside yourself" equaled worship of
a mystery god; the concept of prayer itself does not appear to have been

objectionable.[65] While accepting Allah's alteration of the text, Prince would also complain of Five Percenters attempting to remove the words "Muslim" and "Islam" from lessons.

Prince's legacy remains the cause of argument. For Wakeel Allah, who had studied under him at the Allah School, Prince provides a proper lineage, connecting the Allah Team's pro-Islam views to the origins of the Five Percenter movement. Wakeel Allah describes Prince as "the ranking Elder" of the community, who "knew more about Allah's teachings and history than any other Five Percenter. He was an actual firstborn who started with Allah from the very beginning."[66] Debating on Islam with Five Percenters in an online discussion group, Wakeel Allah builds upon Prince's authority to give Islam a place within the Five Percent:

> 1st Born Prince was the kind of God that would pull you to the side and teach you certain things if he felt you were ready for it. I was very impressed with his knowledge of the Holy Quran, the Prophet Muhammad's history and the teachings of Orthodox Islam. . . . A few years ago we were in front of the Allah School. I believe I was outside with Shabazz Adew Allah and the God was speaking on the Quran. 1st Born Prince walked outside and Adew mentioned that 1st Born Prince was the one who taught him some of the Quran including some of the prayers or ayats of the Quran. We then scooted over to 1st Born Prince and he started touching on the teachings of the Holy Quran. I was very impressed because although I heard Gods build on the Quran and seen plus lessons on the Quran I never seen a God speak on it as thoroughly as he did. He even knew the Arabic words and build on what they meant. I was very impressed with his build and remember saying to myself . . . damn, I want to know it like that. Although at that time I wasn't really as heavy into the Quran or Arabic but his build made me want to study it more.[67]

Prince's authority, for what it means to the Allah Team's project, cannot be touched. Wakeel Allah writes, "In reference to theological disputes, Firstborn Prince set the record straight when asked about what he knew to be Allah's teachings"; he then quotes Prince as stating that Allah's plan for the Five Percenters "is in the 120 and has been revealed in the Kitab [Qur'ān] and Bible!"[68] It is based on Prince's account, supported by two additional First Borns and another elder, that Wakeel Allah claims the Nation of Islam to be the true source of Supreme Mathematics.[69]

Prince was murdered in 2001, perhaps due to conflicts that were significantly related to Islam within the Five Percenter community. Prince's death and the circumstances surrounding it are employed by Wakeel Allah to construct a pro-Muslim narrative. In the Name of Allah, Vol. 2 discusses an Atlanta faction of Five Percenters who "influenced a vast multitude of Gods to be smoke-free, drug-free, crime-free and alcohol-free and promoted jail prevention, higher education and the respect of women"; Wakeel Allah describes these Five Percenters as "Muslim Gods."[70] They are positioned against "Kalimites," Five Percenters associated with God Kalim, an elder who has written confessionally on his battles with drug addiction in the Five Percenter newspaper. According to Wakeel Allah, it was Kalim who first proposed Nation of Gods and Earths for the movement's new name.[71] Kalim, Wakeel Allah writes, was rendered "helpless and homeless" by his demons, and had once greeted an assembly of Five Percenters by declaring, "My name is G. Kalim and I'm an elder, I smoke crack."[72] Wakeel Allah additionally alleges that a group of Kalimites broke into the home of two Muslim Gods and robbed them of valuables, including lessons by Elijah Muhammad.[73] After discrediting Kalim and the NGE, Wakeel Allah then publishes Kalim's critique against Prince and others who compromise their Five Percenter godhood with the unseen "mystery god" of traditional Islam:

These days when I hear brothers say, "He thinks that he is Allah," I wonder who they think they are. Go into yourselves and become One with Allah (God) within you. Which is a best part preserved for self. For what else does being one with Allah make you? First Born Prince relates: in Islam IHSAN—is the worship of Allah as if you see him and although you see him not, surely he sees you.

In other places you are told to get a God or Higher Power, that is other than yourself, but that is the teachings of the 10%, used "To conceal who the true and living God is and make slaves out of the 85% by keeping them blind worshiping something he knows they cannot see (invisible) . . ." a 5% does not believe in the teachings of the 10%, so those who call themselves God should know, we don't do that here.[74]

The Muslim Gods are portrayed as seeking harmony between the factions, even suggesting arbitration by Louis Farrakhan to broker peace with the Kalimites. According to Wakeel Allah, the Muslim Gods' appeal for unity is opposed by vulgar Kalimites, who degrade not only Muslims but even the former Clarence 13X:

> In an attempt to promote peace, Muslim Gods proposed a joint "Unity Meeting" between Min. Farrakhan and the Five Percenters to promote unity instead of division. Shahid M. Allah, who was working with Dr. Khallid Abdul Muhammad, addressed the possibility of the meeting with 5% Elders. Once Shahid M. Allah arrived at the Universal Parliament to make knowledge born, Kalim verbally attacked him as "a trouble maker" and said "The only thing a Muslim can do is bend over so I can fuck him in the @ss!" Shahid objected and was restrained, he then left on his own accord. In rebuttal to the Muslim Gods' anti-drug message, [Kalim] mocked them at the Parliament and dropped the bomb

that "The Father gave me my first hit of cocaine!" Needless to say, the two factions had irreconcilable differences. Muslim Gods were dissuaded from attending Parliaments unless they rebuked their stance.[75]

Treating Prince and Kalim as stand-ins for the Allah Team and its NGE opponents, Wakeel Allah downplays the real complexity of their situation. Presenting a dualism of morally upright "Muslim Gods" and depraved anti-Muslim "Kalimites," Wakeel Allah does not mention that First Born Prince Allah also suffered from drug addiction, had been incarcerated for approximately twenty years for the murder of another Five Percenter, and was exiled from the communty.[76] It should also be noted that despite his Muslim stance and estrangement at the time of his death, Prince retained sufficient standing with the Nation of Gods and Earths that its treasury provided financial support for his funeral. On the other side of the equation, Wakeel Allah's treatment of the Muslim Gods and Kalimites in *In the Name of Allah, Vol. 2* ignores Kalim's praise of the Nation of Islam as the foundation for the Nation of Gods and Earths, cited in the first volume.[77]

In 2001, during an altercation in which God Kalim allegedly attacked First Born Prince Allah, who was confined to a wheelchair at the time, Prince shot Kalim.[78] Wakeel Allah describes the shooting as an act of self-defense.[79] Kalim survived. That same year, Prince was shot to death as he left his apartment. Wakeel Allah writes, "Though the assailants are unknown, G. Kalim left town never to be seen again," and adds that Kalim remains "hiding out of harm's reach of Allah's army."[80]

Wakeel Allah then describes the funeral, which serves as an illustration of Prince's complicated religious life. Knowledge Allah, creator of the Five Percenters' anthem, "The Enlightener," sings it with an unusually mournful tone; First Born Al-Jamel, another of the original Five Percenters, recites *al-Fātiḥa*, the Qur'ān's opening *sura,* in elegant Arabic. Rasul, the former Ebeka, who had become an imām after his stint with the Five Percenters, leads the group in a traditional Sunnī funeral prayer. Rasul mentions to the mourners that he had prayed with Five Percenter elders Shahid and Justice after the first shooting of Allah; this account is duly noted by Wakeel Allah, for whom it further connects Islamic religion to the earliest beginnings of the Five Percent.

While it does not appear to be entirely unreasonable, Wakeel Allah's description of Prince's mourners as a "prayerful congregation of Five Percenters" is a problematic, potentially explosive statement, for its attribution of prayer to all Five Percenters present.[81] It is implied not only that every Five Percenter present chose to participate in the prayer, but also that each Five Percenter interpreted the prayer with the same Muslim perspective through which it was presented by Rasul. Prince's funeral, while apparently an example of Muslims and Five Percenters coming together respectfully in shared grief, has also become a rhetorical instrument in the most divisive issue faced by the Five Percenter community.

While some navigation is required around difficult aspects of his life and thought, Prince has been treated with respect in the Nation of Gods and Earths tradition. His plus-lessons, "Lost-Found Muslim Lesson No. 3, the Third Prophecy" and "9 Pertinent Points of Islam," failed to enter the NGE canon, but his "Principles of Learning" article—which contains no references to Islam—is published posthumously in *Knowledge of Self*. The short piece is accompanied by a photo of the elder wearing his *kiffeyeh*, and his bio names him as one of the First Born.[82] One of the anthology's editors has dedicated the book to his memory. Saladin Quanaah' Allah, a member of the Nation of Gods and Earths, has issued a statement on YouTube stating that Five Percenters are not Muslims; but he also remembers Prince fondly on his blog, asking Five Percenters to "reflect upon how valuable that our Elders are."[83] His commentary on Prince references the 120, in which the Original Man—as owner of the planet Earth—knows the "best part," the usable land, and also the "poor part," which he leaves to the devil: "We must preserve the best part of everything they say while they are here with us. May Peace and Blessing be upon The God."[84] The statement can be read to imply that Prince's words also had a poor part, which is not to be remembered.

In his life, teachings, and death, First Born Prince Allah navigated between opposing elements of the Five Percenter culture, at times bridging or widening the gap. While acknowledging that Allah did not consider himself to be a Muslim, Prince regarded himself as heir to Allah's teachings even as he attended Friday prayers in mosques. Prince was known not only as a Muslim God but specifically as "the Sunnī God," a label that is so ironically un-Sunnī, and also un-Five Percenter, that it perfectly sums up the contradictions that he sought to reconcile.

First Born Prince Allah, 1990s

He shocked Five Percenters at the Allah School with his Arab headdress and performance of *salāt*, but his orthopraxy was not an expression of

orthodoxy; in the masjid on a Friday afternoon, Prince's Sunnī brothers would have been stunned by his inner transgressions, the secret
of his prayer. Though Prince complained of Five Percenters editing
the Islamic element out of their history, it might have been the Five
Percent's rejection of Islam that made his own Muslim-ness possible.
With the Nation of Gods and Earths' declaration "We are not Muslims"
came an unconditional release from the demands that could be placed
upon Five Percenters by any other group. Knowledge of self means that
your mind belongs to you. With such self-empowerment clearly stated,
someone like Prince could step into a mosque not as a follower or submitter but rather as Islam's maker and owner.

Prince found his Islam in the same anarchic soup of discourses that
would produce the Five Percenters. He claimed that he had realized the
essential Five Percenter truth, that the black man is God, while engaged
in *wudhu*, washing for traditional Islamic prayer. Glancing into the bath-
room mirror, it dawned on him that he was only praying to himself. The
wudhu episode would serve as an instructional parable later in Prince's
life, as he attempted to bring his Five Percenter beliefs and Sunnī practices into harmony with each other. Rather than move beyond Islam, as
many Five Percenters would view their culture's development, Prince saw
himself as penetrating deeper *into* Islam, to its hidden core.

Prince's writings, while verging on the mystical at times, do not display
a deliberate engagement of Ṣūfism. Nonetheless, it is tempting to speculate
as to whether Prince's ongoing study of Islam ever led him to al-Ḥallāj,
the martyred tenth-century saint who was alleged to have exclaimed,
"*Ana al-Ḥaqq*"—calling himself by God's Name, "the Reality." Perhaps
Prince had even encountered the suggestion that al-Ḥallāj was the basis
for Masonic lore's Hiram Abiff character, whom Prince describes as "our
brother."[85]

When read alongside the paradigm of Ten Percenters ("bloodsuckers of the poor," religious elites, priestly classes), Eighty-Five Percenters ("blind, deaf, and dumb, slaves to mental death and power") and

Five Percenters ("poor righteous teachers," enlighteners of the masses), would al-Ḥallāj have helped First Born Prince Allah to understand his own place within Islam? He might have imagined his teacher, the former Clarence 13X, as a modern al-Ḥallāj, exiled from the mosque and martyred for his unveiling of Islam's secret. For those of us reading Prince after his own assassination, the "Sunnī God" heresy may render Prince an inversion of al-Ḥallāj: a unique religious thinker who, among men calling themselves Allah, proclaimed, *"Anā Muslim."*

Among the textual sources that were important to Prince, we can include the 1936 work *Religion of Islam* by Maulana Muhammad Ali, a prominent scholar in the Ahmadiyya community. In this volume, the Maulana explains that the Qur'ān's descriptions of God through various Names "are really meant for the perfection of human character. The Divine attributes really serve as an ideal to which man must strive to attain."[86] For God to be described as "Fosterer and Nourisher of the worlds," he writes, means that every human must maintain this as a personal ideal, and "endeavor to make the service of humanity, even that of dumb creation, the object of his life."[87] Because God is the Merciful, we must be merciful to each other. God is described as the Wise, the Maulana tells us, and thus "the Qur'ān says that the Prophet was raised to teach wisdom."[88] God is the Lord and Master, and "Man is told again and again that everything in the heavens and in the earth has been made subservient to him."[89] To be fully human is to display the Names of the Creator and Sustainer of the Universe. I can imagine how this text mingled with the teachings of Mosque No. 7 and Harlem's Allah, how new Islams and old Islams might have integrated for a young god.

In a 1991 letter, Prince quoted from the discussion of God's Attributes in *Religion of Islam* to explain his first righteous name: *al-Jabbār* signified the "One who sets things alright by Supreme Power."[90] Like al-Ḥaqq, al-Jabbār is a name reserved for God; to avoid appearing blasphemous, an orthodox Muslim is far more likely to call himself Abdul-Jabbār, "Slave of al-Jabbār." When Prince first became Muslim, he took

Al-Jabbar as his name; even before he met the former Clarence 13X, he was calling himself God.

When Allah called for sweeping changes to illustrate the Five Percenters' full break from Islam, Al-Jabbar was incarcerated in Auburn.

When I returned to the free cipher Allah was teaching that we should give up our Muslim names because we are not Muslims. That we should be more original and create our own names and not copy the names of other people. He also said that some brothers would never change their names. He told me to go in the school and sign the Book for my Flag and that I not sign Al-Jabbar. So I signed Al-Jabbar Allah Love.[91]

He did not come up with a new name until June 16, 1969—just four days before his birthday, and three days after Allah's assassination. "Blackman," he writes, "before then I couldn't think of a name. It just came to me at the Rally that day. It was a clear revelation."[92] He became Prince Allah, heir to the Father's kingdom.

In his later years, when Prince was the elder sought by young gods for his wisdom, he would justify his Sunnī practices by explaining that Allah was okay with gods engaging any wisdom tradition—as long as they understood that the black man was the supreme being. The external form was not as vital as the truth that it conveyed. For the so-called Sunnī God, the journey from Al-Jabbar to Prince Allah did not imply a rejection of one dogma for another. "I did not change the meaning of the name," he wrote, "only the name itself."[93]

NINE

ASSUMING THE TRAITS OF GOD

The difference between man and God is the same as the difference between writing a letter in a straight or in a curved handwriting.

The wise knew, he himself became God, O friend!
—Mullah Shah (d. 1661)[1]

ORTHODOX ISLAM HOLDS the most serious doctrinal offense to be *shirk*, the identification of created things with the Creator. In the eyes of many Muslims today, this is the chief crime of the Nation of Islam. Far from apologizing for his encounter with God-as-Fard, Elijah Muhammad answered that orthodox Muslims were "ignorant" and "spooky minded" for their belief in a formless, transcendent spirit: "I would not give two cents for that kind of God, in which they believe."[2]

As with whiteness, the term "orthodoxy" expresses nothing but power and privilege. We should see the word for what it is: a polite way of describing whichever branch of a religion dominates its rivals at a given moment. At Muḥammad's tomb in Medina, policemen stand between the bodily remains and the pious pilgrims, holding sticks and ready to smack anyone whose love for the Prophet goes too far; in this sense, "orthodox Islam" indeed opposes the deification of human beings.

Questions of orthodoxy aside, Muslims throughout history have taught of Allāh's appearance in human form. Though Alī, the Prophet's beloved son-in-law, was said to have executed a man for calling him God, devotion to Alī would inspire numerous *ghuluww* ("exaggeration") sects, which recognized the Prophet's household and its descendents as divine. The *ghuluww* tradition survives in contemporary communities such as the Bektashis and Alawīs.

During the caliphate of al-Manṣūr (d. 775), a movement called the Rawandiyya regarded al-Manṣūr to be Allāh incarnate, while Ustād Sīs claimed to be God in Khurāsan. During the reign of al-Manṣūr's successor, al-Mahdī (d. 785), a figure known as al-Muqanna' ("the Veiled"), wearing a golden mask, declared himself God. In a theology comparable to the Nation of Islam's succession of "best knowers," al-Muqanna' taught that Allāh had appeared in the person of every prophet from Adam to Muḥammad, then in Alī, then Alī's sons, followed by Abū Muslim and finally al-Muqanna' himself. Similar doctrines among the Druze have encouraged speculation that Master Fard Muhammad came from a Syrian background. Fazlallāh Astarābādī, founder of Hurūfism, was also regarded as the incarnation of Allāh, with his tomb in Azerbaijan functioning as a Ka'ba for his followers.

The deification of humans within an Islamic setting often built upon that particular environment's pre-Islamic heritage. In northwestern Iran and Anatolia after the Mongol invasions, *ghuluww* tendencies spread among converted nomadic tribes that mixed their newfound Islam with shamanistic beliefs.[3] Persia's ancient god-king tradition survived into Islam with the Safavid dynasty's worship of its first monarch, Shah Ismā'īl I, as God. In medieval Bengal, Islamic literature equated the Arabic word for prophet, *nabī*, with *avatar*, the Sanskrit term for a deity's incarnation—allowing both for treatments of Krishna as a messenger of God, and Muḥammad as an "incarnation of God himself" or "manifestation of his own self."[4] North Indian mysticism blended with Ibn al-'Arabī's Ṣūfī teachings to produce the Mughal philosopher-king Akbar, whose preferred salutation of *Allāhu Akbar* carried a

potential double meaning: either "God is the Greatest," or more specifically, "God is Akbar." In post-Depression Detroit, Elijah Muhammad comprehended his encounter with Fard not only through what he
knew as Islam, but also through his Christian background, which had
prepared him to see God as a man. This is not expected to satisfy a certain canonical Islam, which would dismiss the doctrines surrounding
these figures as bid'a, "innovation," the corruption of Islam with outside
sources.

While Elijah's deification of Master Fard Muhammad appears to
violate Allāh's perfect unity (tawhīd), through Fard he could at least
retain a locus of divine power and the semblance of monotheism; orthodox Muslims might compare his deviance to that of Christians. The
apparent blasphemy of Five Percenters reads as an even greater departure from Islam, having democratized Elijah Muhammad's understanding of godhood and scattered the divine power.

There is no mystery god; the only true and living god is the Original Man, the Asiatic Black Man. Beyond this, the 120 gives no theology, leaving Five Percenters to sort out their godhood for themselves.
Remembering Allah B's advice, "How you see it, that's how it is," I wondered whether these traditions were completely beyond reconciliation.

AS MUSLIMS INSIST to Five Percenters that man cannot be identified
with Allāh, some Five Percenters would counter that the Qur'ān does
this itself. The Qur'ān describes Allāh in very human terms, speaking
and moving while possessing body parts that apparently correspond to
human anatomy.

Whether a literal reading of the Qur'ān actually depicts a man-
shaped god depends on just how "literal" Muslims want to get. Some
early interpreters argued that because the Qur'ān describes Allāh as
having a face, we know that Allāh has a face; but because the Qur'ān
does not explicitly say that Allāh also has a head, to assume that Allāh

has a head would mean that we have blasphemously inserted our own conjecture into the Qur'ān. One group that Sherman Jackson describes as "proto-Islamic," the Bayānīyya, read the Qur'ān's promise that everything in the universe perishes except for God's face (55:26–27) to literally mean that God's face will survive when the rest of his body is destroyed.[5]

The eighth-century rise of Abbāsid power and the establishment of Baghdad as a center of learning led to a famed translation movement, exemplified in Hārūn al-Rashīd's *Bayt al-Ḥikma* ("House of Wisdom"), through which Muslim thinkers engaged classical Greek, Persian, and Indian philosophies. Exchanges between these systems would leave a permanent impact upon Islamic conceptions of God. For Islam's blossoming science of speculative theology (*kalām*), the Qur'ān's mention of divine anatomy and attributes threatened to corrupt *tawhīd*, rendering Allāh a composite being who could be broken up into separate parts. Mentions of Allāh's activities were also difficult: to say that Allāh settled upon a throne, as in verse 7:54, could violate Allāh's perfect transcendence by defining Allāh within space and time. Practitioners of *kalām* pondered alternative meanings, considering that Allāh's "hands" could signify not physical hands but "power," while the act of "breathing" life into Adam could illustrate the act of creation, and the "throne" could represent "mastery." For the "Allāh has a face but not necessarily a head" school, these interpretations were outright denials of what the Qur'ān had clearly stated. *Ḥadīth* literature, collections of Muhammad's sayings and actions, offered even more difficulties, with accounts of Allāh appearing to the Prophet in an explicitly human form. Famed jurist Imām Aḥmad ibn Ḥanbāl (780–855), a staunch opponent of *kalām*, accepted the authenticity of such reports, including a narration in which the Prophet said, "I saw my Lord in the form of a young man, beardless with short curly hair and clothed in a green garment."[6] The reconciliation proposed by Ibn Ḥanbal and others, further developed by theologian al-Ash'arī (874–936) and his school, would neither discredit the clear meaning of a Qur'ānic verse or Prophetic report nor refuse the possibility of unknown meanings: the acceptance of difficult statements *bi-lā kayf*, "without asking how." Such a phrase might raise red flags for the Five Percent, whose lessons teach against accepting religious content on face value (9:40).

For my project, dwelling on God's body parts was not all that useful; Muslims who believed that Allāh in fact possessed an arm, leg, leg, arm, and head would still have been horrified by the Five Percent. While Allah Team scholar Wesley Muhammad/True Islam writes on Allāh's corporeality within early Islam, this is more relevant for the Nation of Islam's deification of Master Fard Muhammad than for the Five Percent's deification of self. For the Five Percent, an anthropomorphic view of God would be less important than a theomorphic view of man; portraying Allāh as a man is not the same as holding man to be Allāh. For Allāh to appear to the Prophet Muḥammad as a beardless youth dressed in green, or to Elijah Muhammad as Master Fard, still reinforces the idea of Allāh as Other, a being witnessed as separate from the witness. Whether as physical body or formless spirit, a mystery god is still a mystery god, and fails to de-Other the Divine in a way that works for the Allah School.

Of more interest to me was the Ṣūfī tradition, which has produced a vast body of literature filled with provocative and bewildering statements about the relationship between Creator and created. Abū Yazīd al-Bisṭāmī (d. 874), ecstatic Persian mystic, is said to have told Allāh, "If men knew about you as I know, they would not worship you," to which Allāh replied: "If they knew about you as I do, they would pelt you with stones."[7] These two secrets might be one and the same: what al-Bisṭāmī knows about Allāh, the secret that would destroy religion, is exactly Allāh's secret for which religious men would destroy al-Bisṭāmī. The mystic's experience of Absolute Reality *(al-Ḥaqq)* has torn down the illusions of separation between it and himself, enabling al-Bistāmī to proclaim, "Praise be to me, I am al-Ḥaqq, I am the True God: I must be celebrated by Divine praises."[8]

Needless to say, this poses problems for a more disciplined "orthodox" monotheism, best illustrated by the legend of al-Ḥallāj's execution in 922 for having similarly called himself al-Ḥaqq. It should be mentioned that there's no evidence of al-Ḥallāj having ever said, "I am al-Ḥaqq"; the saint was actually killed for his assertion that Muslims could perform the rituals of pilgrimage without going to Mecca (he had built his own Ka'ba in his yard).[9] Regardless of its historicity, the *Anā al-Ḥaqq* legend took on tremendous importance for Ṣūfism, as thinkers of all persuasions were forced to confront a saint's apparent self-identification with God. The idea that a Ṣūfī could call himself by God's Name, and suffer a brutal punishment at the hands of those entrusted with protecting God's religion, produced a variety of responses. Some celebrated the divine union that al-Ḥallāj had claimed, and sought his advanced station for themselves; others condemned him as an apostate, justifying his murder in the name of keeping Muslims from a sure road to hellfire. Between these responses, there were also commentators who took a third position: al-Ḥallāj was right in what he said, but wrong for saying it, at least in public. In order to protect the community's spiritual welfare, according to this view, al-Ḥallāj should have refrained from such an irresponsible statement. Ibn Khaldūn (1332–1406) accepted that al-Ḥallāj had revealed the "divine mystery" (*sirr Allāh*), but felt that a declaration as wild as *Anā al-Ḥaqq* should have been said only to the initiated, as most people would have misunderstood its true meaning. In his opinion, the death sentence was justified. Allowing that both the mystic and his killers were equally well intentioned and sincere Muslims, this compromise redeems the esoteric and exoteric dimensions of Islam; but it wouldn't fly in the entirely separate moral territory of the Five Percenters, for whom concealing the truth of God is always a mark of the wicked.

Al-Ghazālī wrote, "The one who said, *Anā al-Ḥaqq* was wrong." He saw great danger in Ṣūfīs such as al-Ḥallāj and al-Bistāmī who advanced far enough on the path to have self-annihilating mystical experiences, but were not able to responsibly articulate their stations to others. Al-Ghazālī suggested that while in the spiritually intoxicated state, such figures "may think that there has occurred a conjunction [with God] and express it in terms of incarnation [*hulūl*] . . . they may think that there has occurred a union [*ittiḥād*]: they have become [God] himself and the two have become one . . . when this intoxication gives way to sobriety they understand that they have been in error."[10] Al-Ghazālī allowed two possible exceptions. First, al-Ḥallāj might have been saying that he existed only by virtue of al-Ḥaqq, and possessed no existence of his own. In this case, al-Ḥallāj was not identifying himself with Allāh, but only pointing to the poverty of his own being. Second, al-Ḥallāj could have meant that he had become so consumed with the Ḥaqq, his self-annihilating passion for Allāh left no room for consciousness of anything else; he was al-Ḥaqq in the sense that a lover's identity dissolves into his/her beloved.

Though calling themselves by Allāh's Name might appear compatible with the 120, al-Bistāmī and al-Ḥallāj could be problematic as bridge builders between Muslims and Five Percenters; ecstatic mysticism isn't a good look at the Allah School. Within the intellectual discourse of Ṣūfism, however, there have been conceptions of God and the universe that seemed to blur the line between human beings and the Absolute. Despite his warnings, al-Ghazālī held the highest knowledge of Allāh to verge on this dangerous field of so-called drunken Ṣūfism: at the greatest level of advancement on the spiritual path, a seeker recognizes Allāh as the only existent. For al-Ghazālī, the truest understanding of *tawḥīd* leads one to say, "There is nothing except God." In the vision of "singularity" (*al-fardāniyya*), the many things are revealed to be one.

This could be the truth of a Qur'ānic verse revealed after the Battle of Badr, where Muḥammad had thrown dust in the eyes of his enemy:

"It was not you who threw when you threw, but Allāh threw" (8:17). In his commentary on 8:17, al-Ghazālī confesses to the difficulty of a verse saying both that Muḥammad threw and that he did not. Concluding that the external contradiction can only truly be resolved through mystical intuition, he suggests, "If one's entire life is spent seeking the unveiling of secrets of this meaning . . . one's life will perhaps be exhausted before fully knowing all that follows that meaning."[11]

In his *Iḥya 'Ulum ad-Dīn,* al-Ghazālī mentions the story of Allāh telling Moses, "I feel ill, because you did not visit me." When Moses asks how this is possible, Allāh responds, "My slave so-and-so became sick, and you did not visit him. If you had visited him, you would have found me in his place."[12] From there, al-Ghazālī discusses advancement on the path of spiritual devotion, quoting Allāh's statement regarding the perfected seeker, "I am his hearing through which he hears and his sight through which he sees, his tongue through which he speaks." However, al-Ghazālī then comes to an abrupt halt: "As for this subject, I must stop the pen here."[13] When refuting the idea of God's incarnation within mystics in his *Mishkāt al-Anwār,* al-Ghazālī again references both the Moses story and the "I am his hearing" quote, but immediately adds, "But now I must stop the explanation here."[14] He shows us the cliff and teases like he might jump, but always steps back.

For centuries, al-Ghazālī has been accused of diplomatically shifting his positions for various audiences; one contemporary scholar asks whether al-Ghazālī maintained a "secret doctrine he espoused amongst an inner circle, a doctrine he repudiated in public in his role as pillar of the scholarly community."[15] Another writes that al-Ghazālī's "caution to keep a distance between God and man" might have damaged his standing in later Ṣūfism, but that he had to be cautious to avoid "much trouble with conventional religious scholars."[16] The 120 could have words for this.

Ibn al-'Arabī, known alternately as the "Greatest Shaykh" (*shaykh al-akbar*) or "Most Blaspheming Shaykh" (*shaykh al-akfar*), depending

on who you ask, has remained a controversial figure in part for threatening normative Islam's clear separation of God from the created
universe. The Shaykh's teachings are described with the term *waḥdat
al-wujūd* ("unity of being"), though this exact phrase does not appear in
his works. The Arabic *w-j-d* root can be read to mean not only "being"
but also the act of "finding," which makes a precise translation into
English impossible. "If, for English speakers," William C. Chittick tells
us, "'existence' has no necessary connection with awareness, this is not
the case for Ibn al-'Arabī. To speak of *wujūd* is to speak of finding and
what is found, and finding is meaningless without knowledge and consciousness."[17] Existence is Allāh's own journey of "self-finding."[18] While
everything in the universe serves this purpose of Allāh's disclosure to
Allāh, Allāh's knowledge of self finds its greatest realization in perfected
human consciousness.

Waḥdat al-wujūd could have something to say to my experience of
the Five Percent, since the idea led Ibn Taymiyya to accuse Ibn al-'Arabī
of teaching that God and man were the same. According to Ibn Taymiyya,
for whom proper monotheism required a clearer line to be drawn
between God and humanity, Ibn al-'Arabī was among the vanguards of
ad-Dajjāl, the Islamic antichrist figure who would call himself God.[19]
Ibn al-Qastallānī (d. 1287) lumped Ibn al-'Arabī and al-Ḥallāj together
among monists and "adherents of nothingness" (*laysiyya*).[20] According to al-Taftazānī (1322–1390), Ibn al-'Arabī was simply a drug addict
whose feelings of oneness with God and the universe were brought on
by hashish.[21]

"Due to Ibn al-'Arabī's books and the excessive belief in him," wrote
Ibn al-Ahdal (d. 1481), "the city of Zabīd in Yemen has become an arena
for severe trouble and temptation at the hands of the ignorant Ṣūfīs.
They nurture strange, unheard of beliefs that explicitly state that they
have achieved union with God."[22] Ibn al-Ahdal's report mentions that
these Ṣūfīs would address each other as "Your Greatness," and if one
member of the group cursed another, he would be rebuked for having

cursed God.[23] The founder of Zabīd's Ṣūfī community, Ismāʾīl al-Jabartī (d. 1403), was regarded by his followers as a "personification of the divine attributes"; some even called him Allāh.[24] It is possible that Ibn al-Ahdal's account, intended as anti-Ṣūfī propaganda, exaggerated the offenses in Zabīd. In the event that these Ṣūfīs did take Ibn al-ʿArabī's thought to such extremes, scholar Alexander Knysh exonerates the Shaykh of liability, suggesting that the "relatively recent implantation" of Ṣūfism in Yemen rendered Ibn al-ʿArabī vulnerable to misreadings.[25]

Misreading or not—and if we read Ibn al-ʿArabī the way that he read the Qurʾān, what's a misreading?—it looked to me as though the Shaykh's teachings had produced Five Percenters in fourteenth-century Yemen. This could make Ibn al-ʿArabī the perfect moderator for a dialogue.

ACCORDING TO Elijah Muhammad, the black man created himself when, seventy-six trillion years ago, the Black Mind manifested itself as a physical body. The body was formed out of the "triple stages of darkness," the primeval nothingness, and his skin matched the blackness of that deep space. It is only after this self-creation that the black man willed the universe, our solar system, the Earth, and the Original people into existence.

Strictly speaking, there is no Five Percenter cosmology, since the details of the Black Mind and triple darkness are not covered in the 120, and Allah himself did not appear to be too concerned with the matter. This leaves the field wide open for Five Percenters. Some naturally refer to Elijah Muhammad's commentaries on Fard's teachings, while others might investigate other traditions or attempt to build their own systems.

Though not canonical on the same level as the 120, *The Great Understanding*, a Five Percenter "plus-lesson" of unknown authorship possibly dating back to the 1960s, gets into the nature of God and physical existence:

Allah is not a spirit. Allah is the Black Man of Asia. When he comes, he comes not as a spirit, but as a black man of Asia. Allah is eternal, having neither beginning nor end. Man was not always here as man, but man was always here.

In the beginning, there was no beginning. Something was always here; even though it is a speck of dust, it existed and therefore was existence. Existence is life; existence is eternal, for something always existed, but never a spirit. Life is Allah, and Allah is the universe. Therefore, Allah always existed, but never as a spirit.

That speck of existence became the universe, because it was the universe; and the universe is all which exists. As it had no beginning, neither shall it end, for something always will exist; this is the law of nature.[26]

An excerpt from the text is quoted by Rakim in his 1997 song "The Mystery":

Bear witness that Allah gave birth to all, for Allah was all, and therefore life itself. And the universe gave birth to man; the universe was man. Man was the universe, the universe was all which existed, existence was life, life was Allah, and Allah had no beginning because he is what always was.[27]

The Great Understanding presents existence as a triangle, its three points being Allāh, the universe, and human beings. While there is a sequence of procession, they are identified with one another. For me to read *The Great Understanding* alongside Ibn al-'Arabī's cosmology, the Five Percent started to look like an indigenous American adaptation of *wujūdī* Ṣūfism. As Masataka Takeshita writes:

Ibn Arabī . . . suggests that as man exists in the image of God, so does God in the image of man . . . by the single act of seeing His own image, He sees man who is created in His image and the universe which is in turn created in man's image. By the single act of knowing Himself, He knows both man and the universe. . . .

The universe exists in the image of man, and man in the image of the universe, and because of this correspondence, man's self-knowledge amounts to his knowledge of the universe . . . man's knowledge of the universe amounts to his knowledge of himself, and this self-knowledge is nothing else but his knowledge of God. In this way, man's knowledge of the universe, of himself, and of God coincide.[28]

Perhaps the 120's "poor righteous teachers" are to be counted among Ibn al-'Arabī's "realized selves" (*muḥaqqiqūn*). One could read the saying of Muḥammad, "Even though I am a son of Adam in form, in him I have an essence of my own which testifies that I am his father"[29] in light of *The Great Understanding*:

God is eternal, and so bear witness that the original man himself is God in his eternity. Original man cannot trace himself to his origin. And he who seeks to find what was never there is a fool. God accepts himself as God . . . What fool would seek beyond God? . . . Truth has no origin. . . . You have been shown that man is the universe and existence itself. Therefore it is but the absolute truth that man is God-Allah.[30]

A contemporary voice in the culture, Saladin Quanaah' Allah has written on cosmology from a Five Percent perspective, in which Allāh/man is self-created from the womb of Triple Darkness. This state of Nothingness was also "all things simultaneously," and represented by the number zero—which, in Supreme Mathematics, is seen to express totality and comprehensiveness. "This state of Nothingness caused

Allah (Self) to realize Self, therefore 'Nothing' (inactivity) created Allah (Me)," he explains on his *Allah School in Atlantis* blog. "I, Allah always was and always will be and no birth record can be ascribed to me, Allah (The Universal Mind)."[31]

To shed light on the materialization of this Universal Mind into human form, Saladin Quanaah' Allah appropriates the Qur'ānic narrative of Adam's creation, in which Allāh decrees, "I am setting in the earth a vicegerent [*khalīfa*]" (2:30). In historical Islam, this verse has been taken to mean that human beings represent the will of God on Earth. Ibn al-'Arabī compares the human *khalīfa* to the setting of a seal, the place at which a king marks and protects his treasures; Adam was Allāh's seal, by which Allāh signed the world.[32] In a modern reading, Amina Wadud interprets *khalīfa* as human moral agency, the "responsibility of each human being to establish social justice, as a representative of the divine will or cosmic harmony."[33] Saladin Quanaah' Allah reworks *khalīfa* to suit a Five Percenter worldview, in which he represents both sides of the God/human relationship:

> Through this evolutionary process and establishment of LAWS, I, Allah eventually manifested a Terrestrial Home called the Planet Earth (Pangea). Essential to this, I, Allah needed to manifest a conduit Self as the Khalifah within my Creation. I, Allah evolved a physical form or conduit of Consciousness in order to experience Self (Creation).[34]

In these terms, Five Percenter godhood and more traditional monotheism do not seem entirely incompatible. "The likelihood of just one atom simply phasing into existence by chance is so remote that it can't be calculated fairly," writes Supreme Understanding Allah in *Knowledge of Self.* "The evidence for intelligent design is great. However, it doesn't point to the immaterial, invisible God of the Creationists, but to the

234 WHY I AM A FIVE PERCENTER

culmination of God on Earth, the Black man, as its source."[35] Supreme
compares the universe to a computer program written by the "Black
mind, present in the ultimate (final) Black man."[36]

Before the creation of the physical universe, Allah was present as
the creative intelligence that spawned itself and began developing
all life and matter from an initial atom. This first ATOM, imbibed
with the innate intelligence of God, was Allah The Original Man.
The Sun replaced this atom as the representation of the Black man
until ultimately God himself could take dominion over the earth
in the flesh. . . . This universal, infinite intelligence is active in its
highest form in the individual mind of the Black man. The Black
man is the primary conduit for the intelligence that once created
the universe, as he is the Creator himself.[37]

The question of Five Percenter theism can go either way, since I've
seen some gods make reference to al-Ḥallāj and others quote pop atheist writer Richard Dawkins. At times, the mystery god appears as little
more than a matter of one's personal sensibility: some might suggest
that Five Percenters do not *technically* believe in a mystery god, while
Ibn al-'Arabī *technically* does. What now? What does God do after finding himself, except *be* God? After putting down the Bibles and Qur'āns,
this is the real work of the Five Percent: the adventure of perfecting
one's own character to properly express divine attributes, showing and
proving Allāh's self-realization.

> *If we were made in his image*
> *Then call us by our Names*
>
> —Erykah Badu, "On and On"[38]

There's a reason for my earlier statement that First Born Prince Allah
did not display a *deliberate* engagement of Ṣūfism; the commentary on

Divine Names that he found in Maulana Muhammad Ali's *Religion of Islam,* while not presented as "Ṣūfī" thought, was nonetheless covered in Ṣūfī fingerprints. Prince might have been unaware that through reading this Ahmadiyya text, he was digesting Ṣūfism. Just as Muslims strive to follow the sublime example (*sunna*) of the Prophet Muḥammad, the Divine Names reveal Allāh's *sunna,* adherence to which becomes a path of *ta'alluh,* "becoming God." Ibn al-'Arabī's understanding of *ta'alluh,* writes scholar Sajjad H. Rizvi, renders each human a "theomorphic being."[39]

Al-Ghazālī quotes the Prophet as saying, "You should be characterized by the characteristics of God most high," and "Given that God is characterized by the ninety-nine [Names], whoever is characterized by one of them enters paradise."[40] Al-Ghazālī also mentions a Ṣūfī shaykh who taught that God's ninety-nine Names become attributes of the seeker on his path. In his commentary on the Names, al-Ghazālī writes that God's Attribute as *al-Ghaffār* (He Who is Full of Forgiveness) is best reflected by one who conceals the ugliness of others while calling attention to their best qualities; al-Ghazālī provides an example in the Ṣūfī parable of Jesus, who, upon finding the stinking carcass of a dog by the road, complimented it for having beautiful teeth. *Al-Khabīr* (the Totally Aware) is actualized by the seeker who, "aware of his lower self and experienced in it," remains vigilant against his own heart's deceptions.[41] A person reflects God's Attribute as *al-Mujīb* (Answerer of Prayers) by "assisting every beggar in whatever they ask him, if he is able to do it; or with a kind response if he is unable to do so."[42] *Al-Mu'min* (the Faithful) is displayed in the person from whom all creatures are safe. "Moreover," adds al-Ghazālī, "every fearful person can anticipate help from him in keeping harm away from them."[43]

In his reading of the Name worn by First Born Prince Allah, *al-Jabbār* (the Compeller), al-Ghazālī writes that sharing in the Name means that the aspirant is "too high to be a follower and has attained the level of one followed; and is distinguished by the elevation of his rank in such a way that his life and his manner compels creatures to emulate him, and to follow him in his character and his conduct."⁴⁴ Al-Ghazālī's understanding of God's Name *al-Bā'ith* (Raiser of the Dead) is somewhat compatible with Elijah Muhammad's view of resurrection. Though al-Ghazālī did believe in a physical resurrection of the dead, and had famously defended this Islamic tenet against the *falāsifa,* he also suggested that human beings imitate God as al-Bā'ith through raising up the *mentally* dead: "Ignorance is the greatest death and knowledge the noblest life ... Whoever lifts another out of ignorance to knowledge has already created him anew and revivified him to a blessed life."⁴⁵

Someone who realizes his share of *al-Mālik* (the King) rules his kingdom—whether a literal empire with soldiers and subjects, or the kingdom of his own self, in which desires and emotions are his soldiers, and his subjects are his limbs and bodily organs. "If he rules them and they do not rule him," writes al-Ghazālī, "and if they obey him and he does not obey them, he will attain the level of a king in this world."⁴⁶ In a possible Five Percent reading, to represent al-Mālik through self-mastery would mean realization of the 120's 14:36 degree, "His own self is a righteous Muslim." "Man's control of his body," writes Takeshita, "resembles the Creator's control over the universe."⁴⁷ To the extent that the mind brings the body to offer submission (*islām*), the human being represents both God and the submitter to God.

Self Born Allah, author and poet, has written similar examinations of the Names from a Five Percenter perspective. On the thirteenth day of the month, he contemplates Allāh's thirteenth Name, *al-Muṣawwir* (the Shaper and Bestower of Forms), and thus incorporates Knowledge (1), Understanding (3), the letter M (13), Culture (1 + 3 = 4), and the fourth letter of the alphabet, D (signifying "Divine" in Supreme Alphabets) into his interpretation:

> Knowledge and Understanding are One and the same; this is what
> allows one the capacity to be Master of self; it is an expression of

Culture (or Freedom), the Divine right to show and prove that we
are who we say we are.[48]

Seeing humanity as personifying the Shaper and Bestower of Forms,
he writes, "Who names the creation? Where's the manual that cata-
logued all that there is to be known and understood? This is Us, shap-
ing from that primordial chaos to manifest cosmos, which is order." To
manifest al-Muṣawwir is to recognize how your perceptions give form
to your world, the extent to which you are "shaper of your own book
(qur'an, his/her story)."[49]

As scholar Toshihiko Isutzu explains, every happening in existence
is an "actualization of a Divine Name, that is to say, a self-manifestation
of the Absolute through a definite relative aspect called Divine Name."[50]
Rather than limit Allāh to the ninety-nine Names in the Qur'ān, Ibn
al-ʿArabī holds the Divine Names to be as countless as Allāh's manifestations in the universe.[51] One Name that does not appear among the
Qur'ān's Attributes for God, but can be found in works of Islamic theology,
is al-Fard (the Solitary/Unique).[52] None of these Names describe God in
totality; God is more than al-Mālik or al-Muʾmin. The most comprehensive Name for God, expressing the sum of all Divine Names, is Allāh. This
all-encompassing Name also represents what it means to be human, as
the human being—a microsm of the universe—stands above everything
else in creation in his/her capacity for expressing every Divine Name.
According to Chittick, our ability to manifest all Names is displayed by
the seemingly limitless range of human behaviors and emotions:

> If Adam had been created not in the form of God, but in the form
> of the All-Compassionate, no human being could be angry or
> cruel. If he had been created in the form of the Vengeful, no one
> would ever forgive his enemy . . . since human beings were cre-
> ated in the form of all names, they can make manifest any con-
> ceivable attribute.[53]

"Each human individual," Chittick writes, "reflects every divine attribute to some degree. But during the course of a human life, the divine names manifest themselves in all sorts of intensities, combinations, and interrelationships."[54] The challenge of our lives as humans is to bring our expressions of Allāh's often contradictory Names into balance: to exist simultaneously as "Merciful" and "Conqueror," "Forgiving" and "Terrible in Punishment," carrying these paradoxes within us while giving each Name its appropriate due.

The previously mentioned approach to the Qur'ān's "wife-beating verse" offered by Laury Silvers is rooted in this idea of Allāh's infinite self-disclosures commanding us to a path of moral and ethical development.[55] If our purpose is to progress toward the appropriate synthesis of Divine Names, then someone who works to degrade humanity, steering people away from Allāh's self-knowledge, can be called a devil. One could say that white supremacist patriarchy displays excess in Allāh's Names relating to punishment, dominion, and destruction but deficiency in the Names relating to justice, nourishment, and compassion. Such a gross imbalance leads both the oppressor and oppressed away from knowledge of the divine self.

If, on the other hand, someone walks among the degraded, manifesting Allāh's Names in their right balance—acting as the Friend to the friendless, the Merciful to those who had been denied mercy, Bestower of Lordship and Power to the powerless, the Guide to those who had been misguided, and the Avenger upon their enemies—perhaps we could say that Allāh appeared in that person, without resort to an incarnationist doctrine that would violate both Islamic *tawhīd* and Five Percenter rejection of mystery gods. Such an individual has reached the final stage of personal development, the level of *al-Insān al-Kāmil,* the Perfect or Complete Human—*al-Ayn al-Maqṣūda,* "the Sought-after Entity," the highest being in material existence, the reason for creation, sibling to the Qur'ān, and God's most comprehensive self-realization.

The Perfect Human has progressed beyond the Animal Human to the point of fulfilling Ṣūfism's purpose, "assuming the character traits of God."[56] This Perfect Human, writes Chittick, functions as the "ontological prototype of both man and the universe" and the "locus of manifestation for the Name 'Allāh.' "[57]

Ibn al-'Arabī's teachings on *al-Insān al-Kāmil* would be further developed by Abd al-Karīm al-Jīlī (d. 1428), who came to Yemen from India and became a student of al-Jabartī. Among the Ṣūfīs of Zabīd, who are described by Knysh as adhering to a "rather bizarre mixture of the Ṣūfī doctrine of the Perfect Man, incarnationalism, and the messianic texts of the 'extreme' Shi'a," al-Jīlī came to recognize al-Jabartī as a manifestation of the Prophet Muḥammad.[58] As Knysh compares the apparent worship in this student-teacher dynamic to Rūmī's love for Shams-i Tabrīz and al-Shādhilī's devotion to Ibn Mashīsh, we can begin to properly contextualize Elijah Muhammad's understanding of his own teacher within the larger Islamic tradition.

> You know well that all this is but heresy, atheism, and forsaking the Islamic religion.
>
> —al-Taftazānī[59]

> Idolatry and Unity are both but one essentiality.
>
> —Maḥmūd Shabistārī (1288–1340)[60]

For a moment, let's accept the charges from canonical Islam at face value, and consider Elijah Muhammad and the Five Percenters as idol worshipers for having made gods of Master Fard and themselves. This would disqualify them from Islam as we generally know it, but part of Islamic orthodoxy's problem with Ibn al-'Arabī has been his apparent refusal to condemn idolaters. As Chittick mentions in his work *Imaginal Worlds: Ibn al-'Arabi and the Problem of Religious Diversity,* "That 'religious diversity' is a 'problem' may not be obvious to everyone. Certainly, it is not a problem for Ibn al-'Arabi himself or for the school of thought that he established."[61]

For Ibn al-'Arabī, the diversity of God's self-disclosures in physical creation, as well as the capacity for human beings to express Allāh's Names, is mirrored by the diversity of ways in which humans conceptualize and worship Allāh. The unity of existence is matched by a unity of theological positions, and Ibn al-'Arabī recognizes Allāh as the source of all belief systems within the cosmos.[62] Adherents of these various traditions all recognize God in some form, but fail to capture Allāh in totality. Ibn al-'Arabī thus distinguishes between the Absolute Reality (al-Ḥaqq) and "God as created in various religious beliefs."[63] Each of us worships Allāh in the form that we recognize, but we fail to recognize Allāh as seen by others. What the Muslim contemplates as God is actually a reflection of his/her own self in God's mirror.[64] As Isutzu comments: "Each man has his *own* god, and worships his *own* god, and naturally denies the gods of other people. God whom each man thus worships as *his* god is the Lord (*rabb*) of that particular man."[65] To know the Absolute in its Absoluteness lies beyond the limits of human power.[66] Regardless, a seeker is "deceived by his own imagination and strives in vain to reach his imagined God."[67]

"THAT WHICH IS worshiped by every tongue, in all states and at all times, is the One," wrote Ibn al-'Arabī, adding that "Every worshiper, of whatever kind, is the One."[68] One wonders what the Shaykh might have done with a movement advocating deification of the self, in which the central idea seems to swing between idolatry and atheism. A possible answer lies in the Shaykh's exegesis of the Qur'ān's story of Noah, where he comments upon Islam's relationship to idolatry. Ibn al-'Arabī's understanding of Noah, which he employs with the intention of reconciling polar opposites, actually becomes one of the most polarizing aspects of his *tafsīr*. Scholar R. W. J. Austin describes Ibn al-Arabī's interpretation of Noah as "incomprehensible and extraordinary," "at best, reckless, and at worst, flagrantly heretical," and "most outrageous, since he seems indeed to be suggesting meanings diametrically opposed to those usually accepted."[69]

In Ibn al-'Arabī's reading, Noah and his people represent Islam's crisis of *tanzīh* and *tashbīh*: the question of how Allāh remains both unknowable and knowable, transcendent and immanent. *Tanzīh*, meaning "transcendence" or "keeping something away from anything making impure," implies that God's absolute unity (*tawḥīd*) requires an equally absolute separation from comparison or association with anything in creation.[70] The most extreme advocates of *tanzīh* in early Islamic thought were the Mu'tazila, for whom God's unity meant rejection of not only embodied anthropomorphism but also the Names. According to the Mu'tazila, instances of the Qur'ān calling Allāh the "Creator" or "Provider" are not to be taken literally. Mu'tazilism has been described as regarding Allāh more as an impersonal "dharmic force," as opposed to the "personal deity" of normative monotheism.[71]

Tanzīh-heavy theologies derive largely from the fusion of Neoplatonism into Islamic thought, while the god of *tashbīh* could be seen as more classically Abrahamic. *Tashbīh*, translated as "making something equal to something else," is *tanzīh*'s opposite, "ascribing human or worldly characteristics to God."[72] In contrast to *tanzīh*'s abstraction, contemplating Allāh exclusively through *tashbīh* produces a highly anthropomorphic mystery god, Allāh as the curly-haired young man appearing to Muḥammad.

Both sides of the *tanzīh-tashbīh* tension claim support in the Qur'ān: *tanzīh* in verses such as 112:4 ("And there is none like unto him") and *tashbīh* in 20:5, when Allāh sits upon a throne. Nonetheless, these concepts of divinity have often been treated as incompatible.[73] The setting in which Ibn al-'Arabī was born, Spain during the rule of the Almohad caliphate, favored *tanzīh* to the point of fanaticism. The founder and first caliph of the Almohads, Ibn Tūmart, had named his faction "Those Who Declare *Tawhīd*" (*al-Muwaḥḥidīn*, i.e., Almohads).[74] For Ibn Tūmart, affirmation of God's unity meant the emphatic disavowal of all anthropomorphism.[75] Scholar Madeline Fletcher describes Ibn Tūmart's theology as a "denial of the similarity between God and man to the point that he says more about what God is *not* than about what He is."[76] Integrated into the caliphate's political ideology, discourse of *tanzīh* reached such fervor that on the battlefield, "Anthropomorphists!" (*Mujassimūn!*) became the taunt that Ibn Tūmart's soldiers would shout at their opponents.[77]

Preaching a religion in which Allāh is abstract and purely transcendent, Noah represents the *tanzīh* position; but his tribe, worshiping the divine presence within things of this world—whether celestial bodies, acts of nature, prophets of past generations, or idols of their own construction—practices a religion of *tashbīh*. Noah attempts to convert them but is rejected and mocked. As the Qur'ān reports, God issues a clear verdict, destroying Noah's people in the flood and then burning them in eternal hellfire. Ibn al-'Arabī's reading, however, appears to side *with* the idolaters *against* the prophet. Noah has erred with a misreading of monotheism; when Allāh commands humanity to worship no false deities, Allāh actually means that to do otherwise is impossible, since everything in creation exists only as a self-disclosure of the Absolute. A pantheon of idols, to the Shaykh, is capable of representing the "diversity of the Names";[78] in some cases, smashing idols actually denies Allāh. Ibn al-'Arabī thus argues that Noah's people *did* worship Allāh, but in forms that Noah failed to acknowledge. (This would also be the mistake of Moses, who couldn't see that the golden calf represented Allāh.[79]) In his uncompromising, *tanzīh*-only religion, Noah ignored the truth in *tashbīh*, and was therefore unable to present Islam in terms that the idolaters would understand. "Had Noah combined the two aspects in summoning his people," the Shaykh writes, "they would have responded to his call."[80] The Qur'ān reports that Noah complained bitterly to Allāh, pleading that he had preached to the people constantly; but Ibn al-'Arabī somehow suggests that in his complaint, Noah secretly praised them.[81] That they denied Noah does not mean that God denied them, since Ibn al-'Arabī interprets their fates of Flood and Fire as allegory: being "true knowers" of Allāh, bewildered by Allāh's gathering of opposites, Noah's people chose to "drown" and "burn" in the wisdom of their perplexity.[82]

The issue of Noah provided devastating ammunition for Ibn al-'Arabī's adversaries. In addition to the apparent insult toward a prophet and rejection of the Qur'ān's clear meaning, Ibn Taymiyya would accuse Ibn al-'Arabī of breaking down any distinction between Muslims and unbelievers, and attempting to exempt the worshipers of idols from their deserved punishments in this world and the next.[83] Another opponent charged Ibn al-'Arabī with degrading Allāh through anthropomorphic doctrine, while suggesting that the real author of the Shaykh's commentary was none other than the Devil himself.[84]

The Shaykh also had his supporters, and the spread of waḥdat al-wujūd throughout the cultures of Islam encouraged the appearance of ostensibly pro-idol themes in Islamic poetry and mystical literature. The defense of religious diversity by poet-saint Muḥammad Lāhījī (d. 1507) even accuses idolatry's opponents of rejecting Islam! For Lāhījī, true blasphemy would be to regard anything as possessing reality apart from the Reality:

If you—who make claims to Islam and religious piety—perceive naught but the idol's visible form and do not envision God hidden behind the veils of its determined form . . . you properly and legally also cannot be called a Muslim. In fact, you are an infidel (kafr) because you have veiled God's theophany appearing in the idol.[85]

The themes of Noah's mission as interpreted by Ibn al-'Arabī, and the polemical antagonism that developed around it, would later be reflected in discord between the American Muslim community and Five Percenters. For Muslims, Five Percenters degrade and dishonor God by claiming God's Names as their own; for Five Percenters, Muslims remain blind to their own divinity, choosing instead to worship a phantom that does not actually exist.

When Noah demanded that his people reject their idols and worship only his abstract god, a man identified as the "chief of the unbelievers" raised objections. He insisted that Noah was a mortal man like anyone, and that his claim to prophethood was only an attempt to gain superiority over the people. If Noah's unseen god wanted to instruct them, the chief of the unbelievers argued, the god would have sent angels from heaven rather than a mere human who could not prove the truth of his words. Finally, the chief of the unbelievers reminded his people that this new religion of transcendent monolatry was not the way of their ancestors. These arguments would match Five Percenter critiques of religion: that no human being should mentally enslave himself/herself to another; no supernaturalist belief system has yet proven itself by actually delivering the supernatural; and finally, to discard ancestral wisdom in favor of an alien theology would make one "other than his own self." The chief of the unbelievers exposes Noah as a Ten Percenter asserting power over the masses through an affiliation with spirits.

In acknowledgment of idolatry's secret, it is possible that Ibn al-ʿArabī would sympathize with the Five Percenters. Recognizing God's self-disclosure, he could come to Harlem, find the Allah School on Seventh Avenue, walk in, and proclaim that yes, the black man is God. When Five Percenters give themselves names like Beloved Allah or Divine Justice Allah, Ibn al-ʿArabī might see them as paragons of *tajallī*, the "shining through" of Allāh's Names, simply highlighting the reality of existence in which we are all walking, talking Names of Allāh. As Ibn al-ʿArabī regarded Allāh as disclosed to all people through forms that they would recognize, he could perhaps sympathize with oppressed peoples identifying with Allāh through Names such as Powerful and King.

At first glance, the Five Percenters' association of divinity with humanity would make them adherents of *tashbīh*, but it can also be said that Five Percenters take *tanzīh* even further than Noah. Stripping Allāh of all description until even calling Allāh a "thing" that "exists" is impossible, the apophasis of *tanzīh* could lead to rational agnosticism or atheism. "Arm Leg Leg Arm Head" might be described best as *tanzīh* with the consequences of *tashbīh*. Because we cannot comprehend or prove the existence of a Creator—"The son of man has searched for that mystery god for trillions of years and was unable to find a mystery god"—our search begins and ends with the human mind; "so they have agreed that the only God is the son of man" (10:40).

The Shaykh holds that *tanzīh* and *tashbīh* can each claim only half the truth of the Absolute; one remains mindful of Allāh's unknowable Essence, while the other works with Allāh's knowable Attributes. Those who emphasize *tanzīh* to the point of excluding *tashbīh* have done to God exactly what they oppose: the placing of restrictions. "To deny all limitation," Ibn al-'Arabī tells us, "is itself a limitation, the Absolute Being limited by his Own Absoluteness."[86] Meanwhile, those who deny *tanzīh* are polytheists, in the Shaykh's view, for attributing an existence to things independent of the Absolute.[87] A distinction is made between "high" and "low" idolatry; the idol worshipers are correct in their worship so far as they recognize that they are only worshiping Allah's self-disclosures in these forms, and not the forms themselves.

Rather than make excesses in either direction, Ibn al-'Arabī advocates a middle way in which one looks with "both eyes" and witnesses both *tanzīh* and *tashbīh* in harmony.[88] He writes: "If you maintain both aspects you are right, an Imām and a master in the spiritual sciences."[89] The Shaykh describes his middle way with the term *qur'ān*, which in this case does not refer to Islam's scripture. In another example of his play with language, Ibn al-'Arabī derives *qur'ān* not from the Arabic verb *qara'a* ("to read"), as in the holy book, but *qarana*, "to link." This *qur'ān*, linking the oppositional concepts of transcendence and immanence, is for the Shaykh the most comprehensive and mature approach to Allāh.[90] The human being lives out the paradox of *huwa/lā huwa*, "he/not he," in which contemplation of Allāh does not lead us to "abstract him from creation," and contemplation of creation does not mean that we "invest it with what is not the Reality."[91] With *huwa/lā huwa*, Ibn al-ʿArabī could be placed between Muslims and Five Percenters and satisfy either everyone or no one—Ibn Taymiyya called Ibn al-ʿArabī an atheist, while Five Percenters might accuse the Shaykh of believing in a mystery god.

As a human being participating in this universe, I am a Name of the Black Mind/al-Ḥaqq. I am not separate from the Black Mind, because the Black Mind has no place where it is *not*. But I'm also a distinct entity, Mike Knight, and other distinct things exist independently of me, so I can't *be* the Black Mind. *Huwa/lā huwa* means that I can greet Allah B with "Peace, god," and then visit Cee Allah next door and say "Peace, god," to him too, and some Five Percenters can say "Peace, god," to me, and none of us are polytheists or idolaters. It might work because I've never known a Five Percenter solipsist, a god who believed that all of creation existed specifically within *his* individual mind, that the world was exclusively a creation of *his* consciousness, and that other gods were not as real as he is. If gods share their godhood with one another, then no one's the Absolute in full Absoluteness, the Black Mind alone. Ibn al-ʿArabī tells us that *al-Insān al-Kāmil* is "only ʿa truth' (ḥaqq), not ʿthe Truth' (al-Ḥaqq)."[92] Whether a Five Percenter's ideas of God sound like mystical pantheism or pragmatic atheism, it doesn't seem to me that anyone who comes in the Name of Allah is really trying to be Allāh in the traditional Islamic sense. No one's claiming to have supernatural powers; the common naysayer's challenge to a Five Percenter, "If you're God, let's see you levitate," is meaningless. For a human being to identify with the mind of the universe does not mean that s/he can defy natural laws, even within one's own body. When we express the Names, it is to the degree of human capacity, within the boundaries of human existence. *Huwa/lā huwa* means that I can have it both ways.

IT'S STILL HARD to place Ibn al-'Arabī in relation to the Five Percent. The Shaykh produced a large amount of material, and it's near impossible to pin him down—which has allowed his teachings to proliferate without the guiding structure of an official "Ibn al-Arabī order." In Ibn al-'Arabī's descriptions of his mystical experiences, I found a single paragraph in which he could be interpreted as taking Ten, Five, and Eighty-Five Percenter positions:

> In this night journey I gained the meanings of all the Divine Names. I saw that they all go back to a single Named Object and a Single Entity. That Named Object was what I was witnessing, and that Entity was my own existence. So, my journey had been only in myself. I provided no indications of any but myself. It was from here that I came to know that I am a sheer servant and that there is nothing whatsoever of lordship within me.[93]

In this night journey I gained the meanings of all the Divine Names. Because not everyone's going to have this privileged knowledge, and such knowledge would entitle the knower to a degree of authority over others, the Shaykh reads as vintage Ten Percent here. Unfortunately, Ṣūfism is not exempt from the dynamics of "bloodsuckers" and "slaves to mental death and power." Ibn Taymiyya rightly warned of the danger in Ṣūfī claims of hidden saintly hierarchies. Ibn al-'Arabī's primary instruction came from his encounters with unseen spiritual beings, which is certainly a Ten Percent road to power, and others have used his concept of the Perfect Human as a template for their own political and economic gain. Alexander Knysh points out that despite Ibn Taymiyya's legitimate criticism, we should also remember the political consequences of Ibn Taymiyya's own thought, which has been frequently cited as an influence on modern "Wahhābī" revivalism, the form of Islam that presently dominates in Saudi Arabia.[94] With Ṣūfīs boasting privileged mystical knowledge, and orthodox *ulama* claiming ownership of Islam's legal tradition, we have competing arguments for power that can produce Ten Percenters on both sides.

I saw that they all go back to a single Named Object and a Single Entity. That Named Object was what I was witnessing, and that Entity was my own existence. So, my journey had been only in myself. I provided no indications of any but myself. In this section, Ibn al-ʿArabī might read as Five Percent, as the self is identified with the sum of Allāh's Names. The Shaykh's career also provides an example of the masterless tradition of *Uwaysī* Ṣūfism, which would make him a more mystical kind of Five Percenter. Though Ibn al-ʿArabī did have teachers, writes scholar Gerald T. Elmore, this does not mean that he put himself in complete submission to a master: "It is all too obvious that Ibn al-ʿArabī's spirit would not allow him to willingly submit to human authority for any length of time, and there is really no indication that he ever did so."[95]

It was from here that I came to know that I am a sheer servant and that there is nothing whatsoever of lordship within me. Here's where Five Percenters would take issue. Five Percenters and Ṣūfīs may appear to reach similar conclusions, but they arrive by different paths. One system says that man is divine because God does not exist outside of man; the other says that man is divine because man does not exist outside of God. One seeks to build the self; the other seeks to make the self disappear. *Huwa* and *lā huwa* may both be true, but they can act as veils over each other, one concealing the knowledge of its opposite. Whether at the mosque or the Allah School, *huwa/lā huwa* both qualifies and disqualifies me, as my own truth rests on the "/" between terms.

WRESTLING OPPOSING IDEAS of God into agreement might be easier than doing the same with modes of knowledge, the ways that Ṣūfīs and Five Percenters know what they know.

Ṣūfīs have made use of rational argument, and al-Ghazālī is seen as having reconciled Islam's separate paths of philosophy and mysticism, but both al-Ghazālī and Ibn al-ʿArabī privileged mystical modes of knowing (*dhawq*, "tasting") over pure intellect (*ʿaql*). Ibn al-ʿArabī was not opposed to seeking God through rational speculation, but also saw this as a *tanzīh*-only path limited by its lack of *tashbīh*. Ibn al-ʿArabī additionally claimed that he was not the author of his *Fuṣūṣ al-Ḥikam* but its receiver; every word had been delivered to him in a vision from the Prophet Muḥammad, just as the angel Gabriel had brought words to Muḥammad centuries earlier. The Shaykh's visionary adventures would also include conversations with everyone from prophets such as Adam and Moses to saints such as al-Ḥallāj and Junayd. Needless to say, Five Percenters aren't into angels or dead bodies flying around—especially when, if a Ṣūfī master sees with God's Eyes and thus knows what we don't know, these visions become a source of social or political advantage.

There are ways in which Five Percenters can place value on mystical experiences and even prophetic revelation while maintaining their crucial distance from supernaturalism. When I had a dream in which Master Fard Muhammad appeared to me, some gods were willing to discuss it seriously without believing that I had experienced a literal encounter with Fard's ghost; even as a production of my own brain, the vision could still have meaning and value for my personal path. Ibn al-ʿArabī believed that when the seeker received knowledge, it manifested in forms of the seeker's own active imagination; the angel Gabriel thus appeared as Muḥammad's manifestation to himself.[96] Al-Ghazālī's conception of prophethood, argues scholar Frank Griffel, leads to the idea that even if Muḥammad experienced genuine divine revelation, he nonetheless had to form the specific words of the revealed text himself (though Griffel admits that al-Ghazālī "never expressed that openly"[97]).[98] The prophetology formulated by Islamic philosophers, placing emphasis on Muḥammad's supremely developed rational and imaginative faculties, "challenges the traditionally held view that God is the author of the Qur'ān."[99]

Indian mystic Muḥibb Allāh Ilāhābādī (d. 1648) taught that Gabriel was within Muḥammad, and regarded Allāh's Tremendous Throne (al-'arsh al-aẓīm) as Muḥammad's own tongue.[100] I'm going to take that Ṣūfī thought and misread it with Five Percenter thought, and it might get me somewhere. His name sounds so Five Percent already—I can imagine him walking into the cipher at a parliament saying, "Peace, I come in the name of Muḥibb Allāh."

COMMENTING ON Maḥmud Shabistarī, a Persian Ṣūfī poet influenced by the Shaykh, scholar Leonard Lewisohn mentions Shabistarī's view that being Muslim requires one to recognize Allāh in other traditions: "enter into their belief-systems and try to comprehend their God, however alien to reality or your own concept of divinity this may be."[101] Even if Ibn al-'Arabī wasn't exactly a Five Percenter, his thought and legacy opened portals through which I could explore Five Percent ideas while maintaining a classically Islamic center of gravity.

I made a trip to the Allah School with high hopes of sharing what I had found in Ṣūfism. On the sidewalk in front of the school, I started getting into it with a god, presenting all of the mind-blowing quotes and fancy Arabic terms that I had collected. I built on the Muḥammadan Reality, the notion of Muḥammad's "light" as a cosmic principle, with a Five Percenter spin: we were *all* prophets when Adam was between the water and the mud. The god heard my spiel with an open mind, but told me that in the Five Percent, it was key to avoid thoughts of God and self as abstract entities; if we're not talking about flesh and blood, it's not all that useful. An elder god then stepped into our cipher, holding his infant daughter or granddaughter, and listened as I attempted to link Five Percenter self-deification with tajallī, the "shining through" of Allāh's Names in our persons.

"Listen," he interjected. "I *met* Allah. He was standing in front of me like you are now. And you know what he told me?"

"What did he tell you?" I asked.

"'Stay away from religion.'" The man gestured to the baby in his arms. "Religion's not going to feed her. Religion's not going to put clothes on her. Drop all that talk about religion."

This put an end to the discussion. The god had instantly and effortlessly shot down my nerded-out *bāṭinī* style, and rightly so. Treating my tall stacks of Ṣūfī literature as an amusement park, I had ignored the real point of the Five Percent: the realization that despite every effort by society to degrade you, the universe is yours and you can accomplish anything. The older god telling me to drop religion was like Allah (Allāh?) himself showing up and slapping me awake. It is not merely belief in the mystery god that allows for oppression and injustice, but those "trillions of years" that the 120 says have been wasted searching for that mystery god. Nat Turner and John Brown believed in the mystery god, but did not lose any time being theologians. If you have the freedom and access to read nine thousand pages on Ṣūfism, your life must already be pretty good; but running around Harlem with that *tanzīh/ tashbīh* stuff isn't feeding babies. What Five Percenters sometimes call "high science" is not to be attained at the expense of real-life concerns; "I see brothers quote Math plus degrees," says GZA in "Swordsman;" "Look at professor ass niggas can't feed they own seeds."[102] Perhaps this should be a good place to note that both al-Ghazālī and Ibn al-ʿArabī had abandoned their homes and families to embark on navel-gazing truth quests. One *alif* is all you need.

TEN

UNIVERSAL FLAG: A FIVE PERCENTER AT HARVARD

My whole life has been a chronology of changes—I have always kept an open mind, which is necessary to the flexibility that must go hand in hand with every intelligent search for truth.

—Malcolm X[1]

He and people like him . . . are restless and they do not adhere to one firm view, because they have such intelligence and craving that they long to discover the method of the elect.

—Ibn Taymiyya, describing al-Ghazālī[2]

HARVARD'S CAMPUS IS COVERED in American religious history. The first Bible published in North America, John Eliot's translation into the Massachusett language, was printed here in 1663, at the present site of Matthews Hall.

In 1838, Ralph Waldo Emerson gave his famous Harvard Divinity School address, in which he declared the slow death of old Christianity and called for an emphasis on the beauty and goodness of the natural world over theology and scripture. No miracles, no Christ as Divine Other; Jesus was only a human who realized his own potential (which

242   WHY I AM A FIVE PERCENTER

would be the potential within all of us) to know the divine self and
"expand to the full circle of the universe."³ Emerson told the senior
class that it was not through institutional religion but "only by coming
again to themselves, or to God in themselves," that they could "grow
forevermore."⁴

Malcolm X spoke here three times: first in 1961, as the Nation of
Islam's star minister; then in March 1964, just after he broke with his
mentor but still praised him as the *Honorable* Elijah Muhammad; and
finally in December 1964, shortly after returning from a trip to Africa
and just two months before his assassination. During the first of those
visits, Malcolm glanced through a window and realized that he was fac-
ing the direction of his old burglary gang's hideout. "Standing by that
Harvard window," he recalls in his *Autobiography*, "I silently vowed to
Allah that I never would forget that any wings I wore had been put on
by the religion of Islam."⁵

In 1971, when Mary Daly became the first woman to deliver a sermon at Harvard Memorial Church, she spoke of the women's movement as an "exodus community" that must break free of its captors:
"Singing sexist hymns, praying to a male god breaks our spirit, makes
us less than human. The crushing weight of this tradition, of this power
structure, tells us that *we do not even exist*." Then she led hundreds of
women in a walkout, leaving their bondage in the church for "a future
that will be our *own* future."⁶

There are two rituals surrounding the statue in Harvard Yard. Tour-
ists traditionally rub John Harvard's feet for good luck; after tens of
thousands of oily hands upon the metal, they now shine with a bright
polish. As a shadow of this practice, countless students over the years
have considered it a rite of passage to urinate on the statue.

John Harvard's sculptor, Daniel Chester French, was also the creator
of Abraham Lincoln's statue in Washington, and there's a similar feeling
between the two statues: both men are seated, backs straight, staring
flatly across the landscape, their expressions empty enough to produce

whatever meanings you want. John Harvard, a Puritan minister who had been described as "reverent, god-like, and a lover of learning," looks like a king, while President Lincoln looks like a philosopher or prophet.

Tour guides call it the "statue of three lies." Two of the lies are found in the statue's inscription, which reads "John Harvard, Founder, 1638." John was a major financial contributor to the first Harvard College but not the founder; and Harvard was actually founded two years earlier, in 1636.

The third and perhaps most significant lie is the statue's face: it's not John Harvard.

In 1884, when Daniel Chester French fashioned the statue, there were no surviving portraits of John Harvard, so he chose Harvard Law student Sherman Hoar to put on seventeenth-century costume and model as John Harvard's stand-in. For his good looks and social position (Sherman's father, Ebenezer R. Hoar, was himself a Harvard alum and former U.S. Attorney General who had just retired from the school's board of overseers; his uncle was George Frisbie Hoar, also a Harvard Law grad and influential senator), Sherman Hoar became John Harvard, the institution's personified totem.

Contemplating the 120 one morning on my way to Arabic class, I glanced at the John Harvard statue and it flipped a switch in my brain. I stopped directly in front of it, unintentionally blocking a tourist from photographing his daughter with her hand on John Harvard's foot. The statue's third lie expressed the day's degree (5:14), which described the exploitation of Jesus after his death as a shield for the holders of power—highlighting Power (5) as the day's mathematics. This is what religion does: we compensate for a prophet or ancestor's absence by removing him from history, creating an image of him outside of real time. Memory drifts away from fact. Then it gets dangerous, because the dead prophet cannot speak for himself; as a symbol for the tribe and its institutions, his new meaning is decided by the same elites who run everything else, the bloodsucking, slave-making Ten Percenters. So this

John Harvard is really a statue of the Attorney General's son and senator's nephew. By these same processes, Jesus became not only a white man, but the name of the first British vessel carrying slaves to America. The Jesus who had once fought at the edge now sleeps in the center; instead of calling for a better society, he is used to reinforce things as they are.

This also happened with Muḥammad. When it comes to holy sites, the king of Saudi Arabia wears humble titles like "Custodian," but let's be honest: the Prophet is now literally the king's physical property. More than fourteen centuries after his death, I visited the Prophet's remains at his mosque in Medina, roughly two hundred miles from Mecca. The police officers around the tomb are there not only to preserve order and security amidst the devotional fervor, but also to impose the ritual dictates of an extreme Ḥanbalī Sunnism, the religious underpinning for the modern Saudi nation-state and its royal family's claim to authority. By enforcing their definition of authentic Islam, the king upholds the assumption that an "authentic Islam" actually exists, which therefore makes its enforcement necessary, which therefore makes the king necessary. So if a cop has to hit someone with his stick, it's not only his pious Islamic duty; it's patriotism.

Standing before the polished and pissed-on foot of fake John Harvard, the statue expressed what I had taken from 5:14. Gazing up at *whoever*, I understood. This statue could teach me as much about religion as some courses that I've taken here.

I AM PRESENTLY sitting at a table in Harvard's Widener Library and I'm supposed to be writing a paper on al-Ghazālī, doing the knowledge, wisdom, and understanding as to whether al-Ghazālī had remained faithful to the Ash'arī school. Was he merely, as Ibn Rushd charged, "an Ash'arī with the Ash'arīs, a Ṣūfī with the Ṣūfīs, and a philosopher with the philosophers?"[7] Al-Ghazālī himself did not leave us with a clear answer, but it doesn't appear that he would have believed in the question. In response to the matter of whether disagreement with the Ash'arī school amounts to unbelief, al-Ghazālī writes, "Whoever thinks that heresy is defined by opposing the Ash'arī, Mu'tazilī, Ḥanbalī, or any other school of thought, then know that such a person is not stupid! He is a prisoner of authority (*taqlīd*)."[8] Or an Eighty-Five Percenter, as some would say.

Al-Ghazālī had initially made his fame by taking on the philosophers by their own rules, but Ibn Taymiyya repeats a jurist's criticism that al-Ghazālī had "entered the stomach of the philosophers, then when he wanted to come out he could not do so."[9]

To write about a tradition is to be in a certain narrative relation to it, a relation that will vary according to whether one supports or opposes the tradition, or regards it as morally neutral. The coherence that each party finds, or fails to find, in that tradition will depend on their particular historical position.
—Talal Asad, "The Idea of an Anthropology of Islam"[10]

Are you a Five Percenter?

It is not easy for me to answer, because neither my insider-ness nor my outsider-ness is secure. I am always at the gate. I find my inheritance in Five Percenters who themselves aren't always accepted: Azreal, Allah's Irish-American death angel, and First Born Prince Allah, the "Sunnī God." To use a word from the Qur'ān, they are both *barzakh* figures, like the invisible partitions between seas. Azreal and Prince divide categories. Some Five Percenters would call Azreal a devil, and a few would call him a god; for most, he is neither. Prince was too Muslim for the Five Percenters, but too Five Percent for Muslims; in his heart, he was both. While standing firm on my square, the ground feels unsteady.

Yes, I am a Five Percenter. The texts of this culture have answered several important questions to my satisfaction. Its symbols have pulled me in with a genuine magnetic power, and I speak its language; having crawled into the Five Percent's stomach, I cannot get out. Perhaps most important, the community has treated me as a member of its family.

No, I am not a Five Percenter. To claim membership is also to claim ownership—both that I own it and am owned by it—and this is impossible. I am only inside because I have shown respect for the fact that I can never be inside. My legitimacy as a Five Percenter is injured at the moment that I actually call myself a Five Percenter.

I have my own idea of what it means to be a Five Percenter, and an idea of what it means to be Muslim, but it doesn't always seem that these visions exist outside my fantasy. So holding my Allah pin, fidgeting with it between my fingers and making click sounds with the catch, rubbing over the face and name with my thumb like it's a lucky coin, my eyes start to tear up but for reasons that are only mine. I don't know if I can translate these reasons into identification with a movement or "nation."

While trying to write my al-Ghazālī paper, I am wearing the Five Percenter emblem, the Universal Flag, on my shirt. The wearing of this flag includes a number of statements—on race, on America and our terrible shared history, on religion, on the search for meaning. These statements intersect in ways that might confuse outsiders, those more outside than me; but concealed by a button-up, the flag is a communication exclusively to myself.

"Are you able to show and prove on this Flag that you bear?" asks King Sun in his song "Universal Flag." "Each element of sun, moon, and star? And what that 7 means?"[11] For me to wear the Universal Flag may be an act of theft, or even violence—an especially troubling one, when we return to the question of *particular historical positions.* But I am also a small part of the life of this flag. I have engaged in the process called "subjectification" by anthropologist Gannath Obeyesekere, in which "cultural patterns and symbol systems are put back into the melting pot of consciousness and refashioned,"[12] allowing them to "produce, and thereafter justify, innovative acts, meanings, or images that help express the personal needs and fantasies of individuals."[13] The Universal Flag, its history, and the personalities and literature related to it have become tools for me to illustrate my own thought. To be something other than a Five Percenter means erasing them from my memory, pretending that I have never seen the flag or recited its references in RZA lyrics: *I'm the 7 in the center of the sun.*

The Universal Flag itself is an example of subjectification carried out in 1960s Brooklyn by its teen creator, Universal Shaamgaudd Allah. The youth is said to have constructed his new artifact from materials in his environment: the Islamic star and crescent (specifically as it appears on the Nation of Islam flag); the eight-pointed emblem of the Cross Park Chaplains, a gang to which he (and twelve of the other thirteen original Five Percenters in Brooklyn) had belonged; and Supreme Mathematics. The inclusion of symbols relating to the Nation of Islam and gang life are particularly interesting. It would appear that while both had significance to Shaamgaudd, there came a moment—perhaps when Allah forbade membership in gangs and also declared a formal break from the religion of Islam—at which neither could adequately represent him.

The new place that Shaamgaudd occupied as a Five Percenter could only be illustrated with a new symbol, both memorializing and transcending the symbols of his past.

In the reverse of subjectification, which Obeyesekere calls "objectification," the transformed symbols—having been interpreted and reinvented by the individual—are returned into the culture to be accepted and used by others. Objectification occurred when Shaamgaudd showed his flag to Allah, who then used it as a symbol for the movement, leading other Five Percenters to take the new symbol through their own subjectification. Investing their mental power in Shaamgaudd's work, gods produced numerous commentaries on the flag's meaning, interpreting the rhetorical significance of the sun, moon, star, and seven, the sun's eight points, and even the measurements of each angle. In the next stage of objectification, these personal reflections were published in Five Percenter literature or distributed as plus-lessons, becoming the materials from which new understandings would be formed.

In the 1980s, Shaamgaudd himself added layers to the flag's meaning, publishing plus-lessons that explained his own interpretations. He even presented a new version of the flag with a sixteen-pointed sun, and justified his innovation by connecting it to the flag's origin: Allah was said to have approved the design twenty years earlier, but warned him that Five Percenters were not yet ready for it. Shaamgaudd's reprocessing of his own symbol failed to enter the subjectification-objectification cycle, as gods preferred the original eight-pointed sun.

I've recently caught glimpses of a schismatic Five Percent sect, attached to hip-hop artist Vast Aire (aka Vishnu Allah), advocating an increased openness to godhood for all, regardless of race or gender. Its symbol is a transformation of the Universal Flag, recolored red, black, and green out of respect for Marcus Garvey, with the 7 replaced by 9 (the number signifying birth and the letter I, which in Supreme Alphabets signifies "Islam"). "I elaborated on the flag," says Vishnu Allah, "because I have the knowledge to do that."[14] It's too soon to know if this new flag will have any life, but the exchange of subjectification and objectification, the personal and cultural, is unending.

> To make devil, what must you do first?
> To make devil, one must begin grafting from the original.

—31:40

Here is the destructive potential of my wearing the Universal Flag: in our use of symbols, we are all Shaamgaudds in the making. Though already coded with meanings, this flag asks me to create its meaning, to *draw up* its meaning. Wearing the flag, I force the flag to wear *me*, and whatever (mis)readings I impose upon it. For the Universal to be worn by the wrong person threatens the stability of the flag, along with all of the texts attached to it—the growing entourage of commentaries that surround the flag. This is also why any movement, whatever its mission, should distrust writers. To write on a tradition, whether as insider or outsider, committed evangelist or detached observer, is to have a hand in its ongoing creation, intervening in its civil wars and contributing to the cycle—to graft from the original. Though my affection for the Universal Flag is genuine, it sometimes feels as though I am living in a parable from the 120, and should march myself across the hot desert, away from the holy city.

In established readings of the Universal Flag, Five Percenters view the sun as representing the black man, the moon as the black woman, and the star as the black child. In Arabic, however, "sun" (*shams*) is a feminine word, and "moon" (*qamar*) is masculine. English translations of the Qur'ān typically reverse the genders in conformity to Western literary norms, but a precise translation of 91:1–2 reads "By the sun and *her* brightness/by the moon as *he* follows *her*." In pre-Islamic South Arabia, the sun was worshiped as a goddess. There's no reason that this should mean anything to most Five Percenters, but the verses jump out at me when I see the Universal Flag: a moon enclosed within the sun, as though resting in its womb. This in turn leads me to reflect on the Arabic word for "womb" coming from the same r-ḥ-m root letters as Allāh's Names "the Compassionate" and "the Merciful." Though the flag is called "Universal," it has a context, and mixing with other contexts can change what it says. I have taken the Universal to a place far from its origin.

Intertextuality between my Qur'ān and my flag has altered my consciousness of both; the Prophet Muḥammad and Universal Shaamgaudd Allah never saw it coming. Just as my Muslim background directed my reading of the Universal, Five Percenters have also transformed my Qur'ān. In 33:56, Allāh is described as blessing the Prophet, but the Arabic verb for "bless" is also the verb for "pray," perhaps implying that Allāh performs a kind of prayer.[15] For many, this thought would pose an obvious theological challenge, but Ibn al-'Arabī described Allāh as muṣallī, "he who prays."[16] Verse 33:56 now makes me think of First Born Prince Allah and wonder whether he knew enough Arabic to catch it; I imagine Prince at the green-domed Sunnī mosque on 116th Street, Malcolm's old mosque, wearing his kiffeyeh in the front row at Friday prayers, and he prays because Allāh prays.

My being both Muslim and Five Percenter is good for neither community, at least not for Muslims who need their system to be the one and only "straight path" (sirātul-mustaqīm) and Five Percenters who need to keep their science "right and exact." It's a trend throughout history: the Islamic term for "heretic," zindīq, first appeared in the eighth century as a means of describing Iranian converts to Islam who secretly maintained their own traditions, such as Manichaeism and Mazdakism.[17] Many would see the mixture of two traditions as a corruption of both.

BUT DOES IT have to be that way? In Mughal India, the growing impact of Ibn al-'Arabī's thought became devastating for the borders between systems; as a pantheistic reading of *waḥdat al-wujūd* gained ground, Ṣūfīs found increasing resonance between their own materials and Vedanta philosophy.[18] *Waḥdat al-wujūd's* promotion of "universal brotherhood" and "peaceful coexistence" reached its climax with the reign of Akbar, who had attempted to merge all of India's traditions into his own state religion.[19]

In the first half of the seventeenth century, Akbar's great-grandson Dārā Shikūh joined the Qadīrī Ṣūfī order, of which some branches had grown monistic through contact with Indic philosophy and veneration for al-Ḥallāj.[20] Dārā Shikūh studied *waḥdat al-wujūd* in the works of Ibn al-'Arabī, wrote his own Ṣūfī treatises, and also embarked upon a serious study of Vedanta, becoming the disciple of Baba Lal, head of a minor order.[21] Baba Lal stressed upon Dārā Shikūh the capacity for every religion to produce saints and gnostics who can genuinely further their followers on the path.[22] After engaging scholars and mystics from both Ṣūfī and Indic traditions, Dārā Shikūh arrived at the realization that there was no difference between their understandings of the Truth except in their language and external forms.[23] As a Muslim, Dārā Shikūh regarded *tawḥīd* as the most essential truth; but he also believed this principle to be at the core of what we today call Hinduism.[24] For Dārā Shikūh, Sanskrit and Arabic were equally valid as languages for the Divine Reality.[25] The Ṣūfī declaration "I am al-Ḥaqq" and the Vedantist's "I am the Brahman" conveyed the same experience.[26]

Dārā Shikūh did pursue knowledge of the Qur'ān, but was frustrated in his attempts to uncover the text's *bāṭin* meaning; however, believing that God's sacred books were but commentaries on one another, he used texts from other religions to assist his Qur'ānic study. Along with Jewish and Christian scriptures, he revered the Indic spiritual lexicon as divinely inspired and in full harmony with the Qur'ān, even interpreting the Qur'ānic verse "Most surely it is an honored Qur'ān, in a book that is protected; none shall touch it save the purified ones" as a reference to the Upanishads.[27] While Tasadduq Husain rightly notes that "[s]uch an interpretation could not, of course, be acceptable to Muslim scholars," Dārā Shikūh's view that India must have received divine guidance would be in step with the Qur'ān's claim of prophets sent to every nation.[28] India did receive prophets, Dārā Shikūh asserted, and all four Vedas were revelations.[29]

To better demonstrate this unity of religion, Dārā Shikūh set upon the task of redefining Indic religion in Islamic terms. Mahadeva, Vishnu, and Brahman were equated with Islamic angels, while *Om naman* was translated as *Hu Allāh*.[30] Elsewhere, he identified Brahma with Adam.[31] Dārā Shikūh compiled his interpretations in a tract, *Majmā ul-Bahrain*, "The Mingling of the Two Oceans," described as a "collection of the truth and wisdom of two Truth-knowing groups."[32] In this vision of harmony between the traditions, at the heart of their agreement was a common ground shared by *waḥdat al-wujūd* and Vedanta.[33]

Inspired by these religious mash-ups, I began to think of my own engagements less as a one-person interfaith dialogue and more in relation to groups such as the Satpanthis, a South Asian community that had once venerated Alī as the tenth incarnation of Vishnu. Readily incorporating the Prophet's son-in-law and an Indic deity into their own knowledge of self, Satpanthis only concerned themselves with the question of "Muslim or Hindu" during the colonial period, when British courts and census officers demanded that they categorize themselves as one or the other. As "Islam" and "Hinduism" have become increasingly reified in modern times, defined in opposition to each other and encouraged by competing nationalisms, such traditions as identifying Alī with Vishnu or Fāṭima with Lakshmi have all but disappeared.

Scholars such as Harvard professor Ali Asani have suggested that rather than force groups like the Satpanthis into our modern categories of "Muslim" and "Hindu," we should instead consider them as drawing from a common pool of resources that worked in their setting—a pool in which both Alī and Vishnu were appropriate choices. Describing the

Satpanthis as "syncretic" would be troublesome, since the possibility of "syncretism" first requires "Islam" and "Hinduism" to be clearly defined and separate systems, which has not been the case in every historical context. For people of a certain time and place, Alī was naturally Vishnu; why couldn't he be? It happened for the Satpanthis in Gujarat, and it has happened in America too, when Elijah Poole found his Christ in Master Fard's Mahdī.

The Lakota elder Black Elk blended his people's Sun Dance, which had been banned by the U.S. government, with Christianity, enabling the tradition to survive in a changing environment. "Lakota ritual is very fluid," writes scholar Clyde Holler, "since each holy man has the responsibility and the freedom to interpret traditional religion according to his vision—that is, in response to the situation he is addressing and the spiritual resources available to address it."[34] As First Born Prince Allah believed that a Five Percenter could engage any tradition, as long as the god knew that his own mind was the highest power of that path, he might have understood religions—as Holler theorizes of Black Elk—as "culture-bound symbol systems":[35]

> The essential touchstone of religion for Black Elk was his vision, and as was traditional, he continually modified it throughout his life in response to his unfolding understanding of religious truth and to changing economic and social conditions. The vision is filled with symbols, and there is no reason to assume that Black Elk did not realize that they were symbols.[36]

For me to pay any mind to Sherman "The premium is now on ensuring and preserving *orthodoxy*" Jackson[37] and backhand the Satpanthis or Nation of Islam as "proto-Islamic" would mean that they could only be valuable as a rung on the ladder to something else, and that they had perhaps committed an offense upon the integrity of both Islam and their own souls. I couldn't see these traditions as fundamentally wrong or destructive; religious identities are no more naturally "pure" or necessarily separate than racial ones.

So who's a Muslim? Who's a Five Percenter?

If there's a legitimate reason for concern in my case, it's the always present issue of power. Black Elk's reforms of the Sun Dance constituted a negotiation of the repressed native tradition with both an advancing missionary faith and state power; as a Sunnī Five Percenter, First Born Prince Allah might have performed similar negotiations between concepts of "orthodoxy" and "heresy." These dynamics would be unavoidable in my own journeys as both participant and researcher. Scholar Bruce Lincoln recalls that while explaining his definition of myth as "ideology in narrative form" to a class, he found himself challenged by a student seated in the back of the room. "But isn't that true of scholarship as well?" she asked him. Scholars engage in the same practices as mythmakers, the student suggested, and academic arguments could share some parallels with religious narratives: "Don't scholars tell stories to recalibrate a pecking order, putting themselves, their favorite theories, and their favorite peoples on top?"[38]

It matters. When you're a white Muslim writing about the Five Percenters and recognize what your scholarship does—"myth with footnotes," as Lincoln says—it *really* matters.[39]

DEEP CREASES and stains mark the image as more than a captured moment in time: the photo itself is a captured physical object, preserved as a digital file. It is possible that the original photograph no longer exists, but the jpeg circulates on the Internet. I have it as my desktop background, lying flat under icons for blue file folders with titles like "Ismā'īlism and Supreme Mathematics." They were just kids when this picture was taken, eight teenagers in front of a gated storefront in Brooklyn. They came into the knowledge through a youth named Benjamin, who became Bilal after his encounter with Allah in Harlem,

which they called Mecca. On December 19, 1964, Bilal rode the train
to Brooklyn and taught them for six days and nights. Before returning
to Harlem, he gave them instructions to fast for three days, subsisting
only on water and coffee (no sugar). That was the end of the Cross Park
Chaplains, and the rebirth of Fort Greene as the "head of Medina."

I know their names: Siheem, Bali, Akim, Waleak, Sha Sha, Hasheem
(holding his baby), Mary Ann, and Casheem. With the exception of
Mary Ann, these were their adopted "righteous" names. When the Five
Percenters renounced religious Islam, Waleak would change his name
to Knowledge God. I also know their "honorable" or "government"
names, the names on their birth certificates.

They are now revered as Medina's "First Born," but there was no
such distinction in the 1960s, when they posed for this picture. Nor was
there yet a Universal Flag for them to wear, or an Allah School for them

to visit, or a document like "What We Teach" to lay down catechism, and they might have even identified themselves as Muslims. They could not have known the term "Nation of Gods and Earths," as it would not exist for nearly twenty more years. Some of them look to be wearing kufis, and one has a bow tie.

Nearly fifty years after Bilal's historic *hijra*, a white pseudo-Ṣūfī Ivy League Five Percenter sits in Widener Library and stares at this picture from another universe. I'm working with the same lessons as these young gods, but could the words possibly mean the same? If I stepped into that picture and built on their science with my study of Ibn al-'Arabī, what would they say? At the taking of this picture, was it even possible to be a white Five Percenter—was there yet an Azreal? Even if I could build with them at a parliament today, it would not take us back to the moment of the photo. The moment is gone, and whatever it meant to be a Five Percenter at that moment is also gone. The names of gods have changed, the lessons have changed, the Mathematics has changed. Islam has changed and memories have changed. The community's name has changed, the flag has changed, the Father has been assassinated, the Allah School in Mecca has been opened and burned down and reopened. That first generation of teen gods fathered children who would grow up to read different books.

None of us approach our traditions with an empty cup; I must therefore consider my *particular historical position* when building with the Five Percenters. It's not enough to stop at "white" and "Muslim;" even within the formations of whiteness and Islam, I have particular historical positions. These positions become the lens through which I comprehend the Five Percenters and write books about them.

I was born nearly ten years after Allah's assassination, and would have my first encounter with his community during its fortieth year. This, perhaps more than whiteness or religion, is the first strike against me, the 6 that I can't pass to reach God. For any tradition that builds upon stories of specific events and human lives, the worst enemy is time. My distance from the companions of the Prophet Muḥammad is much greater in years and miles, but still I try to pray like them, read Qur'ān like them, and translate their experiences into a life that they never could have imagined. Any book that I can write, whether on old Islams or new Islams, is stolen property.

In Muhammad ibn Abdul-Wahhab's *Kitāb at-Tawhīd,* I read the following ḥadīth:

> Ahmad reports that Tariq bin Shihāb narrated that Allah's Messenger, peace and blessings of Allāh be upon him, said: "A man entered Paradise because of a fly, and a men entered Hell-fire because of a fly." They (the Companions) asked, "How was that possible, O Messenger of Allāh?" He said, "Two men passed by the people who had an idol by which they would not allow anyone to pass without making sacrifice to it. They ordered one man to make a sacrifice. He said, 'I have nothing to present as an offering.' The people told him, 'Sacrifice something, even if it be a fly.' So he presented a fly (to their idol). They opened the way for him, and thus he entered the Hell-fire. They said to the other man, 'Sacrifice something.' He said, 'I will never sacrifice anything to any other than Allāh, most Majestic and Glorious.' So they struck his throat and killed him; and he, therefore, entered Paradise."[40]

The story comes from a culture in which people regularly sacrificed to idols, and the first Muslim community was comprised entirely of former idolaters. Even after Islam's triumph in Mecca, Muslims would have faced a natural temptation to revert to their old ways. For the Prophet Muḥammad, this was a major problem; but in my own world, the question of whether to make offerings to idols isn't a pressing concern. On top of that, I'm not entirely into the idea of an afterlife; and even if I was, I wouldn't want my mystery god to be such an asshole as to condemn someone to hell for having offered an insect to an inanimate object. For this story to hold relevance in my life, I change its meaning. The idol is no longer a physical statue, but another kind of idol: my greed, my lust, my ego and self-serving ambition, whatever evils whisper from my lower self. The fly represents a tiny step in the wrong direction, while Paradise and the Hell-fire can be natural consequences in this earthly life, the reality of whatever path I choose. Like Five Percenters who produce alternative interpretations for the 14:36 degree ("His own self is a righteous Muslim") or Warith Deen Mohammed in 1975 reinventing 2:10 ("Who is the Colored Man?") to suit his needs—or even the classical *mutakallimūn* who read God's "hands" to mean something besides hands—I've found that the story can relocate its meaning. Producing a new lesson from the narrative, I can stick it onto my refrigerator and strive to live by it. God bless you, Shaykh al-Islam.

It's one thing to do that with old stories; the man that I call Allah did something else.

The lessons were question-answer sessions between Fard and Elijah, in which Fard asked the questions and Elijah gave the answers. After studying the questions and answers, Allah, then known as Clarence 13X, came to the conclusion that he had unlocked the lessons and revealed their ultimate meaning. Teaching on street corners, he broke with the established interpretations and the institution (as well as the *man*) that had delivered and legitimized the lessons in the first place. Imagine the guts—Clarence had a fairly wild claim to make, especially considering that Elijah was still alive; it wasn't a matter of reinterpreting a dead prophet from fourteen centuries ago who can't talk back. This would be more like a Muslim foot soldier in the Prophet Muḥammad's own lifetime starting a new movement on the grounds that he understood Muḥammad's revelations better than Muḥammad himself.

I can admire the spirit, but *wow*; Clarence was the fringe of the fringe. Just a regular guy at the mosques and gambling spots, he had no self-evident authority to proclaim himself the Best Knower. He wasn't a mystic; Fard didn't hover over Harlem in the Mothership and beam Clarence aboard to implant microchips in his brain. He wasn't a scholar; what had he studied, besides the lessons themselves? But Clarence seems to have known something that the kids needed to know, and he gave it to them; for that, he became Allah, and somehow he ended up crossing the line between apostate from the old and founder of the new. Allah rebelled against an institution, but a generation or so after his martyrdom, the rebellion became an institution in its own right. The religious authority that Allah melted has hardened again, and the Five Percent is as much religion as anything.

Some Five Percenters refer to me as an "orthodox Muslim." I wonder what the term means to them; what is it that makes me orthodox? Many of the historical figures who inform my Islam have had their orthodox credentials challenged or taken away; Muslims have been arguing bitterly over Ibn al-'Arabī's "orthodoxy" for centuries. It doesn't even seem to matter whether I subscribe to crucial articles of orthodoxy, such as belief in the Qur'ān as uncreated and supernaturally revealed; I am in need of a category, and one is assigned to me. Perhaps when a Five Percenter calls me orthodox, he's just making sure that I stay on my side of the line, reminding me that what we have is not the same. The label is a setting of boundaries. That's how we create each other; by defining me as an "orthodox Muslim," he also defines himself as an "orthodox Five Percenter."

Exiled to the caves of Widener Library to write my paper, I'm reading Sherman Jackson's translation of al-Ghazālī's *Fayṣal at-Tafriqa Bayna al-Islām wa al-Zandaqa* ("The Decisive Criterion for Distinguishing Islam from Heresy"). It has been suggested that al-Ghazālī wrote the book as a defense against charges that he himself had transgressed the limits of Islam.[41] I remember my encounter with Jackson at the American Academy of Religion conference, when he came up to me and demanded to know why Five Percenters felt entitled to wear stars and crescents if they weren't willing to pay the ideological dues of being Muslims. There's not really a better answer to that line of questioning than "Because they want to, so what?" It seemed that for Jackson, the Five Percent had trespassed upon what he earnestly felt was his rightful territory. Jews and Christians in seventh-century Arabia might have issued the same accusation against the Muḥammad that Jackson and I share for having proclaimed himself an heir to *their* traditions, their Moses and Jesus. But Muḥammad was part of that world with their symbols and stories floating around him; you can't always choose which ones are going to stick.

So Sherman Jackson questions the Five Percenters' right to exist, and not all Five Percenters would respect *my* right to exist. With consideration for everyone's histories, I don't know how to apologize for what I find meaningful, and I can't lose trillions of years worrying about how ninety-five percent of you would read the flag on my shirt. All I have is the confidence to say "I Self Lord And Master." I know who I am and why.

Peace,

Azreal Wisdom

ACKNOWLEDGMENTS

First, my thanks to the Five Percenters who opened the door for me, allowing me to get a taste of the right foods. I owe an eternal debt to Allah B, whose kindness and care help to make the Allah School in Mecca a peaceful and welcoming place for all. I have heard even theologically conservative and "orthodox" Muslims call this man a true saint for God, and I absolutely agree. I must of course acknowledge Azreal and express my hope for this project to be a fitting tribute to his name and our friendship. I will always cherish our journeys through New York, our epic drive from Harlem to Milwaukee, his stories of Allah, and the gift that I had been given in knowing him. To all Five Percenters who have built with me over the years, I offer my respect and appreciation. All praise is due.

In addition, I have to thank individuals outside the Five Percent community whose friendship and support have contributed to my experience of the tradition. Barry Gottehrer shared his time and personal archive with me, and I will always appreciate his support for my work and his sincere affection for the Five Percent. Minister Akbar Muhammad, international representative for the Honorable Minister Louis Farrakhan, helped me to feel welcome within the teachings, and has consistently treated me as his brother in Islam. Sister Dorothy Blake Fardan has my undying respect for her integrity and courage, and has shown me how this path can be lived out.

The experience of these past two years at Harvard has been personally and intellectually transformative, and I am grateful for the professors and fellow students who have contributed to my thought. I feel especially blessed for the chance to have worked with Ali S. Asani, whose insights on the formation of religious identity have placed me in his permanent debt.

Salaams to Laury Silvers, who still has the sharpest sword.

Special thanks to Mitch Horowitz for believing in this project, and also to Gabrielle Moss, David Walker, and everyone at Tarcher/Penguin.

Much appreciation to Phyllis Wender, Susan Cohen, and Allison Cohen at Gersh Agency.

Finally, peace to my family and friends. It's not easy to be close to a writer, and I've been given more patience than I deserve.

NOTES

1. S. Hayy, *Asian Ideas of East and West: Tagore and His Critics in Japan, China, and India* (Cambridge, MA: Harvard University Press, 1970), 333.

1. DEVIL IN DEEP SPACE

1. RZA, "A Day to God Is 1,000 Years," *Birth of a Prince*, Wu/Sanctuary Urban/BMG Records, 2003.
2. Jay-Z, "Jigga My Nigga," *Vol. 3 . . . Life and Times of S. Carter*, Roc-A-Fella/Def Jam, 1999.
3. Lil Wayne, "Tha Heat," *The Carter*, Cash Money/Universal, 2004.
4. Michael Muhammad Knight, *The Five Percenters: Islam, Hip-Hop, and the Gods of New York* (Oxford: Oneworld Publications, 2007), 90.
5. Susan Friend Harding, *The Book of Jerry Falwell: Fundamentalist Language and Politics* (Princeton, NJ: Princeton University Press, 2000). 34.
6. Ibid., 57.
7. Ibid., 58.
8. Ibid.
9. Clifford Geertz, *The Interpretation of Cultures* (New York: Perseus Books, 1973), 90.
10. Ebrahim Moosa, *Ghazālī and the Poetics of Imagination* (Chapel Hill: University of North Carolina Press, 2005), 84.
11. Joseph Prabhu, *The Intercultural Challenge of Raimon Panikkar* (Maryknoll, NY: Orbis Books, 1996), 5.

2. KILL ALL THE WHITE MEN

1. Rakim, "Holy Are You," *The Seventh Seal*, Ra Records, 2009.
2. Nina G. Jablonski, "The Evolution of Human Skin and Skin Color," *Annual Review of Anthropology* 33 (2004): 585–623.
3. Ibid.

4. Ibid.
5. Nell Irvin Painter, *The History of White People* (New York: W.W. Norton & Company, Inc., 2010), 395.
6. Ol' Dirty Bastard, "Rawhide," *Return to the 36 Chambers: The Dirty Version,* Elektra Records, 1995.
7. Walter Ben Michaels, *The Trouble with Diversity: How We Learned to Love Identity and Ignore Inequality* (New York: Henry Holt and Company, LLC, 2006), 28.
8. Jablonski, "The Evolution of Human Skin and Skin Color."
9. Michaels, *The Trouble with Diversity,* 30–31.
10. Bruce David Baum, *The Rise and Fall of the Caucasian Race: A Political History of Racial Identity* (New York and London: New York University Press, 2006), 213.
11. Kenneth A. R. Kennedy, *God-Apes and Fossil Men: Paleoanthropology of South Asia* (Ann Arbor: University of Michigan Press, 2000), 364.
12. Luigi Luca Cavalli-Sforza and Francesco Cavalli-Sforza, *The Great Human Diasporas: The History of Diversity and Evolution* (New York: Perseus Books, 1996), 230–34.
13. Baum, *The Rise and Fall of the Caucasian Race,* 213.
14. Alan R. Templeton, "Human Races: A Genetic and Evolutionary Perspective," *American Anthropologist* 100.3 (1998): 632–50.
15. Steve Olson, *Mapping Human History: Genes, Race, and Our Common Origins* (New York: Mariner Books, 2003), 43.
16. Jablonski, "The Evolution of Human Skin and Skin Color," 585–623.
17. Templeton, "Human Races," 632–50.
18. Michaels, *The Trouble with Diversity,* 29–31.
19. Faye V. Harrison, "Expanding the Discourse on 'Race,'" *American Anthropologist* 100.3 (1998): 609–31.
20. Benjamin Isaac, "Proto-Racism in Graeco-Roman Antiquity," *World Archaelogy* 38. 1 (2006): 32–47.
21. Zainab Bahrani, "Race and Ethnicity in Mesopotamian Antiquity," *World Archaelogy* 38.1 (2006): 48–59.
22. Ibid.
23. Ibid.
24. Ibid.
25. Ibid.
26. Ibid.
27. Jaz, "The Originators," *To Your Soul,* Capitol Records, 1990.
28. Isaac, "Proto-Racism in Graeco-Roman Antiquity," 32–47.
29. Ibid.
30. Ibid.
31. Ibid.
32. Cavalli-Sforza and Cavalli-Sforza, *The Great Human Diasporas,* 228.
33. Painter, *The History of White People,* 44.
34. Thomas R. Trautmann, "Introduction" in *The Aryan Debate,* ed. Thomas R. Trautmann (Oxford: Oxford University Press, 2010).

35. Kennedy, *God-Apes and Fossil Men,* 67–81.
36. Burjor Avari, *India: The Ancient Past: A History of the Indian-Subcontinent from 7000 BC to AD 1200* (New York: Routledge, 2007), 61–63.
37. Kennedy, *God-Apes and Fossil Men,* 83.
38. Trautmann, "Introduction," in *The Aryan Debate.*
39. Kennedy, *God-Apes and Fossil Men,* 67–81.
40. Ibid., 366–72.
41. Avari, *India: The Ancient Past,* 61–63.
42. Baum, *The Rise and Fall of the Caucasian Race,* 92.
43. Ibid.
44. Painter, *The History of White People,* 42.
45. Matthew Frye Jacobson, *Whiteness of a Different Color: European Immigrants and the Alchemy of Race* (Cambridge, MA: Harvard University Press, 1998), 41.
46. Ibid., 44.
47. Ibid., 46.
48. Cynthia Skove Nevels, *Lynching to Belong: Claiming Whiteness Through Racial Violence* (College Station: Texas A&M University, 2007), 115.
49. Painter, *The History of White People,* 204.
50. Skove Nevels, *Lynching to Belong,* 84.
51. Ibid.
52. Painter, *The History of White People,* 254–55.
53. Jacobson, *Whiteness of a Different Color,* 239–40.
54. F. Hancy Lopez, *White by Law: The Legal Construction of Race* (New York: New York University Press, 1996), 81.
55. Ibid., 83.
56. Ibid., 85.
57. Ibid., 89.
58. Ibid., 148-149.
59. Ibid., 90.
60. Ibid., 92.
61. Ibid., 90.
62. Jacobson, *Whiteness of a Different Color,* 93.
63. Ibid., 84.
64. "Eugenics in Ancient Greece," *British Medical Journal* 2.2762 (1913): 1502–03.
65. Lopez, *White by Law,* 87.
66. Jacobson, *Whiteness of a Different Color,* 91.
67. Ibid., 92.
68. Ibid., 96.
69. Painter, *The History of White People,* 81.
70. Ibid., 80.
71. Ibid.
72. Baum, *The Rise and Fall of the Caucasian Race,* 221.
73. Ibid., 224.

74. Ibid.
75. Ibid.
76. Ibid.
77. Ibid., 230.
78. Alastair Bonnett, *The Idea of the West: Culture, Politics, and History* (New York: Palgrave Macmillan, 2004), 57.
79. Ibid.
80. Ibid., 58.
81. Ibid., 57.
82. Baum, *The Rise and Fall of the Caucasian Race*, 228.
83. Ibid., 231.
84. Ibid., 229.
85. Noel Ignatiev and John Garvey, eds., "Abolish the White Race by Any Means Necessary," *Race Traitor*, 1996.
86. Ibid.
87. Michaels, *The Trouble with Diversity*, 45.
88. Jeru the Damaja, "Scientific Madness," *The Sun Rises in the East*, PayDay Records, 1994.
89. Robert E. Birt, "The Bad Faith of Whiteness," in *What White Looks Like: African-American Philosophers on the Whiteness Question*, ed. George Yancy (New York: Routledge, 2004).
90. Tim Wise, *Speaking Treason Fluently: Anti-Racist Reflections from an Angry White Male* (Berkeley, CA: Soft Skull Press, 2008), 239.
91. Michael Muhammad Knight, *Blue-Eyed Devil: A Road Odyssey Through Islamic America* (Berkeley, CA: Soft Skull Press, 2006), 148.
92. Tim Wise, "Membership Has Its Privileges: Thoughts on Acknowledging and Challenging Whiteness," in *White Privilege: Essential Readings on the Other Side of Whiteness*, ed. Paula S. Rothenberg (New York: Macmillan, 2007).
93. Ignatiev and Garvey, "Abolish the White Race by Any Means Necessary."
94. Ibid.
95. Wise, "Membership Has Its Privileges,"

3. WONDERBREAD GODS

1. Allah, *Wisdom of Allah the Father*.
2. Michael Muhammad Knight, *The Five Percenters: Islam, Hip-Hop, and the Gods of New York* (Oxford, England: Oneworld Publications, 2007), 233.
3. Public Enemy, "Fear of a Black Planet," *Fear of a Black Planet*, Def Jam Recordings, 1990.
4. Jablonski, "The Evolution of Human Skin and Skin Color," 585–623.
5. F. Scott Fitzgerald, *The Great Gatsby* (New York: Simon & Schuster Inc., 1925, 1995), 17.
6. Ernest Allen, Jr., "When Japan Was 'Champion of the Darker Races': Satokata Takahashi and the Flowering of Black Messianic Nationalism," *Black Scholar* 24.1 (1994): 23–46.

7. Elijah Muhammad, *Supreme Wisdom* (MEMPS), 18.

8. Herbert Berg, *Elijah Muhammad and Islam* (New York and London: New York University Press, 2009), 111.

9. Ibid., 115.

10. Elijah Muhammad, *Theology of Time: the Secret of the Time* (Secretarius MEMPS, 2004). 3.

11. Albert Raboteau, *Slave Religion: The "Invisible Institution" in the Antebellum South,* 2nd ed. (Oxford: Oxford University Press, 2004), 4.

12. Valerie Melissa Babb, *Whiteness Visible: The Meaning of Whiteness in American Literature and Culture* (New York: New York University Press, 1998), 21.

13. Gary Taylor, *Buying Whiteness: Race, Culture, and Identity from Columbus to Hip-Hop* (New York: Palgrave Macmillan, 2005), 194.

14. Ibid., 198.

15. Theophus H. Smith, *Conjuring Culture: Biblical Formations of Black America* (New York: Oxford University Press, 1994), 103.

16. Taylor, *Buying Whiteness,* 198.

17. Peter H. Wood, *Strange New Land: Africans in Colonial America* (Oxford: Oxford University Press, 2003), 32.

18. Smith, *Conjuring Culture,* 103.

19. Raboteau, *Slave Religion,* 103.

20. Ibid., 169.

21. Ibid., 147.

22. Wood, *Strange New Land,* 63.

23. Raboteau, *Slave Religion,* 213.

24. Ibid., 291.

25. Ibid., 295.

26. Ibid., 313.

27. David Walker and Henry Highland Garnet, *Walker's Appeal with a Brief Sketch of His Life* (UK: Echo Library, 2007), 20.

28. Waldo E. Martin, *The Mind of Frederick Douglass* (Chapel Hill, NC: University of North Carolina Press, 1986), 178.

29. Raboteau, *Slave Religion,* 314.

30. Martin, *The Mind of Frederick Douglass,* 85.

31. Ibid.

32. Ibid., 116–17.

33. Ibid.

34. Edward T. Blum, "There Won't Be Any Rich People in Heaven: The Black Christ, White Hypocrisy, and the Gospel According to W.E.B. Du Bois," *Journal of African American History* 90.4 (2005): 368–86.

35. Ibid.

36. Ibid.

37. Michael Muhammad Knight, *The Five Percenters: Islam, Hip-Hop, and the Gods of New York* (Oxford: Oneworld Publications, 2007), 16.

38. Nathaniel Deutsch, "The Proximate Other: The Nation of Islam and Judaism," in *Black Zion: African American Religious Encounters with Judaism,* ed.. Yvonne Chireau and Nathaniel Deutsch (New York: Oxford University Press, 2000).

39. Louis Farrakhan, *Put on the New Man,* DVD, Final Call, Inc., 2010.

40. Elijah Muhammad, *Message to the Blackman in America,* 2nd ed. (Atlanta: MEMPS, 1997), 55.

41. Robert Terrill, *Malcolm X: Inventing Radical Judgment* (East Lansing: Michigan State University Press, 2004).

42. Bi'Sana Ta'Laha El'Shabazziz Sula Muhammadia and Master Tu'Biz Jihadia Muhammadia, *The Holy Book of Life, Volume Two: Spiritual Government* (Detroit: Harlo, 1975), 123–30.

43. Farrakhan, *Put on the New Man.*

44. Lord Jamar, interview by author, 2009.

45. Elijah Muhammad, "Old World Going Out with a Great Noise," *Muhammad Speaks,* November 26, 1971, 16–17.

46. W. D. Muhammad, "The Destruction of the Devil," *Muhammad Speaks,* July 11, 1975, 13.

47. "First Official Interview with the Supreme Minister," *Muhammad Speaks,* March 21, 1975, 12.

48. Ibid.

49. Mattias Gardell, *In the Name of Elijah Muhammad: Louis Farrakhan and the Nation of Islam* (Durham, NC: Duke University Press, 1996), 105.

50. Gardell, *In the Name of Elijah Muhammad,* 114.

51. Ibid., 116.

52. Ibid., 117.

53. Clifton E. Marsh, *From Black Muslims to Muslims: The Transition from Separatism to Islam, 1930-1980* (London: Scarecrow Press, 1984), 97.

54. Gardell, *In the Name of Elijah Muhammad,* 118.

55. David Walker, *David Walker's Appeal to the Coloured Citizens of the World, but in Particular, and Very Expressly, to Those of the United States of America* (New York: Hill and Wang, 1995), 16–17.

56. *The Usual Suspects,* directed by Brian Singer (Gramercy Pictures, 1995).

57. Faye V. Harrison, "Expanding the Discourse on 'Race,'" *American Anthropologist* 100.3 (1998): 609–31.

58. Sherman Jackson, *Islam and the Blackamerican: The Third Resurrection* (Oxford : Oxford University Press, 2005), 14.

59. Dorothy Blake Fardan, *Yakub and the Origins of White Supremacy.* (Bensenville, Ill.: Lushena Books, 2001), 16. Print.

4. ELIJAH MUHAMMAD VS. MARSHALL MATHERS

1. "Eminem featuring D12, "Quitter Hit 'Em Up (Everlast Diss)," *YouTube,* http://www.youtube.com/watch?v=Zuvwq0zgwAg.

2. Eminem, "Yellow Brick Road," *Encore,* Shady/Aftermath/Interscope, 2004.

3. Ol' Dirty Bastard, "Harlem World," *Return to the 36 Chambers: The Dirty Version,* Elektra Records, 1995.

4. Valerie Babb, *Whiteness Visible: The Meaning of Whiteness in American Literature and Culture* (New York: New York University Press, 1998), 21.

5. Talal Asad, *Formations of the Secular: Christianity, Islam, Modernity* (Palo Alto, CA: Stanford University Press, 2003), 168.

6. Albert J. Raboteau, *Slave Religion: The "Invisible Institution" in the Antebellum South,* 2nd ed. (Oxford: Oxford University Press, 2004), 4.

7. *Who Was Master Fard?* DVD.

8. Public Enemy, "Fight the Power," *Fear of a Black Planet,* Def Jam Recordings, 1990.

9. Public Enemy, "Black Steel in the Hour of Chaos," *It Takes a Nation of Millions to Hold Us Back,* Def Jam Recordings, 1988.

10. Alex Haley and Malcolm X, *The Autobiography of Malcolm X* (New York: Ballantine Books, 1999), 347.

11. George Breitman and Malcolm X, *Malcolm X Speaks: Selected Speeches and Statements* (New York: Grove Press, 1990), 213.

12. Jack Kerouac, *On the Road,* 5th ed. (New York: Penguin Books, 1991), 180.

13. KRS-One, "MCs Act Like They Don't Know," *KRS-One,* Jive, 1995.

14. Annalee Newitz, "When Will White People Stop Making Movies Like 'Avatar?'" *io9,* December 18, 2009, http://io9.com/5422666/when-will-white-people-stop-making-movies-like-avatar.

15. Robert H. Abzug, *Cosmos Crumbling: American Reform and the Religious Imagination* (Oxford: Oxford University Press, 1994), 138–44.

16. Ibid.

17. Melvin Gibbs, "ThugGods: Spiritual Darkness and Hip-Hop," in *Everything but the Burden: What White People Are Taking from Black Culture,* ed. Greg Tate (New York: Broadway Books, 2003).

18. Eminem, "Role Model," *The Slim Shady LP,* Aftermath, 1999.

19. Craig Watkins, *Hip Hop Matters: Politics, Pop Culture, and the Struggle for the Soul of a Movement* (Boston: Beacon Press, 2005), 91.

20. Devon W. Carbado, "Privilege," in *Black Queer Studies,* ed. E. Patrick Johnson and Mae G.. Henderson (Durham, NC, and London: Duke University Press, 2005).

21. Linda Alcoff, *Visible Identities: Race, Gender, and the Self* (New York: Oxford University Press, 2006), 217.

22. "Declaration of War Against Exploiters of Lakota Spirituality," in *A Documentary History of Religion in America: Since 1877,* ed. Edwin Scott Gaustad and Mark A. Noll (Grand Rapids: Wm. B. Eerdmans Publishing Co., 2003).

23. Ibid.

24. Dorothy Blake Fardan, *Lonesome Road: Journey to Islam and Liberation* (Lumumba Publishing Company, 2009), 140–41.

25. Ibid., 292.

26. Ibid., 552.

27. Ibid., 409.

28. Ibid., 551.

29. Ibid.

30. Ibid., 122.

31. Amir Fatir, "Mothership Connection," *Amir Fatir,* http://amirfatir.tripod.com/sitebuildercontent/sitebuilderpictures/Mothership.htm.

5. POWER AND REFINEMENT

1. Allah, *Wisdom of Allah the Father.*

2. Erykah Badu, "Me," *New Amerykah, Part One,* Universal Motown, 2008.

3. Ian Almond, *Sufism and Deconstruction: A Comparative Study of Derrida and Ibn Arabi* (London: Routledge, 2004), 15.

4. William Chittick, *Ibn Arabi: Heir to the Prophets* (Oxford: Oneworld Publications, 2005), 76–77.

5. Ibid., 112–13.

6. Brand Nubian, "Ain't No Mystery," *In God We Trust,* Elektra Records, 1992.

7. Esther J. Hamori, *"When Gods Were Men": The Embodied God in Biblical and Near Eastern Literature* (Berlin: Walter de Gruyter, 2008), 46–47.

8. Amina Wadud, *Inside the Gender Jihad: Women's Reform in Islam* (Oxford: Oneworld Publications, 2006), 213–14.

9. Bruce B. Lawrence, *The Qur'an: A Biography* (New York: Atlantic Monthly Press, 2006), 127.

10. Allah, *Wisdom of Allah the Father.*

11. RZA, "A Day to God Is 1,000 Years," *Birth of a Prince,* Wu/Sanctuary Urban/BMG Records, 2003.

12. G. S. Hodgson, *The Venture of Islam: Conscience and History in a World Civilization* (Chicago: University of Chicago Press, 1974), 198.

13. Erdmann Doane Beynon, "The Voodoo Cult among Negro Migrants in Detroit," *American Journal of Sociology* 43 (1938): 896–97.

14. Michael A. Gomez, *Black Crescent: The Experience and Legacy of African Muslims in the Americas* (Cambridge: Cambridge University Press, 2005), 186–87.

15. Michel Foucault and Jeremy R. Carrette, eds. *Religion and Culture* (New York: Routledge, 1999), 107.

16. Elijah Muhammad, *Theology of Time: The Secret of the Time* (Atlanta: Secretarius MEMPS, 2004), 19, 272.

17. Mikhail Alexandrovich Bakunin, *God and the State* (Cosimo, 2009), 16.

18. Ibid.

19. Ibid., 17.

20. Ibid.

21. Claude Andrew Clegg III, *An Original Man: The Life and Times of Elijah Muhammad* (New York: St. Martin's Press, 1997), 130.

22. Heather Hendershot, *Shaking the World for Jesus: Media and Conservative Evangelical Culture* (Chicago: University of Chicago Press, 2004), 25.

23. Mara Einstein, *Brands of Faith: Marketing Religion in a Commercial Age* (New York: Routledge, 2008), 190.

24. Ibid., 161.

25. Ibid., 158.

26. David Chidester, *Authentic Fakes: Religion and American Popular Culture* (Berkeley and Los Angeles: University of California Press, 2005), 140.

27. Einstein, *Brands of Faith,* 137.

28. Ibid., 145.

29. Bakunin, *God and the State,* 20.

30. Benjamin E. Mays, "The Negro's God as Reflected in His Literature: Ideas of God Involving Frustration, Doubt, God's Impotence, and His Non-Existence," in *By These Hands: A Documentary History of African American Humanism,* ed. Anthony B. Pinn (New York and London: New York University Press, 2001).

31. *The Problem Book.*

32. Wallace D. Muhammad, "Self-Government in the New World," *Bilalian News,* March 19, 1976, 23–26.

33. Chidester, *Authentic Fakes,* 230.

34. Louis A. DeCaro, Jr., *On the Side of My People: A Religious Life of Malcolm X* (New York: New York University Press, 1996), 269.

35. Allah, *Wisdom of Allah the Father.*

36. Elijah Muhammad, *Message to the Blackman in America,* 2nd ed. (Atlanta: MEMPS, 1997), 6.

37. Ebrahim Moosa, "The Debts and Burdens of Critical Islam," in *Progressive Muslims: On Justice, Gender, and Pluralism,* ed. Omid Safi (Oxford: Oneworld Publications, 2003).

38. Ibid.

39. Barry Gottehrer. Interview by author, 2005.

6. BATTLEFIELD EARTH

1. Sojourner Truth, "Ar'n't I a Woman?" in *The Radical Reader: A Documentary History of the American Radical Tradition,* ed. Timothy Patrick McCarthy and John McMillian (New York: New Press, 2003).

2. Elizabeth Frost-Knappman and Kathryn Cullen-DuPont, *Women's Suffrage in America,* 2nd ed. (New York: Facts on File, 2005), 40.

3. Robert H. Abzug, *Cosmos Crumbling: American Reform and the Religious Imagination* (Oxford: Oxford University Press, 1994), 214.

4. "Declaration of Sentiments and Resolutions," in *Race, Class, and Gender in the United States: An Integrated Study,* comp. Paula S. Rothenberg (New York: Worth Publishers, 2007).

5. Ibid.

6. Gerda Lerner, *The Grimké Sisters from South Carolina: Pioneers for Woman's Rights and Abolition* (New York: Oxford University Press, 1998), 201.

7. Frost-Knappman and Cullen-DuPont, *Women's Suffrage in America*, 175.

8. Sally Gregory McMillen, *Seneca Falls and the Origins of the Women's Rights Movement* (New York: Oxford University Press, 2008), 162–67. Print.

9. William L. O'Neill, *Everyone Was Brave: A History of Feminism in America* (New York: Quadrangle/New York Times Book Co., 1976), 17.

10. Lori D. Ginzberg, *Elizabeth Cady Stanton: An American Life* (New York: Hill and Wang, 2009), 121–22.

11. Ibid.

12. Zillah Eisenstein, "Hillary Is White," in *Who Should Be First? Feminists Speak Out on the 2008 Presidential Campaign,* ed. Beverly Guy-Sheftall and Johnnetta Betsch Cole (Albany: State University of New York Press, 2010).

13. Dwight A. McBride, "Straight Black Studies: On African American Studies, James Baldwin, and Black Queer Studies," in *Black Queer Studies,* eds. E. Patrick Johnson and Mae G. Henderson (Durham and London: Duke University Press, 2005).

14. Sherman Jackson, *Islam and the Problem of Black Suffering* (Oxford: Oxford University Press, 2009), 205.

15. Mary Daly, *Beyond God the Father: Toward a Philosophy of Women's Liberation* (Boston: Beacon Press, 1985), 8.

16. Sojourner Truth, "Ar'n't I a Woman?"

17. Abzug, *Cosmos Crumbling,* 224.

18. Ibid., 215.

19. Ibid., 222.

20. Frederick Douglass and Phillip Sheldon Foner, ed. *Frederick Douglass on Women,* 2nd ed. (Cambridge, MA: Da Capo Press, 1992), 118.

21. Susan Jacoby, *Freethinkers: a History of American Secularism* (New York: Henry Holt and Company, 2004), 197.

22. "Declaration of Sentiments and Resolutions."

23. Elizabeth Cady Stanton, *The Woman's Bible* (Albany: Arno Press, 1972), 12.

24. Margot Adler, *Drawing Down the Moon: Witches, Druids, Goddess-Worshippers and Other Pagans in America,* 4th ed. (New York: Penguin Group, 2006), 204.

25. Mary Daly, "After the Death of God the Father," in *Womanspirit Rising: A Feminist Reader in Religion,* ed. Carol P. Christ and Judith Plaskow (New York: HarperSanFrancisco, 1992).

26. Ibid.

27. Carol P. Christ, "Why Women Need the Goddess: Phenomenological, Psychological, and Political Reflections," *Womanspirit Rising: A Feminist Reader in Religion,* ed. Carol P. Christ and Judith Plaskow (New York: HarperSanFrancisco, 1992).

28. Ibid.

29. Eleanor L. McLaughlin, "The Christian Past: Does It Hold a Future for Women?" in *Womanspirit Rising: A Feminist Reader in Religion,* ed. Carol P. Christ and Judith Plaskow (New York: HarperSanFrancisco, 1992).

30. Christ, "Why Women Need the Goddess."

31. Ann-Louise Keating, "Making 'Our Shattered Faces Whole': The Black Goddess and Audre Lorde's Revision of Patriarchal Myth," *Frontiers: A Journal of Women's Studies* 13.1 (1992): 20–33. Print.

32. Ibid.

33. Audre Lorde, *Sister Outsider: Essays and Speeches*, 2nd ed. (Berkeley: Crossing Press, 2007), 66–72.

34. Ibid.

35. Lord Jamar, "Supreme Mathematics," *The 5% Album*, Babygrande Records, 2006.

36. Jerrold S. Cooper, "Enki's Member: Eros and Irrigation in Sumerian Literature," in *Dumu-e2-dub-ba-a: Studies in Honor of Ake W. Sjoberg*, ed. Hermann Behrens, Darlene Loding, and Martha T. Roth (Philadelphia: University of Philadelphia Museum Press, 1989).

37. Ibid.

38. Knowledge Scientific Cipher, "The God in Man: Allah's Self-Creation," in *Knowledge of Self: A Collection of Wisdom on the Science of Everything in Life*, ed. Supreme Understanding Allah, C'BS ALife Allah, and Sunez Allah (Atlanta: Supreme Design Publishing, 2009).

39. Supreme Understanding Allah, "Why Is the Black Man God?" in *Knowledge of Self: A Collection of Wisdom on the Science of Everything in Life*, ed. Supreme Understanding Allah, C'BS ALife Allah, and Sunez Allah (Atlanta: Supreme Design Publishing, 2009).

40. Supreme Understanding Allah, C'BS ALife Allah, and Sunez Allah, eds., "FAQ," in *Knowledge of Self: A Collection of Wisdom on the Science of Everything in Life.* (Atlanta: Supreme Design Publishing, 2009).

41. Supreme Understanding Allah, C'BS ALife Allah, and Sunez Allah, *Knowledge of Self*.

42. Emblem of Justice, "The Power of the Queen in Chess," in *Knowledge of Self: A Collection of Wisdom on the Science of Everything in Life*, ed. Supreme Understanding Allah, C'BS ALife Allah, and Sunez Allah (Atlanta: Supreme Design Publishing, 2009).

43. Amina Wadud, *Inside the Gender Jihad: Women's Reform in Islam* (Oxford: Oneworld Publications, 2006), 27–28.

44. Ibid.

45. King Sun, "Universal Flag," *Righteous but Ruthless*, Profile, 1991.

46. Michael Muhammad Knight, *The Five Percenters: Islam, Hip-Hop, and the Gods of New York* (Oxford: Oneworld Publications, 2007), 219.

47. Jonathan Walton, *Watch This!: The Ethics and Aesthetics of Black Televangelism* (New York: New York University Press, 2009), 190.

48. Ibid., 191.

49. Cornel West, *Race Matters* (Boston: Beacon Press, 1993), 24.

50. bell hooks, *Outlaw Culture: Resisting Representations* (New York: Routledge, 1994), 19.

51. bell hooks, *Yearning: Race, Gender, and Cultural Politics* (Boston: South End Press, 1990), 16.
52. Devon W. Carbado, "Privilege," in *Black Queer Studies,* ed. E. Patrick Johnson and Mae G. Henderson (Durham and London: Duke University Press, 2005).
53. Marable, *Malcolm X,* 66.
54. Jonathan Walton, *Watch This!: The Ethics and Aesthetics of Black Televangelism* (New York: New York University Press, 2009), 119–21.
55. Ibid., 197.
56. Ibid., 217.
57. Ibid., 130.
58. Knight, *The Five Percenters,* 222–23.
59. Ibid., 125-126.
60. Malcolm X and Alex Haley, *The Autobiography of Malcolm X* (New York: Ballantine Books, 1999), 230.
61. hooks, *Outlaw Culture,* 187.
62. Ibid., 192.
63. Ibid., 193.
64. Ibid., 189.
65. Amy Goodman, "Manning Marable on 'Malcolm X: A Life of Reinvention,'" *Democracy Now! The War and Peace Report,* May 21, 2007, http://www.democracynow.org/2007/5/21/manning_marable_on_malcolm_x_a.
66. Ibid., 188.
67. Sherman Jackson, *Islam and the Blackamerican: The Third Resurrection* (Oxford: Oxford University Press, 2005), 168.
68. Norm R. Allen, Jr., "Humanism in Political Action," in *By These Hands: A Documentary History of African American Humanism,* ed. Anthony B. Pinn (New York and London: New York University Press, 2001).
69. X and Haley, *Autobiography of Malcolm X,* 428.
70. Daly, "After the Death of God the Father."
71. Wadud, *Inside the Gender Jihad,* 28.
72. R. W. J. Austin, "The Feminine Dimensions in Ibn Arabi's Thought." *Journal of the Muhyiddin Ibn Arabi Society* II (1984): 5–14.
73. Cyrus Ali Zargar, *Aesthetic Principles of Islamic Mysticism: Beauty and the Human Form in the Writings of Ibn Arabī and Irāqī,* dissertation, University of California, Berkeley, 2008, 86.
74. Souad Al-Hakim, "Ibn Arabī's Twofold Perception of Woman: Woman as Human Being and Cosmic Principle," *Journal of the Muhyiddin Ibn Arabi Society* XXXIX (2006): 3–13.
75. Truth, "Ar'n't I a Woman?"
76. Knight, *The Five Percenters: Islam, Hip-Hop, and the Gods of New York,* 220–21.
77. Prince A. Cuba, *Culture Essays and Wisdom Poems,* 6.
78. Knight, *The Five Percenters: Islam, Hip-Hop, and the Gods of New York,* 220–21.
79. Ibid.
80. Cuba, *Culture Essays and Wisdom Poems,* 3.

7. GODS OF THE WORD

1. Ian Almond, *Sufism and Deconstruction: A Comparative Study of Derrida and Ibn Arabi* (London: Routledge, 2004), 67.
2. James K. A. Smith. *Jacques Derrida: Live Theory* (New York: Continuum, 2005), xi.
3. Almond, *Sufism and Deconstruction*, 84.
4. William C. Chittick, *Ibn Arabi: Heir to the Prophets* (Oxford: Oneworld Publications, 2005), 124–25. Print.
5. Laury Silvers, "'In the Book We Have Left Out Nothing': The Ethical Problem of the Existence of Verse 4:34 in the Qur'an," *Comparative Islamic Studies* 2.2 (2008): 171–80.
6. Ibid.
7. Toshihiko Izutsu, *Sufism and Taoism: A Comparative Study of Key Philosophical Concepts*, 2nd ed. (Berkeley and Los Angeles: University of California Press, 1983), 232.
8. Salman H. Bashier, *Ibn al-Arabī's Barzakh: The Concept of the Limit and the Relationship Between God and the World* (Albany: State University of New York, 2004), 3.
9. Jacques Derrida, *Margins of Philosophy*, 2nd ed. (Chicago: University of Chicago Press, 1982), 320.
10. Stephen Hirtenstein, *The Unlimited Mercifier: The Spiritual Life and Thought of Ibn Arabī* (Oxford: Anqa Publishing, 1999), 119.
11. Ibid.
12. Joshua Kates, *Fielding Derrida: Philosophy, Literary Criticism, and the Work of Deconstruction* (New York: Fordham University Press, 2008), 22.
13. Almond, *Sufism and Deconstruction*, 133.
14. Wallace D. Muhammad, "Who Is the Original Man?" *Muhammad Speaks*, August 21, 1975.
15. Ibid.
16. Ibid.
17. Raymond Sharrieff, "Supreme Minister to Update Lessons," *Muhammad Speaks*, July 11, 1975.
18. Wallace D. Muhammad, *As the Light Shineth from the East* (Chicago: WDM Publishing Co., 1980), 146–47.
19. Manning Marable, *Malcolm X: A Life of Reinvention* (London: Viking, 2011), 469.
20. Almond, *Sufism and Deconstruction*, 76.
21. Terry Eagleton, *Literary Theory: An Introduction* (Minneapolis: University of Minnesota Press, 1983), 138.
22. *The Problem Book*.
23. Ibn al-Arabī, and Cecilia Twinch and Pablo Beneito, trans. *Contemplation of the Holy Mysteries and the Rising of the Divine Lights* (Oxford: Anqa Publishing, 2008), 17.
24. Jeremy Black and Anthony Green, *Gods, Demons and Symbols of Ancient Mesopotamia: An Illustrated Dictionary* (Austin: University of Texas Press, 1992), 144–45.
25. Gershom Scholem, *Kabbalah* (New York: Penguin Books, 1978), 337.

26. Black and Green, *Gods, Demons and Symbols of Ancient Mesopotamia*, 162.

27. Annemarie Schimmel, *The Mystery of Numbers* (New York: Oxford University Press, 1993), 129–131.

28. L. I. Conrad, "Seven and the Tasbī: On the Implications of Numerical Symbolism for the Study of Medieval Islamic History" *JESHO* 31 (1988): 42–73.

29. Farhad Daftary, *A Short History of the Ismailis* (Edinburgh: Edinburgh University Press, 1998), 53–58. Print.

30. Ibid, 11.

31. William C. Chittick, *The Self-Disclosure of God: Principles of Ibn al-Arabī's Cosmology* (Albany: State University of New York Press, 1998), xxxi.

32. Hirtenstein, *The Unlimited Mercifier*, 231.

33. Abū Yaʿqūb al-Sijistānī, "Kitāb al-yanābīʿ," in *An Anthology of Ismaili Literature: A Shiʿi Vision of Islam*, ed. Hermann Landolt, Samira Sheikh, and Kutub Kassam (London: I.B. Tauris Publishers, 2008).

34. Carl W. Ernst, "Muḥammad as the Pole of Existence," in *The Cambridge Companion to Muḥammad*, ed. Jonathan E. Brockopp (Cambridge: Cambridge University Press, 2010).

35. Annemarie Schimmel, *Islam in the Indian Subcontinent* (Leiden: E. J. Brill, 1980), 92.

36. James A. Bellamy, "The Mysterious Letters of the Koran: Old Abbreviations of the Basmalah," *Journal of the American Oriental Society* 93.3 (1973): 267–85.

37. Mahmoud Ayoub, *The Qurʾan and Its Interpreters* (Albany: State University of New York Press, 1984), 56.

38. Ibid., 57.

39. Ibid., 59.

40. Ibid., 57.

41. Keith Massey, "A New Investigation into the 'Mystery Letters' of the Quran," *Arabica* 43.3 (1996): 497–501.

42. Shahzad Bashir, *Fazlallah Astarabadi and the Hurufis* (Oxford: Oneworld Publications, 2005), 50.

43. Ibid., 55.

44. Ibid., 65.

45. Ibid., 71.

46. Ibid., 72.

47. Ibid., 75.

48. Ibid., 72.

49. Derin Terzioglu, *Sufi and Dissident of the Ottoman Empire: Niyāzī-i Miṣrī (1618–1694)*, dissertation, Harvard University, 1999, 408.

50. Ibid., 372.

51. Ibid., 373.

52. Juan R. I. Cole, "The World as Text: Cosmologies of Shaykh Ahmad al-Ahsaʾi," *Studia Islamica* 80 (1994): 145–163.

53. Mitch Horowitz, *Occult America: The Secret History of How Mysticism Shaped Our Nation* (New York: Bantam Books, 2009), 53.

54. Ibid., 208, 224.

55. Jonathan Walton, *Watch This!: The Ethics and Aesthetics of Black Televangelism* (New York: New York University Press, 2009), 226.

56. Bulleh Shah and Saeed Ahmad, *Great Sufi Wisdom: Bulleh Shah (1680–1752)* (Rawalpindi: Adnan Books, 2005), 9–16.

57. Masataka Takeshita, *Ibn 'Arabi's Theory of the Perfect Man and Its Place in the History of Islamic Thought*, dissertation, University of Chicago, 1986, 129–31.

58. Ibn al-Arabī, Pablo Beneito, trans., and Stephen Hirtenstein, trans., *The Seven Days of the Heart: Prayers for the Nights and Days of the Week* (Oxford: Anqa Publishing, 2000), 18.

59. Javad Nurbakhsh, *Sufi Symbolism XIII: Scribes, Pens, Tablets, Koranic Letters, Words, Discourse, Speech, Divine Names, Attributes and Essence* (London and New York: Khaniqahi-Nimatullahi Publications, 1998), 22.

60. Sachiko Murata, *Chinese Gleams of Sufi Light: Wang Tai-yu's Great Learning of the Pure and Real and Liu Chih's Displaying the Concealment of the Real Realm* (Albany: State University of New York Press, 2000), 18–19.

61. Ibid.

62. Annemarie Schimmel, *Deciphering the Signs of God: A Phenomenological Approach to Islam* (Albany: State University of New York Press, 1994), 226.

63. Hirtenstein, *The Unlimited Mercifier*, 116–17.

8. SUNNĪ GODS

1. Gang Starr, "2 Deep," *Daily Operation*, Chrysalis/EMI Records, 1992.

2. Les Matthews, "Hint of War Among Five Percenters," *New York Amsterdam News*, November 20, 1976, B1.

3. "The Fivepercenters: Youth Gang or Social Workers?" *New York Amsterdam News*, September 18, 1976, B2.

4. John B. Henderson, *The Construction of Orthodoxy and Heresy: Neo-Confucian, Islamic, Jewish, and Early Christian Patterns* (Albany: State University of New York Press, 1998), 10.

5. Michael Muhammad Knight, *The Five Percenters: Islam, Hip-Hop, and the Gods of New York* (Oxford: Oneworld Publications, 2007), 187–207.

6. Ibid.

7. Ibid.

8. Ibid.

9. Ibid.

10. Ibid.

11. Ibid.

12. Ibid.

13. Ibid.

14. Ibid.

15. Ibid.

16. Ibid.

17. Ibid.

18. Ibid.

19. Ibid.

20. Ibid.

21. Supreme Understanding Allah, C'BS ALife Allah, and Sunez Allah, eds., "FAQ," in *Knowledge of Self: A Collection of Wisdom on the Science of Everything in Life* (Atlanta: Supreme Design Publishing, 2009).

22. Wilfred Cantwell Smith, "The Crystallization of Religious Communities in Mughul India," in *Yād—Nāme-ye hāni-ye Minorsky*, eds. Mojtaba Minovi and Iraj Afshar (Tehran: University of Tehran, 1969).

23. Ibid.

24. Fred M. Donner, *Muhammad and the Believers: At the Origins of Islam* (Cambridge, MA, and London: Belknap Press of Harvard University Press, 2010), 205–6.

25. John D. Caputo, ed., *Deconstruction in a Nutshell: A Conversation with Jacques Derrida* (New York: Fordham University Press, 1997), 6.

26. Wakeel Allah, *In the Name of Allah: A History of Clarence 13X and the Five Percenters*, 2 vols. (Atlanta: A-Team Publishing, 2008), 297.

27. Ibid, 294.

28. Most High "The Science Guy," "The Debate: Islam vs. Pseudo-Africentricity," online posting to *The Nation of Gods and Earths*, October 15, 2009.

29. Supreme Understanding Allah, C'BS ALife Allah, and Sunez Allah, eds., "FAQ," in *Knowledge of Self*.

30. Supreme Understanding Allah, C'BS ALife Allah, and Sunez Allah, eds., "Contact Directory," in *Knowledge of Self*.

31. Popa Wu, "Free the Dumb," in *Knowledge of Self*.

32. I Majestic Allah, "Is the NGE a Muslim Community?" in *Knowledge of Self*.

33. Supreme Understanding Allah, "Why is the Black Man God?" in *Knowledge of Self*.

34. Shaikhi Teach Mathematics Allah, "The Build: The Whiteman is the Devil," in *Knowledge of Self*.

35. Almighty Supreme Scientist, "Knowledge vs. Belief: Which Side Are You On?" in *Knowledge of Self*.

36. I Medina Peaceful Earth, "What's in a Name: Self-Definition,." in *Knowledge of Self*.

37. Lord Jamar, *The 5% Album*, Babygrande Records, 2006.

38. Knight, *The Five Percenters*, 198–200.

39. Ibid.

40. Ibid.

41. First Born Prince Allah, Letter to Knowledge Born Azee Allah, August 16, 1991.

42. Knight, *The Five Percenters*, 198–200.

43. Ibid., 42–43.

44. Ibid., 52.

45. Ibid.

46. Ibid., 42–48.

47. Ibid.

48. Donald Lee Grant and Jonathan Grant, *The Way It Was in the South: The Black Experience in Georgia* (Athens: University of Georgia Press, 2001), 167.
49. Allah Education, "Our Story (His-Story)," *Supreme Team,* October 8, 2008.
50. First Born Prince Allah, Letter to Knowledge Born Azee Allah.
51. Ibid.
52. Knight, *The Five Percenters,* 164.
53. Ibid., 188–90.
54. Ibid.
55. First Born Prince Allah, 120.
56. Wakeel Allah, "Re: [The Nation of Gods and Earths] Re: 5% Teachings," online posting to *The Nation of Gods and Earths, December 24, 2004.*
57. First Born Prince Allah, *Lost-Found Muslim Lesson No. 3, The Third Prophecy.*
58. Ibid.
59. First Born Prince Allah, "9 Pertinent Points of Islam."
60. Ibid.
61. Ibid.
62. Ibid.
63. Ibid.
64. First Born Prince Allah, 120.
65. Knight, *The Five Percenters,* 204.
66. Wakeel Allah, *In the Name of Allah,* 368.
67. Wakeel Allah, "Re: [The Nation of Gods and Earths] Re: 5% Teachings."
68. Wakeel Allah, *In the Name of Allah,* 368.
69. Ibid., 96–97.
70. Ibid., 367.
71. Ibid., 364.
72. Ibid., 366.
73. Ibid., 367.
74. Ibid., 366–67.
75. Ibid., 367–68.
76. Knight, *The Five Percenters,* 241.
77. Wakeel Allah, *In the Name of Allah,* 295.
78. Ibid., 368.
79. Ibid.
80. Ibid.
81. Ibid.
82. First Born Prince Allah, "The Principles of Learning," in *Knowledge of Self: A Collection of Wisdom on the Science of Everything in Life,* eds. Supreme Understanding Allah, C'BS ALife Allah, and Sunez Allah (Atlanta: Supreme Design Publishing, 2009).
83. Saladin Quanaah' Allah, "First Born Prince Allah," *Allah School in Atlantis,* September 29, 2005.
84. Ibid.

85. First Born Prince Allah, *9 Pertinent Points of Islam*.
86. Maulana Muhammad Ali, *Religion of Islam* (Lahore: the Ahmadiyyah Anjuman Isha'at Islam, 1936), 163.
87. Ibid.
88. Ibid.
89. Ibid., 127.
90. First Born Prince Allah, Letter to Knowledge Born Azee Allah.
91. Wakeel Allah, *In the Name of Allah*, 244.
92. Ibid.
93. First Born Prince Allah, Letter to Knowledge Born Azee Allah.

9. ASSUMING THE TRAITS OF GOD

1. Saiyid Athar Abbas Rizvi, *Muslim Revivalist Movements in Northern India* (Agra: Agra University, 1965), 349.
2. Herbert Berg, *Elijah Muhammad and Islam* (New York and London: New York University Press, 2009), 115.
3. Colin Turner, *Islam Without Allah? The Rise of Religious Externalism in Safavid Iran* (Richmond, VA: Curzon Press, 2000), 57.
4. Asim Roy, *The Islamic Syncretistic Tradition in Bengal* (Princeton, NJ: Princeton University Press, 1983), 95.
5. Sherman Jackson, *Islam and the Blackamerican: The Third Resurrection* (Oxford: Oxford University Press, 2005), 45.
6. Wesley Williams, "Aspect of the Creed of Imam ibn Hanbal: A Study of Anthropomorphism in Early Islamic Discourse," *Middle East Studies* 34 (2002): 441–63.
7. S. A. Q. Husaini, *The Pantheistic Monism of Ibn Al-Arabi*, 2nd ed., (Lahore: Sh. Muhammad Ashraf, 2006), 238.
8. Ibid., 21.
9. Ahmet T. Karamustafa, *Sufism: The Formative Period* (Berkeley and Los Angeles: University of California Press, 2007), 25–26. Print.
10. Alexander Treiger, *The Science of Divine Disclosure: Gazālī's Higher Theology and Its Philosophical Underpinnings*, dissertation, Yale University, 2008, 290.
11. Muhammad Abul Quaseem, "Sufi Interpretation of the Qur," in *Encyclopaedic Survey of Islamic Culture*, ed. Mohammed Taher (New Delhi: Anmol Publications, 1997).
12. Masataka Takeshita, *Ibn 'Arabi's Theory of the Perfect Man and Its Place in the History of Islamic Thought*, dissertation, University of Chicago, 1986, 28.
13. Ibid., 28.
14. Ibid., 41.
15. Caner K. Dagli, *From Mysticism to Philosophy (and Back): An Ontological History of the School of the Oneness of Being*, dissertation, Princeton University, 2006, 15.
16. Takeshita, *Ibn 'Arabi's Theory of the Perfect Man and Its Place in the History of Islamic Thought*.
17. William C. Chittick, *The Self-Disclosure of God: Principles of Ibn al-Arabi's Cosmology* (Albany: State University of New York Press, 1998), xix.

18. Ibid.
19. Alexander Knysh, *Ibn Arabi in the Later Islamic Tradition: The Making of a Polemical Image in Medieval Islam* (Albany: State University of New York, 1999), 232–33.
20. Ibid., 169.
21. Ibid., 151.
22. Ibid., 232–43.
23. Ibid.
24. Ibid., 244–45.
25. Ibid., 243.
26. Allah Jihad, *The Immortal Birth* (Drewryville, VA: Ubus Communications Systems, 2007), 436–37.
27. Rakim, "The Mystery," *The 18th Letter*, Universal Records, 1997.
28. Takeshita, *Ibn 'Arabī's Theory of the Perfect Man and Its Place in the History of Islamic Thought*.
29. Michael Chodkiewicz, *Seal of the Saints: Prophethood and Sainthood in the Doctrine of Ibn Arabī* (Cambridge, UK: Islamic Texts Society, 1993), 67.
30. Jihad, *The Immortal Birth*, 438.
31. Saladin Quanaah' Allah, "Triple 'Sages' of Darkness," *Allah School in Atlantis*, January 31, 2007.
32. Chodkiewicz, *Seal of the Saints*, 67.
33. Amina Wadud, *Inside the Gender Jihad: Women's Reform in Islam* (Oxford: Oneworld Publications, 2006), 35.
34. Saladin Quanaah' Allah, "Triple 'Sages' of Darkness."
35. Supreme Understanding Allah, "Why Is the Black Man God?" in *Knowledge of Self: A Collection of Wisdom on the Science of Everything in Life*, ed. Supreme Understanding Allah, C'BS ALife Allah, and Sunez Allah (Atlanta: Supreme Design Publishing, 2009).
36. Ibid.
37. Ibid.
38. Erykah Badu, "On and On," *Baduizm*, Kedar/Universal, 1997.
39. Sajjad H. Rizvi, "Mysticism and Philosophy: Ibn Arabī and Mullā Ṣadrā," in *The Cambridge Companion to Arabic Philosophy*, ed. Peter Adamson and Richard C. Taylor (Cambridge: Cambridge University Press, 2005).
40. Abū Ḥāmid Muḥammad Al-Ghazālī and David Burrell, trans., *Al-Ghazali on the Ninety-Nine Beautiful Names of God* (Cambridge, UK: Islamic Texts Society, 1992), 149.
41. Ibid., 98.
42. Ibid., 115.
43. Ibid., 63.
44. Ibid., 66.
45. Ibid., 123.
46. Ibid.

47. Takeshita, *Ibn 'Arabī's Theory of the Perfect Man and Its Place in the History of Islamic Thought*.
48. Asukile Bandele, "Knowledge Understanding: Al Musawwir," Facebook.
49. Ibid.
50. Toshihiko Izutsu, *Sufism and Taoism: A Comparative Study of Key Philosophical Concepts*, 2nd ed. (Berkeley and Los Angeles: University of California Press, 1983), 103.
51. William C. Chittick, *Imaginal Worlds: Ibn al-Arabī and the Problem of Religious Diversity* (Albany: State University of New York Press, 1994), 21.
52. Gerald T. Elmore, *Islamic Sainthood in the Fullness of Time: Ibn al-Arabī's Book of the Fabulous Gryphon* (Leiden: E. J. Brill, 1998), 248.
53. Ibid., 32.
54. Ibid.
55. Larry Silvers, "'In the Book We have Left out Nothing': The Ethical Problem of the Existence of Verse 4:34 in the Qur'an," *Comparative Islamic Studies* 2.2 (2008): 171–80.
56. William C. Chittick, *The Sufi Path of Knowledge: Ibn al-Arabi's Metaphysics of Imagination* (Albany: State University of New York Press, 1989), 283.
57. William C. Chittick, "The Perfect Man as the Prototype of the Self in the Sufism of Jāmī," *Studia Islamica* 49 (1979): 135–57.
58. Alexander Knysh, *Ibn Arabi in the Later Islamic Tradition: The Making of a Polemical Image in Medieval Islam* (Albany: State University of New York, 1999), 248–51.
59. Leonard Lewisohn, *Beyond Faith and Infidelity: The Sufi Poetry and Teachings of Maḥmūd Shabistarī* (London: Curzon Press, 1995), 290.
60. Ibid.
61. Chittick, *Imaginal Worlds*, 4–5.
62. Ibid.
63. Izutsu, *Sufism and Taoism*, 83.
64. Takeshita, *Ibn 'Arabī's Theory of the Perfect Man and Its Place in the History of Islamic Thought*.
65. Izutsu, *Sufism and Taoism*, 83.
66. Ibid., 23.
67. Ibid., 71.
68. Stephen Hirtenstein, *The Unlimited Mercifier: The Spiritual Life and Thought of Ibn Arabī* (Oxford: Anqa Publishing, 1999), 25.
69. Ibn al-Arabī and R. W. J. Austin, trans., *The Bezels of Wisdom* (Ramsey, NJ: Paulist Press, 1980), 71–73.
70. Haji Muhammad Bukhari Lubis, *The Ocean of Unity: Waḥdat al-Wujūd in Persian, Turkish and Malay Poetry* (Kuala Lumpur: Dewan Bahasa dan Pustaka, 1994), 40.
71. Khalid Blankinship, "The Early Creed," in *Cambridge Companion to Classical Islamic Theology*, ed. Tim Winter (Cambridge: Cambridge University Press, 2008).
72. Lubis, *The Ocean of Unity*, 40.
73. Ibid., 42.
74. Ibid.

75. Ibid.
76. Ibid.
77. Ibid.
78. Izutsu, *Sufism and Taoism*, 57.
79. Knysh, *Ibn Arabi in the Later Islamic Tradition*, 216.
80. Ibn al-Arabī and Austin, *The Bezels of Wisdom*.
81. Izutsu, *Sufism and Taoism*, 58.
82. Ibn al-Arabī and Austin, *The Bezels of Wisdom*.
83. Knysh, *Ibn Arabi in the Later Islamic Tradition*, 106.
84. Ibid., 124.
85. Lewisohn, *Beyond Faith and Infidelity*, 293.
86. Lubis, *The Ocean of Unity*, 44.
87. Ibid., 42.
88. William C. Chittick, *Ibn Arabi: Heir to the Prophets* (Oxford: Oneworld Publications, 2005), 19.
89. Lubis, *The Ocean of Unity*, 42.
90. Izutsu, *Sufism and Taoism*, 58.
91. A. E. Affifi, *The Mystical Philosophy of Muhyid Din-Ibnul Arabi* (Lahore: Sh. Muhammad Ashraf, 1964), 42.
92. John T. Little, "Al-Insān al-Kāmil: The Perfect Man in Ibn al-Arabī," *Muslim World* 77 (1987): 43–54. Print.
93. Chittick, *Ibn Arabi*, 25.
94. Knysh, *Ibn Arabi in the Later Islamic Tradition*, 110.
95. Elmore, *Islamic Sainthood in the Fullness of Time*, 105.
96. Affifi, *The Mystical Philosophy of Muhyid Din-Ibnul Arabi*, 118.
97. Frank Griffel, "Muslim Philosophers' Rationalist Explanation of Muḥammad's Prophecy," in *The Cambridge Companion to Muḥammad*, ed. Jonathan E. Brockopp (Cambridge: Cambridge University Press, 2010).
98. Frank Griffel, "Al-Gazālī's Concept of Prophecy: The Introduction of Avicennan Psychology into As'arite Theology," *Arabic Sciences and Philosophy* 14 (2004): 101–44.
99. Griffel, "Muslim Philosophers' Rationalist Explanation of Muḥammad's Prophecy."
100. G. A. Lipton, *Muḥibb Allāh Ilāhābādī's* The Equivalence between Giving and Receiving: *Avicennan Neoplatonism and the School of Ibn Arabī in South Asia*, dissertation, University of North Carolina, 2007, 84–85.
101. Lewisohn, *Beyond Faith and Infidelity*, 292.
102. GZA, "Swordsman," *Liquid Swords*, Geffen/MCA Records, 1995.

10. UNIVERSAL FLAG

1. Alex Haley and Malcolm X, *The Autobiography of Malcolm X* (New York: Ballantine Books, 1999), 347.
2. Ahmad Dallal, "Ghazali and the Perils of Interpretation," *Journal of the American Oriental Society* 122.4 (2002): 773–87.

3. Barry Maxwell Andrews, *Emerson as Spiritual Guide: A Companion to Emerson's Essays for Personal Reflection and Group Discussion* (Boston: Skinner House Books, 2003), 36–38.

4. Ibid.

5. Haley and Malcolm X, *The Autobiography of Malcolm X*, 293.

6. Cynthia Eller, *Living in the Lap of the Goddess: The Feminist Spirituality Movement in America* (New York: Crossroad, 1993), 47.

7. Arthur Hyman and James Jerome Walsh, *Philosophy in the Middle Ages: The Christian, Islamic, and Jewish Traditions* (Indianapolis: Hackett Publishing Company, 1983), 310.

8. Ebrahim Moosa, *Ghazālī and the Poetics of Imagination* (Chapel Hill: University of North Carolina Press, 2005), 158.

9. Dallal, "Ghazali and the Perils of Interpretation."

10. Talal Asad, "The Idea of an Anthropology of Islam," *Center for Contemporary Arab Studies (CCAS)—Georgetown University,* Center for Contemporary Arab Studies, Georgetown University, 1986, http://ccas.georgetown.edu/87058.html.

11. King Sun, "Universal Flag," *Righteous but Ruthless,* Profile, 1991.

12. Gananath Obeyesekere, *Medusa's Hair: An Essay on Personal Symbols and Religious Experience* (Chicago: University of Chicago Press, 1981), 169.

13. Ibid., 137.

14. "Who Is the 5 Series 3/25/2010," *Allah Team Radio.*

15. Kimberly C. Patton, *Religion of the Gods: Ritual, Paradox, and Reflexivity* (Oxford: Oxford University Press, 2009), 283–306.

16. Ibid.

17. Derin Terzioglu, *Sufi and Dissident of the Ottoman Empire: Niyāzī-i Miṣrī (1618–1694),* dissertation, Harvard University, 1999, 358.

18. Stephen Hirtenstein, *The Unlimited Mercifier: The Spiritual Life and Thought of Ibn Arabī* (Oxford: Anqa Publishing, 1999), 119.

19. Sir H. A. R. Gibb, *Encyclopedia of Islam* (Leiden: E. J. Brill, 1953), 545.

20. Annemarie Schimmel, "The Martyr-Mystic Al-Ḥallāj in Sindhi Folk-Poetry: Notes on a Mystical Symbol," *Numen* 9.3 (1962): 161–200.

21. Tasadduq Husain, "The Spiritual Journey of Dārā Shikūh," *Social Scientist* 30.7/8 (2002): 54–66.

22. Saiyid Athar Abbas Rizvi, *Muslim Revivalist Movements in Northern India,* (Agra: Agra University 1965), 355.

23. Ibid., 366.

24. Husain, "The Spiritual Journey of Dārā Shikūh."

25. Rizvi, *Muslim Revivalist Movements in Northern India,* 360.

26. Husain, "The Spiritual Journey of Dārā Shikūh."

27. Rizvi, Saiyid Athar Abbas, *Muslim Revivalist Movements in Northern India* (Agra: 1965), 360. Print.

28. Husain, "The Spiritual Journey of Dārā Shikūh."

29. Ibid.

30. Ibid.
31. Ibid.
32. Rizvi, *Muslim Revivalist Movements in Northern India*, 356.
33. Husain, "The Spiritual Journey of Dārā Shikūh."
34. Clyde Holler, *Black Elk's Religion: The Sun Dance and Lakota Catholicism* (Syracuse, NY: Syracuse University Press, 1995), xxxi.
35. Ibid., 215.
36. Ibid.
37. Sherman Jackson, *Islam and the Problem of Black Suffering* (Oxford: Oxford University Press, 2009), 8.
38. Bruce Lincoln, *Theorizing Myth: Narrative, Ideology, and Scholarship* (Chicago: University of Chicago Press, 1999), 207.
39. Ibid., 209.
40. Muhammad bin Abdul-Wahhab, *Kitab At-Tauhid: The Book of Monotheism* (Riyadh: Dar-us-Salam Publications, 1996), 52.
41. Frank Griffel, *Al-Ghazālī's Philosophical Theology* (Oxford: Oxford University Press, 2009), 105.

INDEX

Azreal *(cont.)*
 as white Five Percenter, 65, 71, 91–92, 245
 on whites as gods, 64

Badu, Erykah, 97, 222
Bakunin, Mikhail, 107–8, 112
Baldwin, James, 46, 72, 124, 125
Bambaataa, Afrika, 114–15
Bashir, Shahzad, 165–66
Beloved Allah, 180
Berg, Philip S., 111
Bilal (later First Born ABG), 7, 12–13, 254–55
Bistāmī, Abū Yazīd al-, 213–14
Black Elk, 253, 254
black godhood, 6–7, 12, 55–56, 156
Blood Brothers, 192
Blumenbach, Johann Friedrich, 39
"Bomb, The" (Five Percent), 182–84, 190
Brooklyn (Medina), 7, 12–13, 254–55
Buddhism, 102, 103
Bulleh Shah, 170

Carbado, Devon W., 86
Caucasians, 35–36, 39–42, 83–84
Cavalli-Sforza, Luigi Luca, 28
Chaos Crumbling (Abzug), 128
Chinese Gleams of Sufi Light (Murata), 176–77
Chittick, William C., 99, 150, 217, 225–29
Christ, Carol P., 130
Christianity, 56–60, 102–3, 107, 108, 110–11,
 138–39
Cipher, Knowledge Scientific, 133
Cone, James, 141–42
Cosell, Howard, 55
Cuba, Prince Allah, 145–46, 181, 189–90

Daly, Mary, 127, 129–30, 142, 242
Dārā Shikūh, 251–52
Davis, Angela, 135–36
Davis, Ossie, 139
"Debts and Burdens of Critical Islam" (Moosa), 118
degrees. *See* 120 degrees *(as though spelled "one
 hundred twenty degrees")*
Derrida, Jacques, 149, 151, 152–53, 157, 185–86
"Destruction of the Devil, The" (Warith Deen
 Mohammed), 155
Divine Names, 223–27, 235
Dollar, Creflo, 138
Donner, Fred M., 185
Douglass, Frederick, 59, 81, 108, 123–24, 128
Dow, George, 35
Du Bois, W.E.B., 60

Dumar Wa'de Allah, 181
Durkheim, Émile, 172

Eagleton, Terry, 157–58
Earth, I Medina Peaceful, 189
8 Mile (Eminem), 76, 82
Einstein, Mara, 110–11, 112
Elijah Muhammad. *See* Muhammad, Elijah
Elmore, Gerald T., 236
Emerson, Ralph Waldo, 241–42
Eminem, 73–74, 76, 82, 86–87
English Lesson C-1, 61–62, 170, 175
Enki (Mesopotamian deity), 133
"Enlightener, The" (Five Percenter anthem), 172
Equality, Goddess Earth, 145
Exceptional Devils, 80–88, 90

Fard, W. D. *See* Muhammad, Master Fard
Fardan, Dorothy Blake, 48, 66, 92–95
Farrakhan, Louis, 8, 62, 64, 68–69, 94, 156
Fatir, Amir, 95
feminist issues
 antagonism toward black men, 124
 Declaration of Sentiments, 122–23, 128–29
 goddess concept, 130–31
 in Muslim communities, 116–18, 134
 racial injustice and, 121–23, 136–37, 146–47
 religion-based subjugation of women, 127–29,
  138, 242
 suffrage, 122–24
 wife-beating reference in Qur'ān, 150, 172, 226
 women as Five Percenters, 125, 132–35, 137,
  144–47
First Born ABG (formerly Bilal), 7, 12–13,
 254–55
First Born Al-Jamel, 202
First Born, 189–90, 254–56
Five Percenters
 anthem, "The Enlightener," 172
 "Arm, Leg, Leg, Arm, Head" interpretation of
  Allah, 5, 165–66, 182, 233
 Atlanta versus Kalimite factions, 200–202
 beginning and spread of movement, 5–9, 192,
  254–55
 black man as god of own universe, 6–7, 12, 156
 description of, in 16:40 degree, 112
 disassociation from Nation of Islam and
  Muslim identity, 11–12, 18–19, 180,
  182–83, 187–89, 205, 211
 First Born, 189–90, 254–56
 on Five Percent as culture versus religion, 133,
  173, 181, 186–87, 239

Printed in the United States
by Baker & Taylor Publisher Services